The Rattle and Hiss of the Tin gods

The Rattle and Hiss of the Tin gods

Evelyn L. Damore

Writers Club Press
San Jose New York Lincoln Shanghai

The Rattle and Hiss of the Tin gods

Writers Club Press
an imprint of iUniverse, Inc.

For information address:
iUniverse, Inc.
5220 S. 16th St., Suite 200
Lincoln, NE 68512
www.iuniverse.com

All information in this book is based on my research of the issues, and is accurate to the best of my ability.

ISBN: 0-595-22844-5

Printed in the United States of America

Contents

Part II   Drawing a Counterfeit Portrait/Charting the Course

Part III *A Quest for Power*

Part IV *Tyranny of the Gods*

Part V   National Destiny

CHAPTER 13   One Nation Under God 237

Introduction

What prompted me to write this book was the one-sided view the media has subjected us to over the years. It has been discouraging to see a constant belittling of a way of life, principles, and values that I and so many other Americans believe in, and so I decided to focus on the things that either never hit the nightly news, or are significantly played down so as to lose their significance.

As I see it, the basic cultural arguments are generally filtered through the concepts of two major beliefs: Judeo/Christianity and secular humanism. Ironically, Christianity, once widely accepted and taken for granted throughout our history as a guide to live by and a morality marker for justice, became a controversial issue in the 1960's. Just as secular humanism began to rise as a competitor for the hearts and souls of Americans, Christianity was to be shunned almost everywhere. Therefore, I found it necessary to compare the basic tenets of humanism and Christianity, documenting the impact secular humanistic thought has had on all aspects of American life, from movies to politics, an analysis which necessarily entails some focus on the issue of political Christians.

One of the major things I hope to bring to the reader's attention is the blatant strategies to deceive, which various political organizations and media outlets use—things like double standards, hypocrisy, propaganda, liberal rationale, omission of facts (some call lying), and other misrepresentations that are often intended to benefit the left and brandish the right. And let us not forget the rewrite of history so that it favors the liberal's agenda, at the cost of authenticity.

I also wanted to expose the left's end goal for using these deceptive strategies, which is to transform society into a liberalism in the mode of secular humanistic theories. For instance, the scheme to deceive with

1

homey, mom-and-apple-pie euphemisms, to redefine certain words such as "gender," "family," "marriage," and a host of other terms to fit the left's agenda, as well as, changing the subject when the media's favored side is in hot water and by the employment of hyperbole, are all done with the intent to find the "mote in the opponent's eye" in order to draw attention away from the "beam in their own."

I wanted to expose several things which I grew particularly tired of (due to the repetitiveness of it), such as a shallow media that will not rein in one political party that constantly uses children (and senior citizens) as a wedge issue on as many issues as one can possibly stretch the imagination, speaking "nobly" and "compassionately" on their behalf, whether relevant or not to the issue at hand, to get women's votes.

I grew tired of a shallow media that is ever ready to report favorably on the National Organization for Women (NOW), but will not report on Concerned Women for America (CWA) and its positive achievements, most likely because CWA has surpassed NOW's membership. I grew tired of a shallow media that refers to conservative Republicans as "right wingers" and liberal Democrats, just as "Democrats." Their idea is to put Republicans in a box and keep them there, no matter what. I grew tired of a shallow media that pretends to set the record straight by burying the record as a brief footnote on the air, or somewhere deep into a fairly insignificant spot in the newspaper.

Still another reason I wrote this book is just plain nostalgia for a time when neighborhoods and schools were havens of safety for children. Not too long ago, kids could ride their bikes or walk to Little League, to dancing lessons, to the swimming pool, to Saturday afternoon movies, to town with their friends, window shopping or stopping for a soda. Today, parents have to oversee every move their children make away from home, transport them to and from every activity they are involved in, worry about the gangs in schools, the foul language, and whether or not they are getting a good education or being taught outcomes based whatever.

Also, I wrote the book in the spirit of "catch-up" time at the risk of being accused of presenting one political party as the devil incarnate and the other as saints, and the same thing applying to Christians and non-Christians. The truth is that I do recognize noteworthy traits and deeds, as well as flaws in the characters of all people, whether they are conservative, liberal, or something in between, Christian or non-Christian.

I am reminded of a letter on the editorial page of my local newspaper some time after the 1992 Republican Convention, at which time it was unpopular to mention God. The writer complained that Republicans were making the "big grab for God." He wrote: "You can measure a person's love of God by their attitude toward the poor, the weak, and the hungry"—the implication here being Democrats are those who love God, while Republicans only make a pretense of it. If we judge godliness by the writer's measuring stick, then we have to say that no one group has given more real help to the poor than the churches, which of course, includes members of both parties.

The key to understanding the writer's complaint lies in the fact that he did not understand the difference in offering help that strengthens and allows people to maintain their sense of worth and dignity so that they can become self-reliant once again, and help that results in an ongoing dependency and hopelessness. Anyone who does not understand this theory needs to check out a forty-year record of the hard fighting done by liberal congressmen and women, and their special interest organizations for this kind of so-called help to see why so often poor people were not lifted up, but have been held down year after year to life in a rut—nothing kindhearted about that.

However, the writer had an axe to grind and used this complaint to cover his real intention. His aim really was to put Republicans down for publically expressing their belief in God by sarcastically using such terms as "holy" and "righteous" against them and to present them as overbearing pious people. But in doing so, he exposed his own narrowness. He made it apparent to his readers that he did see the connection between moral decay and the exclusion of God from their lives.

However, there should be no complaint from anyone on the subject of "hogging God"—the writer's complaint—as each party is the sole creator of its own speeches and programs, and as such, its members can make the same assertion, if they so desire, and "make the big grab for God," too. Only those few blinded by their own ignorance would suggest or believe God belongs to a particular political group.

This book asks the question: "What, if any, does Christianity play in solving societal problems?" If I have answered that question, or at least given anyone reason to think more seriously about it, then I have accomplished what I set out to do.

PART I

The Impact of Humanism on Society

1

A Path Mis-Taken

o o o o o o o o o o o o o o o o o o o o o o o o o o o o o o o o

"In those days all the people did what was right in their own eyes."—Judges 17:6

Several years ago I read an article by Don Feder, syndicated columnist for the *Boston Herald*, entitled, "The dead-end road to non-judgmentalism." In it he talked about a "value-free America" in which no one takes responsibility. He wrote: "If there is one thing we're good at in America today, it's not assigning blame. Over our public policy debate should be a sign reading 'Excuses R Us'." He went on to quote Senator Daniel Patrick Moynihan (D) of New York, who had described the same dire circumstances Feder spoke of as "moral deregulation" and "defining deviancy down." The Moynihan quote read: "We are defining deviant behavior so that it appears to be normal…. We are getting used to a lot of behavior that is not good for us."

As late as the 50's and early 60's, the majority of Americans would have been in utter dismay over the "moral deregulation" Moynihan talked about. Understandably, the people of "yesterday" would not have believed that in the near future the divorce rate would soar to 50%, that nurseries would be installed in the public schools to care for teenager's babies, that schools would distribute condoms to kids, that drug usage would become commonplace, that school curriculums would be dumbed down so kids could pass, that metal detectors would

7

be installed to detect guns and other weapons carried into school, that an alarming number of kids would kill over a pair of shoes or a difference of opinion, that gangs would flourish in schools, that kids would drive by neighborhoods or business districts, shooting randomly from their cars at anyone (just for the "fun" of it); or, for that matter, that adult American terrorists, who without conscience or remorse, would bomb a federal building, killing and injuring hundreds of people simply because they hated the government. One might easily assume that in the not too distant past, the average person would have said: "Never in America! Maybe somewhere else, but never in America!"

But times did change much more than anyone could have imagined, and the undreamed horrors did come to America. The "deregulators," considering themselves all-knowing in ways to attain ultimate "freedom" for the masses, put forth their agenda to revolutionize American thought, along lines of their idea of a fun-loving and totally free society—a plan executed methodically, subtly, and deliberately in order to insure internalization and acceptance of it.

However, the consequences of their endeavors did not produce the recipe for "utopia," as they imagined, but a steady sordid decline in morals and values. It would take years of documented proof, repeated many times over before reality would begin to sink into the minds of some of these misguided people. The rest of us were left wondering how we could undo the harm performed on nearly two generations of young people, many of whom have been indoctrinated in the new morality of "cultural relativism", so that they really did/do not know right from wrong, and think almost anything they do is okay if it is "right" for them.

The social deregulators are responsible for all kinds of new fads among the teenagers. More details on this issue will be discussed in a later chapter, but for the present, the example of disillusioned teenagers celebrating a mass killer like Charles Manson as their hero, his songs and T-shirts and other paraphernalia, which brought in millions of dollars, is an indication of the far-reaching adverse effects fostered by the new morality movement.

To say the least, the task to stop this downward spiral from reaching the point of no return is HUGE. For thirty years or more, the mainstream media has blatantly dismissed any material that presents a positive, traditional perspective on any of today's issues, or on any view that disagrees with liberal humanistic theories of the "new morality"—the so-called "enlightened path to fulfillment," consisting of "self-actualization," sexual freedom, redefined families, cultural relativism. etc. Although these terms are not often used in the media, the same ideas are generally present as the underlying theme of the "news" and of various talk shows, and needless to say, sitcoms and movies.

With the rapid disappearance of absolutes, maybe it is time to consider what George Barna, author and researcher, had to say about America. He suggests that today's America is a "virtual" America—a poor imitation of a country—"one obsessed with escaping into a false reality." Even if he is right, there are some good reasons for optimism—the slowly rising tide that keeps turning in the direction of common sense, which has grown stronger since September 11, 2001 terrorist attacks on America. One does not necessarily have to be in total agreement with the "surfers" on this tide to see that they do possess a certain amount of wisdom on the issues. We first saw the new tide with the gradual, and deliberate in cause, emergence of several conservative radio-talk shows, and with the preaching, counseling, and praying against the new morality in the churches across America. Still, further evidence of the turning tide happened when *Fox News* came on board, talking about things that the major media would rather the public remain in the dark. *Fox News* has not been totally successful in shunning political correctness, but, because of its more candid and fair and balanced reporting than what the public has been used to for decades, it has outranked the monopoly of the liberal-media biggies of half a century, and is now America's number one choice for the news.

It seems to me that the only way to understand the quagmire we are responsible for is to examine the two belief systems that dominate the majority of American thought—secular humanism and traditional Judeo/Christian philosophies—and then consider the prevailing agendas of each to measure their effectiveness in solving our problems. Hopefully, readers of both persuasions will look beyond the surface gloss of words that have become meaningless to many people for the solutions so desperately needed.

THE POWER

It is human nature to want power, to have the last word, to control events, but when the drive for power is an obsession, it is, more than not, downright mean and destructive. Some argue that secular humanism is the culprit, others say Christianity is, but advocates of both beliefs expound the "virtues" of their own as the only acceptable way to fulfill oneself.

Though the new order presented by the school of secular humanism has its origins in the Middle Ages, it was introduced in the United States in 1933 when John Dewey, known as the "Father of progressive education," joined others of like mind and became the chief designer of the *Humanist Manifesto.* However the new religion was not overtly put into practice until the 1960's. The big revolutionary changes were to promote freer, happier, and more fulfilling lifestyles. Today, the advocates of the humanist doctrine continue to disseminate their ideas more effectively than they did in the 60's. Their revolutionary changes in the name of "freedom", via every conceivable forum—TV, movies, newspapers, educational systems, etc.—are being used almost constantly to convince Americans the secular humanist view is the only way to go.

To verify this statement, one need only recall the vast movement that endorsed the psychology of humanism and its endless stream of literature, which has been written, preached, and sworn by under the guise of two, we might say, people-friendly terms: "self-improvement" and "the power of positive thinking." The popularity of this humanist philosophy is truly phenomenal. It permeates every level of our society; it is taught in the public schools; it is reinforced by university professors; and it is preached in the business world, with numerous companies now paying the tab for their employee's courses in success. In fact, secular humanism is so widely accepted, it has unquestionably become an American institution, as stated in the *Human Manifesto I*: "In every field of human activity, the vital movement is now in the direction of a candid and explicit humanism." It is no wonder this theory is so popular, for its promises are all up-beat and positive, virtually guaranteeing everyone the ability to be his or her best—to attain success, happiness, creativity, etc. Disciples of this philosophy claim: "The humanist outlook will tap the creativity of each human being and provide the vision and courage for us to work together" *(Manifesto I)*.

Now, most of us are for self-help and positive thinking. However, secular humanists have seized the terms as an opportunity to indoctrinate nearly two generations of Americans with the liberal idea that they are entitled to do whatever feels good to them. Self-help and positive thinking to the humanist means the new morality previously mentioned, and all the entanglements that go along with it. In other words, it is a system that largely discards absolutes as obsolete.

Another important characteristic of humanism becomes apparent when we compare it with Christianity, for some of its basic premises are in many ways almost carbon copies of Christian beliefs (here lies the deception). However, these wonderful transformations humanists promised us have not been forthcoming for many people—a fact borne out by the visible decline of standards and values held by our society today that have resulted in a multitude of complex problems, many of which seem almost beyond remedy. Given what appears to be a foolproof blueprint for success, we cannot help but wonder why such a positive endeavor has failed.

What exactly is secular humanism, and are its doctrines really similar to Christian beliefs? To a large extent, the humanist philosophy can be summed up in the belief that there are no bad people, that human beings have an inborn characteristic of goodness. For this reason, humanists focus their attention on the growth of the individual, studying what he is and what he can become. According to noted humanist psychologist, Abraham H. Maslow, an individual following his system of positive thinking eventually becomes "self-actualized," which means he has reached his highest potential and is then able to enjoy a special kind of perception that allows him to be creative. Furthermore, the self-actualized man or woman is not stifled by traditional beliefs and stereotypes, but, instead, searches for new and better ways of doing things. All this speculation sounds good, but problems mount when absolutes are rejected, and nothing but chaos can follow.

The similarity the idea of self-actualization has with Christian doctrine lies in the fact that today most Christian churches place more emphasis on God's love and promises for His people and on their spiritual growth than they do on sin. (This is not to say sin is unimportant.) Christians believe that we are descendants of a loving Spirit-Father, as stated in John 4:24, "God is Spirit," and are destined to grow from birth. However, growth hinges on biblical absolutes, and since we are given a free will, it is up to each person to choose God's way or to reject it—a sort of trial and error process in which one either learns from his mistakes and wants to change, or continues to "bat his head against a stone wall." The growth theme permeates the Bible, but the scripture most of us are probably more familiar with is what Jesus said on this subject in John 10:10: "I am come that they might have life, and that they might have it more abundantly."

This is why Christians attribute their fulfillment and creativeness, not as humanists do to themselves, but through submission to Christ —becoming one with their inner source. Their reward is to "be strengthened with might by His spirit in the inner man" (Eph. 3:16). Reliance on the Holy Spirit as their counselor and guide better equips them to cope with life's adversities, and, at the same time, grow stronger spiritually in the process of working through their problems. (In today's terms, it is called character building.) Paul tells us, "He [God] has not given us a spirit of fear, but of power, and of love, and of a sound mind" (2 Tim. 1:7). As for the non-believers who made the choice to cut themselves off from God, Christians believe that they have opened themselves up to a wide path of disillusionment, that they are more prone in their attempts to escape painful situations to choose various destructive behaviors, ranging from obsessions for status symbols to more serious problems, like drug addictions, alcoholism, criminal behavior, suicide, etc. A biblical explanation of their "reward" might be recorded in Luke 6:45: "An evil man out of the evil treasure of his heart brings forth that which is evil." Further on in Ephesians 4:18–19, Paul says, "They having their understanding darkened, being alienated from the life of God through the ignorance that is in them, because of the blindness of their heart, who being past feeling have given themselves over unto lasciviousness, to work all uncleanness with greediness."

Nevertheless, secular humanists do not accept any part of God. They feel they have the answer to ensure good mental health. Maslow says "It is essential to express one's creative self so that one does not become overly anxious, discouraged, or emotionally disturbed." A similar concept, however, has its origin in the Bible. The apostle Paul spoke specifically of two selves, one positive, the other negative, when he said, "I die daily." In this way he denied his ego-dominated self, the worrying anxious man who relied on the outer world, and put his faith in the inner Christ to gain peace, inspiration, and fulfillment. A training relative to this kind of self-discipline is recorded in Philippians 4:8 where we are encouraged to "think on whatsoever things are true… honest…just…pure…lovely…of good report…."

Judging from these observations, one might assume humanists and Christians are to a large extent in close agreement on some important precepts. However, on closer analysis of the two beliefs, we see fundamental differences that divide them.

THE CONTRAST

One belief in particular, as stated by the late philosopher, Dr. Francis A. Schaeffer, is sufficient to make a meeting of the minds between secular humanist and Christian thought impossible. He said: "The dominant thought of the humanist philosophy is that man is the center of everything, his knowledge comes from whatever finite man is able to obtain."

A Christian, on the other hand, places God at the center of his life and believes he grows in wisdom and knowledge, receiving God's Holy Spirit through prayer and communion with Him. "We speak, not in the words which man's wisdom teaches, but which the Holy Ghost teaches" (1Cor. 2;13). Also, since the humanist has become his own god, he establishes his own moral base and the standards he will live by, thus believing he has absolute control over his destiny. The first tenet in *Manifesto II* reads: "We can discover no divine purpose to providence for the human species…humans are responsible for what we are or will become. No deity will save us; we must save ourselves."

Salvation for the Christian, however, is just the opposite; it means total acceptance of Jesus Christ as his/her Savior. "I am the way, the truth, and the life. No man comes to the Father, but by me" (John 14:6). Also, salvation for the new Christian does not mean he is a "finished" product (quite the contrary). He now embarks on a life-long process of change, letting the Holy Spirit instruct, mold, and counsel him into a resilient, wise, and prosperous person, at peace with himself and God—"a new creature in Christ." (True prosperity is of the soul, but may also manifest materially as well.) Nevertheless, the "new creature" aspect does not mean the Christian's life is a "bed of roses." Jesus said in Matthew 5:45 "…for He [the Father] maketh His sun to rise on the evil and on the good, and sends rain on the just and on the unjust."

In Ephesians 4:24–32, we see some of the many ways in which the transformation from the former corruptive self takes place—"putting away lying, stealing, unforgiveness, all bitterness, selfishness, faultfinding," etc.—to become "strong in the Lord and the strength of His might" (6:10).

Surprisingly, even the humanist's belief, "being one's own god," is seen in the Bible on several occasions, but probably the most notable one is recorded in Genesis 3:7, where we see satan, the "Father of lies," luring his victim into a trap by telling her if she ignores God's laws "Ye [Eve and Adam] shall be as gods." We see this mind-set of individual sovereignty everywhere today and it is very appealing, for it gives one freedom to do what feels good as an individual "right". But Paul says, "Beware lest any man spoil you through philosophy and vain deceit, after the tradition of men, after the rudiments of the world, and not after Christ."

However, this advice doesn't faze the humanist. He merely says his attitude is not selfish, but a means of promoting self-confidence and good self-esteem. According to the *Humanist Manifesto II*, "Humanism can provide the purpose and inspiration that so many seek, it can give personal meaning, and significance to life, [and move one] toward a wider vision of human potentiality." Also, humanists admit their goal is to completely take over, not only the United States but also the world, with their "design for a secular society on a planetary scale."

2

Traveling Deception's Path

o o o o o o o o o o o o o o o o o o o o o o o o o o o o o o

"For men shall be lovers of their own selves, covetous boaster, proud, blasphemers, disobedient to parents, unthankful, unholy." —1 Timothy 3:2

The glaring result of living without absolutes is best seen in a major by-product that comes from following the secular humanistic code—the sexual revolution—which supposedly would free everyone, but instead, every study shows that its major "contribution" to society has been the rapid disappearance of the nuclear family. It has caused the divorce rate to soar, inflicted a heavy price on children who look for love and acceptance outside the home, and sentenced hundreds of thousands of runaway kids to dangerous, degrading life on the streets. The pay-off of unrestrained sex is spelled out almost daily in the media—millions of pregnant teenagers annually (many of whom use abortion as their method of birth control), and the proliferation of prostitution and suicide. All of these problems have resulted in overloaded, understaffed welfare programs, bogged-down court dockets, and shortages of prisons where problems are compounded by ever-increasing numbers of violent criminals—and the list goes on. These societal atrocities are the end result of the psychology of humanism internalized—simply put, the effects of extreme liberalism. The bottom line is, Vice President

Dan Quayle had it right when he said: "When families fail, society fails."

As we have seen from the declarations in the *Humanist Manifesto*, its followers are extremely liberal in their views. One does not need to be a card-caring member of this organization for it to have an impact on his or her life. The movement has been successful in gaining ground through various mediums because of its strategy to indoctrinate and desensitize the public—gradually the unacceptable begins to be "no big deal," and in many instances it has become common place. No matter what Hollywood film producers claim, or do not claim, as their religious affiliation, with few exceptions, they fall into this category. The steady stream of filth they have spewed out for several decades is proof of where they stand on the issues. Occasionally we do get good movies that pretty much steer away from "shock value," and are certainly worthy of applause.

SELLING POOR IMAGES OF CHRISTIANS

Christians often complain that their voices are seldom heard, and when they are, it is presented with bias and hatred by both the entertainment world and from a news standpoint—the former often portraying Christians negatively, the latter usually distorting facts by omitting important information that would in itself shed new light on the truth of the situation. However, since 9/11 with more people going to church and professing their belief in God, and also the fact that we have a religious president in George W. Bush, who boldly confesses himself a believer in Christ, the media's behavior has of late changed somewhat more favorably toward Christians. I'm sure the media realizes to do otherwise at the present time would not sit well with the majority of the public.

However, the fact remains that Hollywood has portrayed Christians in unflattering ways for many years. According to the chairman of the Christian Film and Television Commission (CFTC) Ted Baehr, this is a trend that started in the late 60's and has continued on to the present time. He says further that such bias has caused a growing discontentment among viewers with the film industry, and that the so-called religious movies not only brand Christians as ill-informed, intolerant, fanatical, but also as wicked people who are not in touch with reality. Most Christians probably thought the movie *The Last Temptation of Christ,* which distorted the Bible and the character of our Christian God, a totally unconscionable act, as well as the height of vulgarity; and probably they believed the ruckus this movie caused would end all attempts to demean our Lord—not so.

The loveable, kind, godly men of yesterday, like the priest portrayed by Bing Crosby in *Going My Way,* or Father Flannigan by Spencer Tracy in *Boy's Town,* were replaced by losers, like the role Robert De Nero played as a self-ordained minister who was also a psychopathic killer in *The Night of the Hunter,* or as a different kind of loser, like the priest in *The Exorcist,* whose God is not powerful enough to save him from death at the hands of satan. A more recent attempt to slander men of the cloth is illustrated in the movie *Priests,* which is a story about three priests depicted as the antagonists. One has a mistress, one has an affair with a man, and one is an alcoholic. *Prophesy* goes a step further. In this movie satan is portrayed as the hero, while the priest is the villain. Film critic and talk show host, Michael Medved, explains that Hollywood is not a friend to Christians, and especially not to the Catholic Church. He says that the Catholic Church is "the most visible religious institution in the world, so Hollywood views it as a particularly juicy version of cardinal sin because it came out against homosexual marriages and abortions." And he adds, "It is extremely apparent that the liberal producers are out to get revenge."

Priests aren't the only "wicked" people in the Catholic Church: *Agnes of God* is about a nun who gets pregnant and murders her child. Jane Fonda played the part of an atheist psychiatrist who gave the Mother Superior a hard time, telling her "it is alright to hate God"; *Monsignor* is about a priest involved in the Mafia and has an affair with a nun—while in *Godfather Part III*, the Mafia owns St. Peter's Basilica; and *Household Saints* is about a nun who isn't "playing with a full deck," as she thinks that she plays pinochle with the Trinity.

But it is not just the "religious" movies that have Christians and other conservative people upset. They are opposed to what their children are exposed to on a daily basis: an unhealthy diet of violence at its goriest—sadist, merciless, blood-dripping scenes—and explicit, sexual innuendos and behaviors that permeate television. Most of their role models on the screen are crude and foul mouthed. Story lines promote several myths about sex with the female nearly always taking the seductive lead. The irony of this is that roles for female actresses more and more exhibit the same macho behavior women say they abhor in men.

Also, the depiction of a whole family has fast become an oddity. In fact, statistics show that only about 9 percent of the sex scenes on television are between married couples. Syndicated columnist and talk-show host, Cal Thomas, writes: "A generation has been taught not only that sin no longer exists but that if it did, the only sin left would be suggesting that another person is living the wrong way and that such behavior is not only hurting him or herself but society at large."

But thanks to public outcry, decent family programs are gradually coming back, and thanks also to people like Ted Baehr, Michael Medved, Brent Bozell, the late Steve Allen, and others who do/did more than sit on the sidelines and complain about the situation. These people have worked tirelessly to put some limits on Hollywood and the explicit vulgarity that marks so much of their films and television shows. Unfortunately, Hollywood does not want to step up to the plate and take responsibility toward family entertainment.

Even so, there is good reason for Christians to feel encouraged because of the few movies that do portray Christians in a positive way, such as Ken Wales' production of *East of Eden, Islands in the Stream, Christy, Left Behind, etc.* Also, a significant number of more films are being rated "G" and "PG," and negative references to religion are on the decrease, while positive references are up. Much of the new programing is the result of Christian and Jewish producers working together to honor their respective religious traditions, and to celebrate family life.

As a guest on *The 700 Club* on March 12, 2002, Dr. Bob Getz tells the story of a new film that "explores the ramifications—spiritual, dramatic, and comedic—of a possible Second Coming of Christ to Small-town, America." His friend Philip Anschutz, who is a business man, wanted to create a positive change in the media along the lines of wholesome family entertainment, and asked him to come and work with him as a consultant on a project for television. Dr. Beltz had been a pastor for 30 years, and was ready to try something new. Together they produced the movie *Joshua*, which is based on Joseph F. Girzone's novel, of the same name.

Dr. Beltz speaking of the movie said: "The main character is a charismatic stranger who arrives in town and makes his presence felt in inexplicable ways....Known only by his first name, his particular brand of wisdom and charity soon places him at the center of the town's attention." Dr. Beltz hopes "believers would come away from the film thinking that they have just been in the presence of Jesus, and that the non-churched would leave the film asking to know more about Jesus."

It certainly is hopeful when we see signs that the tide is beginning to turn, but a handful of shows on the order of decency does not a victory make. The culture of depravity runs deep and pervasive, and it is not likely that many of its producers will change their ways. Because music is such a powerful medium to inspire all sorts of feelings, both good and bad, these producers of filth have cast it to play a big part in pollution of the airways.

Much of today's music is directed at the younger generation and goes directly against the values parents try to instill in their children. It sends the message to kids that "sex and violence are right things to do." Most of the popular rap music is either a put-down of authority or of women. But the sickest themes in music are anti-Christian themes such as Marilyn Manson's "Antichrist Superstar," which questions the existence of God, and instead, encourages its listeners to believe in themselves.

Columnist Mona Charen gives one of the more shocking descriptions of Manson's character, his garish dress, self mutilation, grotesque props, Bible shredding, and acts of filth almost beyond imagination, which 40 years ago would have landed him in jail. In response to an article published in the *Washington Post*, (Escaping from our culturaldepravity, May 9, 1997). Charen writes: "The tone of the *Post* story about Manson conveys a great deal about why we have 'entertainment' like this. The tone is ironic and detached throughout. It adamantly refuses to be shocked. Protests against Manson are characterized as a 'rumpus.' His grotesque behavior is said 'sure to offend some sensibilities…but there's a segment of pop music that has moved beyond the furious snarl of punk rock.'" She goes on to say: "Has it never occurred to these folks that adults have a duty to be outraged? Some rebellious teenagers will always push the limits. It is the responsibility of the elders to push back. When teenagers rebel, it's like pushing on a string. And so the rebellion takes more and more outrageous forms in search of a response."

"Portrait of an American Family" is another put down to Christianity in which American Christians are described as "the biggest satan of all". The groups leader told *Guitar Magazine*, "Things need to go to the point of extremism in order to be born again, so we can once again appreciate the little things in life: sex, drugs and rock 'n' roll. It's my job to sort of cleanse the world of its sins." A line from Nine-Inch Nails goes, "He dreamed a God up and called it Christianity; God is dead and no one cares." The group Cannibal Corpse graphically describes killing a woman by strangulation. Lyrics by Ice-T and 2 Live Crew are about killing cops, glorifying violence to women, and the destruction of the female vagina. Among other gross and disgusting lyrics, two of Ice-T's lyrics include gang rape of a younger sister and oral sex performed on a sleeping mother.

There seems to be no end to the examples that illustrate the extent these radical leftists go with their obscenities, which they choose to foist upon teenagers. As bad as "The Coup's" lyrics on "5 million ways to kill a CEO," there are many more that are even worse.

> *5 million ways to kill a CEO*
> *slap him up and shake him up*
> *and then you*
> *Let him off the floor*
> *Then bait him with the dough*
> *You can do it funk or do it disco…*
> *Toss a dollar in the river and when he*
> *jump in*
> *If you find he can swim, put lead boots*
> *on him and do it again*
> *You and a friend videotape and the party don't end*

Along with the aforementioned, add Madonna and Michael Jackson performing before a live audience while having sex with themselves, and you have the ultimate in human degradation.

But what is a common media response to parents who protest the constant bombardment of sex, violence, and profanity on TV, music or any teen entertainment? We saw the typical irresponsibility of just how far secular humanistic programing has impacted one's ability to think rationally on this issue when the organization Concerned Viewers for Quality Television, hoping to get film makers attention, asked people to turn off their TV sets for one day. The typical liberal answer soon came from an anonymous staff member of *The Wichita Eagle*: "It's a meaningless gesture, an ironic substitute for thinking." The writer suggested people should make selective choices on a day-today, program-to-program basis for themselves and their families.

This sort of scrutiny is possible with small children, but an oversimplification to a very difficult problem where teenagers are concerned, as it is an impossible to involve oneself in monitoring everything older children watch without a "private eye". But the liberal left has a way of coming up with the most ridiculous arguments in defense of the garbage they support. They rationalize that movies are a reflection of what is seen in the dominate culture, but just the opposite is true—the culture begins to reflect what is seen in the movies. It seems the bottom line is that producers could care less; they are more interested in boosting ratings based on titillation and shock value, and if they accomplish that, they feel they have a great success.

Apparently, a good many film makers are unaware of the irony of their choices, that is, the most inspiring memorable movies are those of substance, simply because writers of these stories are adept at developing plots and characters and do not need to fill up space with violence, profanity, and explicit sexual scenes (a good indication of one's ineptitude at writing an interesting story). Yet film producers do not seem to recognize this fact. Their usual cop-out has become so redundant that we can anticipate the rationalizations for their own greed and irresponsible behavior—the exercise of the First Amendment rights, or conservative people merely want to stifle creativity and dictate morals.

Judge Robert H. Bork does an excellent job of nailing down the truth about dictating morals in his book, *Slouching Toward Gomorrah*. He writes: "Modern liberals try to frighten Americans by saying that religious conservatives 'want to impose their morality on others.' That is palpable foolishness. All participants in politics want to 'impose' on others as much of their morality as possible, and no group is more insistent on that than liberals. Religious conservatives are not authoritarian. To the degree they have their way, it will be through democratic processes. The culture would then resemble the better aspects of the 1950's, and that would be cause for rejoicing."

Back in the 70's, Frank Capra, three-time Oscar winner, saw the trend Hollywood was taking and decided to get out of the business of making movies. In his autobiography, he wrote: "The winds of change blew through the dream factories of make-believe, tore at its crinoline tatters....The hedonists, the homosexuals, the hemophiliac bleeding hearts, the God-haters, the quick-buck artists who substituted shock for talent, all cried: 'Shake 'em! Rattle 'em!" (And with the support of the major media, they have done just that.)

While this is only a small sampling of what is out there to severely undermine how kids think, and thus influence their values and their actions, a lot of concern and positive actions are being taken from every quarter in attempts to save the kids. Pastors are waking people up to the seriousness of this problem, both in church and on television. Some senators are speaking out on this issue. Senator Joseph Lieberman, (D. Conn.) says that MCA Records should be ashamed to promote Manson's band: "This is the sickest group ever promoted by a mainstream record company." Parents need to get on top of how their kids are "entertaining" themselves. The more the public complains about this kind of trash, the sooner it will diminish in popularity." Sadly, Senator Lieberman caved in on his Hollywood complaint during the 2000 election. Apparently, their money meant more to him than his convictions.

PROGRAMMING KIDS ON THE LIBERAL AGENDA

Why has the brainwash been so successful? It's "entertaining;" it's funny; or maybe it's because a lot of people don't like to think and reason about the point being made, whether it is the news talk shows, TV sitcoms, or movies. Otherwise, TV stations would have been swamped with letters and phone calls in opposition to some of our children's heroes. For instance, note the vulgarity of Madonna, the obscenity on MTV, the sexual escapades of child-doctor Doogie Howser on national television (one instance involving skinny dipping with his mother's boss); the class valedictorian, Andre, a star of "Beverly Hills, 90210," a "card-carrying liberal" who promotes condom distribution in school, and the teen show, "The Becky Bell Story" when it promoted a pro-abortion story line—and this is just a sampling of what is out there to impress impressionable young minds. It doesn't stop with teen shows either. The adult movie *Pretty Woman*, a story that glamorizes a prostitute's lifestyle, was plugged on TV as *The Cinderella Story*.

A poll taken by child advocacy group, *Children Now*, found that shows like "The Simpsons" and "Married With Children" influenced kids to be disrespectful to their parents. In response to the poll, Brent Bozell, chairman of the Media Research Center, had this to say: "Of course [children are] going to be influenced, and Hollywood pretends that there is no cause and effect. It is terribly destructive because television more than any other institution shapes the mind."

Even those shows that appear on the surface to be fairly innocent are usually pushing the left's liberal humanistic agenda. Their stories depict homosexuals, prostitutes, radical feminists, and pro-abortionists as wise, compassionate people pitted against policemen, conservatives, Christians, and pro-lifers as narrow-minded hateful people. Tolerance and political correctness are pushed everywhere. For instance, what could sound homier than the apple pie family-type show, entitled "Picket Fences." But the underlying messages are meant to indoctrinate viewers to think like liberals. In this show, conservatives are always proven wrong, as they are portrayed as less caring, while liberals are portrayed as wiser, nobler, compassionate and more just.

Many of these shows are no longer on the air, but what has replaced them is even more vulgar, so that the older shows may seem almost mild in comparison to them. L. Brent Bozell, III, who is Founder & President of Parents Television Council, gives a shocking list of the latest "entertainment" for children:

—On the WB Network they're giving children shows like "Buffy the Vampire," which contains grisly violence, masturbation and erotic homosexual fantasies.

—On Fox TV, children get shows like "Boston Public" set in a high school, where children will watch teenagers performing oral sex on each other in the hallways, or having sex with their teachers, with no moral consequences.

—On NBC, children see show like "Friends" featuring non-stop sexual innuendo including, this year, the promotion of lesbianism.

—and if they go to UPN Network, they get shows like "WWF Smackdown!—" in my opinion, one of the raunchiest, most violent programs ever produced for children.

The left has always accused conservatives as being abusers of the First Amendment, regarding any complaint they may have on gutter-type programing; but once polls establish that the majority favors a particular side on a given controversy, the left is then ready to take the popular stand. In fact, more than not, they end up claiming it as their own. The irony is that their hypocrisy often helps their opponents, giving them cause to be optimistic. For instance, the letters and phone calls to TV stations, as well as representatives in Congress, began to gradually pay off. Suddenly two favorite series, "Christy," and "I'll Fly Away," appeared on TV guides. Lowell Paxson, owner of several stations, committed himself to wholesome family programing. Some of his productions are "Touched by an Angel," "Promise Land," "Dr. Quinn, Medicine Woman," and "Seventh Heaven," and the word is there is more to come.

Brent Bozell and his organization is doing a tremendous job in trying to clean up the airways. Former Honorary Chairman, the late Steve Allen said, "Dirty shows will disappear from TV when they can't get sponsors," and that is just what Parents Television Council (PTC) is trying to do and with some good results. Bozell writes: "We are putting TV SPONSORS on notice—by putting the spotlight on them, directly and publicly, that every decision they make to sponsor a TV show has consequences. Our campaign is showing results!

"For example, we have taken the lead in convincing TV SPON-SORS to steer clear of some of the most offensive shows in history on network TV such as, 'Temptation Island,' 'Big Brother II,' 'The Howard Stern Show,' 'WWF Smackdown,' and 'Boston Public.'

"The decisions of major TV Sponsors—companies like Coca-Cola, Ford, GM, AT&T, Mars Candy, Wrigley Chewing Gum, Wendy's, and the U.S. Army—to withhold their commercials from shows like these added up to a huge victory for PTC and our members.

"On top of that, the almost-pornographic 'Big Brother II' was moved out of the TV Family-Hour, and 'The Howard Stern Show' sewage fest was canceled altogether!"

Anyone interested in supporting this organization with a donation of any kind, can contact them at this address: Parents Television Council, 707 Wilshire Blvd., Los Angeles, CA 90017.

Also, another possibility for parents is a satellite system called *Sky Angel*, which consists of 33 TV and radio channels featuring Christ-centered and family-friendly programming. It is a 24-hour network with programs for children. "TVU" is a new network, created for teen-agers. Anyone interested can call 1-888-sky-angel for a free informa-tion packet, or look it up on the internet at **www.skyangel.com.**

THE NATIONAL ENDOWMENT OF THE ARTS

The invasion of secular humanistic thinking has had an impact on every level of society, but nowhere has it wrought the depths of cultural destruction as we see in the National Endowment for the Arts (NEA). This organization's disgraceful exhibits are passed off as "art" under so-called "free speech," a popular term with liberals as a coverall for the "right" to express or engage in any sort of immorality.

Nevertheless, one does not have to be an artist to recognize that piles of feces, or a man's head up a rectum, is not art, but the brush rantings of a sick mind. Just as we began to think the human spirit had sunk to its lowest level, we were confronted with an even worse contamination. Apparently, the Christian symbol of Jesus Christ, the crucifix in a jar of urine, was not enough to satisfy someone's twisted mind. The blasphemy against our Christian God as a pedophile, as a man with a woman's body (breast bared) was even more revolting. And the sin is that Christian and non-Christian alike, seemingly without recourse, have been forced to support this cesspool with their tax dollars.

Don Feder gives his opinion of abject art exhibits as nothing more than dirt, hair, excrement, dead animals, menstrual blood and rotting food. He writes: "It has reached the point where all an exhibitionist needs is a warped imagination and multiple grievances to be hailed as an artistic genius...but if everything is art, nothing is art. (As *Time's* critic rhetorically asks, 'Is there any use in choosing anything over anything else'?") Why go to a museum, when the same aesthetic experience can be had peering into a toilet bowl, gaping at road-kills, listening to an Al Sharpton harangue, or visiting a landfill in mid-August?" And husband Ed agrees: "If everything is art, instead of going to a museum, just follow a dog around until he takes a crap."

Then there are columnists like Myrne Roe, recently retired from *The Wichita Eagle*, whose biggest concern on this issue is "a growing antipathy in Congress toward those Americans who strive daily to give the rest of us paintings with green skies and blue grass that challenge our thinking and lift our spirit." She goes on to say that if the NEA's funding is lost because of cost or of unpopular political decisions the organization has made, Congress "will fail Americans who cherish a civilized society to support the arts."

However, there is an important issue Roe did not address: Why are our tax dollars used to subsidize the hedonistic, in-your-face, uncivilized insults passed off as "art"? For instance, besides those examples already mentioned, a few others are Ron Athey's performance, in which he cut designs into a man's back who had AIDS, soaked up the blood with paper towels and threw it out onto the audience, or Tim Miller's act, disrobing before an audience and fondling himself, or Marion Rig's pornographic production of *Tongues Untied*: the blasphemous depictions of Christ, etc.—so much for green grass and blue skies, for lifted spirits cherished by a civilized society. (And I thought we were paying trash collectors to have this kind of garbage taken out of our lives. Why would anyone want to pay to get it back in?") However, things have settled down somewhat in the art industry since the uproar about the *Madonna* painting with its floating female sexual parts.

Why do Americans allow themselves to be deceived, used, insulted, and entertained by such vile stuff? Maybe it is because so many of us have been programmed, brainwashed, and misled by a majority of what we read and see. Much of it comes from the fraudulent technique of the secular humanists who know the persuasive power of commercials, and also how to use the technique to promote their own agenda —the appeal is to our emotional and prideful natures, the promise of success and happiness, and the offer of "new and improved" packaging (but less product at higher prices). In fact, it is hard to find an area of our lives where we are not being"commercialized" with incivility. The secret the programmers use is to bombard us with the images they want eventually to sink into our psyches until we internalize them as "normal." The next step is to bombard again with an even viler image, so that the previous one seems not so bad in comparison. Finally—the fatal attraction—there are no rights or wrongs (sound familiar?). My husband Ed summed it up this way. "One gets the impression that the NEA feels obligated to try to determine just how much trash the public is willing to take, and it is their duty to supply it."

Most conservatives thought that if we could just get a Republican president, the National Endowment for the Arts' (NEA) federal assistance would be significantly cut, but disappointedly, that has not happened with President George W. Bush. Only one grant has been denied in Bush's first year in office, the application to fund an exhibition for artist, William Pope, L. at Maine College of Art. Journalist Julia Duin of The Washington Times writes: 'Pope. L, may be best known for a work in which he walked around the Harlem section of New York City wearing a plastic male sex organ that occasionally deposited an egg onto the sidewalk. The application apparently was approved by the council but rejected by acting Chairman Robert S. Martin, a Bush appointee."

Perhaps the reason we have not seen more progress in the area of denying federal funding for obscene art is that, at the present time, Chairman Martin stands alone in his efforts to put a stop to some of the grosser aspects of the "art" world. The council he works with are holdovers from the Clinton Administration, "half of whom are serving on expired terms because the White House has not yet replaced them....One of six slots on the council for a member of Congress is also vacant. Michael P. Hammond, the Bush nomination for chairman of the NEA, is awaiting Senate confirmation." But given Majority Leader Tom Dashle's record so far, all of Bush's nominations will be delayed as long as he can possibly keep the Senate from voting on them.

EDUCATION

If the "die was cast" in the 60's, are we to be forever imprisoned by the secular humanist mind-set of that period? At times, it looks that way with so many university professors busy for decades pumping our socialist, humanist, fascist ideology with their "commercials" to rewrite and distort history, so that this and future generations will not realize that America's greatness came mainly from the fact it was founded on biblical principles. The tragedy is that this same humanistic agenda has trickled down to the innocent, fertile minds of children, who are now being indoctrinated by these philosophies—kindergarten through twelfth grades.

Lynne Cheney, head of National Endowment for the Humanities during President George H. W. Bush's administration, was concerned over the distortion of history. Apparently the birth of American democracy is not very important to today's "historians." According to Cheney, the new textbooks downplay the work of the founding fathers, making it secondary to the viewpoints of American natives, African-Americans, and peoples of different social classes and religions. Multiculturalism, woman's studies, the Ku Klux Klan, and the social customs of Mansa Musa (13th century) seem to be the big stories now. Men of great accomplishments are barely mentioned or omitted completely from the texts, like one of America's soldiers, General Robert E. Lee, who was considered by military strategists of the day to be a great general, so much so that he was asked to join the Union Army. Also gone from the pages of the new "history" are the contributions of men like Thomas Edison, Alexander Graham Bell, Albert Einstein, the Wright Brothers, Paul Revere, Daniel Webster, and Henry Clay.

Eagle Forum president Phyllis Schlafly in her March, 1995, newsletter spoke out against the revisionist history created by the National History Standards Project (NHSP) at the University of California in Los Angeles, and the institutes strategy to get its version enforced into law by sending out thousands of packets to teachers urging them to write to their congressmen to endorse the new history. Schafly said that the NHSP had recast history into an "entire panorama of one long conflict about race and gender, in which all ethnic groups except white males were portrayed as "victims." She claimed further that the "current crop of academic professionals are determined to drop the Dead White European Males down an Orwellian memory hole and to replace history with "Oppression Studies.'" Also, former American Federation of Teachers chairman, Al Shanker, said in regard to the new history: "If this document embodies a standard, it's a double standard. Practices of non-western civilizations are treated enthusiastically and uncritically. Those same practices, when carried out in the West, are scrutinized and criticized…this is the first time a government has tried to teach children to feel negative about their own country."

Syndicated columnist John Leo raises another question: "Are children being taught to feel negative about their own parents"? He talks about the Miranda program, a health curriculum used in several thousand public schools, in which students are given an assignment to check out their homes for poisons such as alcohol and tobacco, and to confess "problems at home" in secret messages to the teacher. Also, in the "human interaction program in Petaluma, California students are given worksheets to determine whether they live in an "open" or "democratic", or a "closed, authoritarian" family. Leo writes: "In Tucson, high school students were asked in a health class, 'How many of you hate your parents'? Oregon parents testified that in a 'values clarification' program, their children were asked, 'How many of you ever wanted to beat up your parents'"? He goes on to quote from Dana Mack's book, *The Assault on Parenthood: How Our Culture Undermines the Family,* saying that the author "makes the case that the crisis of the public school system is not simply the familiar one of academic failure. It's also that a new ethic, dismissive of parents and traditional values, has descended on the schools. 'At the heart of parents' frustration with the schools is a deep and unbridgeable chasm between vocabulary of moral dictates, rules and authority that parents think are best for children, and the vocabulary of autonomy and 'choices' that emanates from the classroom.'"

The fundamental problem with the left's educational agenda is it is, for one thing, too divisive. It is a system of classification, not unlike tribalism which always causes division and conflict—like Jesus said in Matthew 12:25: "Every kingdom divided against itself is brought to desolation; and every city or house divided against itself shall not stand." With the kind of diversity liberals are after, it is easy to understand why they are so attracted to political correctness—a system that limits freedom of expression and gives them more power and control.

About the subject of political correctness, Vice-President of Intercollegiate Studies Institute, Christopher Long said: "I think political correctness is really that group of tactics that has been used by the left on campus…to silence conservative students and conservative opinion on campus." A study by the national association of English professors, The Modern Language Association, seems to bear Long's view out, showing that approximately 40% of English courses are taught from a Marxist perspective, and 60% from a feminist perspective.

In 1991 two officials at Yale College, Dean Donald Kagan, and President Benno Schmidt, agreed that their professors should prioritize Western Civilization as a core study rather than favoring multicultural studies. Not only did both men have to step down from their positions, but the Western Civilization classes were not extended. In fact, the school returned a $29 million donation given for the purpose of extending that particular class, and then went on to create gay and lesbian classes with other donations. And we wonder what is wrong with education in the schools today.

Another subject that gets a lot of space in classes K-12 is sex education. Thomas Sowell, columnist for *Forbes* magazine, likens the seriousness of the problem of the current sex education program to war. He writes, "If there is anything worse than being in war, it is being in war and not knowing it." He says the claims the left makes that their programs will reduce teen pregnancy, venereal disease, and drug usage are just politically effective ways of getting these programs into the schools—they remain even when hard evidence shows that the problem they were supposed to solve is, in fact, getting worse." He goes on to say, "More is being done in this area with the nation's children than parents realize." He explains further how the brainwashing process is brought into the schools "under such names as 'decision-making,' 'values clarification,' or even 'gifted and talented' programs"—all of which "have little to do with their actual content."

According to Sowell, "The overarching message of these programs is that there is no such thing as right or wrong, that traditional values in general must be discarded as old prejudices, so that the individual can construct his or her own values to reflect his or her own feelings." And we see this kind of thinking perfectly analogous with the psychology of the *Humanist Manifesto II* which says: "In the area of sexuality, we believe that intolerant attitudes often cultivated by orthodox religions and puritanical cultures, unduly repress sexual conduct...the many varieties of sexual exploration should not inthemselves be considered 'evil'."

Sowell's analysis of the "names game" just further validates the fact that secular humanist are prone to operate through deception. Believing the means justifies the end, they deliberately hide the meaning of their intent with words that carry built-in judgments, words that are likely to plant seeds of acceptance in the minds of parents for programs they ordinarily would not accept.

Everyone admits that something is wrong with the educational system, but liberals do not seem to have the capacity to face reality. Their ideas are invariably to get away from basics and go with divisive programs like multiculturalism and situational ethics, and above all to keep throwing money into things proven not to work. The California schoolsystem is a good example of this kind of irrational thinking. The state spends over 45% of its entire budget on education, and yet California students rank 35th in the nation on test scores; its fourth graders finished next to last on a national reading test. Polls show that public school teachers in the state are nearly twice as likely as the general population to choose private schooling for their own children.

However, this dismal record did not stop the California Teachers Association from doing everything in its power to defeat the school voucher initiative when it came up for vote in 1994. The Association assessed its 25,000 members $63 to fund a $6 million media blitz against their opponents, in which they went into overkill with exaggerated claims to scare parents. They inducted school children, giving them campaign literature to take home to their parents to inform them that "witches" and "Aryan supremacist" would be the new teachers of their children, and high school kids were indoctrinated with the Association's posters which were plastered in the hallways of their schools. In other words, if euphemisms aren't enough to sway voters, the liberals way is to use scare tactics.

Well, they have scared us! There is clear evidence that the witches have taken over the curriculum and the hex is in, via a textbook "*Across the Centuries"* (published by Houghton-Mifflin, Boston, MA), which has been adopted throughout the California school systems (Special to ASSIST News Service, or ANS, Jan. 29, 2002). The Byron Union School District puts its 7th-grade students through an intensive three-week study of the Islamic religion. This study goes far beyond teaching ancient culture and history, as the principal of one of the schools, Nancy Castro, would have parents believe. "It is not religion," she says. "We do not endorse any religion. We just make students aware." But the requirements of the course clearly say otherwise. One doesn't have to be a "brain" to see that the lessons are designed to indoctrinate and program innocent minds to embrace the Muslim religion.

For instance, students are required to pretend they are Muslims, pick Muslim names, wear robes, learn the tenets of Islam, memorize scriptures from the Koran, stage their own jihad, and give a report on what a trip to Mecca would be like. Furthermore, the memorization includes 25 Islamic terms, 6 Islamic phrases, 20 Islamic Proverbs, and Five Pillars of Faith and the study of 10 key Islamic prophets and disciples. And that isn't all! Students are taught to pray in the name of "Allah, the Compassionate, the Merciful" and to chant, "Praise to Allah, Lord of Creation."

Absolutely everything in the textbook is biased in favor of a loving and kind Islamic religion. There is no mention of the cruel treatment of women, nor the cruelties inflicted on their own people, such as cutting off hands and feet, or beheading them for "infractions" of the religion. Neither does the text teach that the god Muhammad was man's creation, but that he is the same god as the Christian God. The ANS report goes on to say: "Arabia was a pagan nation that worshiped over 300 gods. One of those was the moon god named, al-ilah....To this day a crescent moon can be found at the front of every mosque, acknowledging that Allah was, and is the moon god." Also, the text portrays Muhammad as an "extremely moral man, but he had multiple wives, a sexual problem, and among his wives, he took a 10-year-old girl for his pleasure (some accounts list her age as 6)." But this so-called history book omitted these important facts.

On the other hand, all references to Christianity are negative and restricted to "The Reformation, Martin Luther, and the Catholic Church." Along with distorting some biblical facts, the text teaches that only one religion persecutes other religions—you guessed it, Christianity…" with events such as the Inquisition, the Salem witch-hunts, etc., highlighted in bold, black type."

Elizabeth Christina Lemings, a 7th-grade teacher in the Byron school district says that students are not allowed to mention Jesus or to wear crosses to school, and yet when she asked the principal if she would allow Christianity to be taught, Nancy Castro said that italready is. But according to Mrs. Lemings, the "Christianity that is taught is brief, taught as a myth, and strictly negative," and the textbook portrays it the same way.

Mrs. Lemings goes on to say: "Can you imagine the barrage of lawsuits and problems we would have from the ACLU if Christianity were taught in the public schools, and if we tried to teach about the contributions of Matthew, Mark, Luke, John and the apostle Paul? But when it comes to furthering the Islamic religion in the public schools, there is not one word from the ACLU, People For the American Way or anybody else. This is hypocrisy."

ANS quotes Omar M. Ahmad, chairman of the board of the Council on American-Islamic relations, in an announcement he made at the Flamingo Palace Banquet Hall: "I urge Muslims not to shirk their duty of sharing the Islamic faith with those who are on the 'wrong-side'." If you choose to live here, you have a responsibility to deliver the message of Islam…Islam isn't in America to be equal to any other faith, but to become dominant. The Koran should be the highest authority in America, and Islam the only accepted religion on earth."

I consider this situation a crisis. Actually, the Islam religion has been taught in the California schools for several years, but parents didn't really wake up to the fact until September 11, 2001. If nothing is done about it in California, it will eventually be in all the states. "Where is the media? Where is the Congress? Where is the outrage? Addresses are as follows for anyone interested in voicing their opinion on this issue:

The California Department of Education; phone (916) 657-2451; e-mail: **destine@cde.ca.gov**

Byron Union School District, 14401 Byron Hwy., Contra Costa, CA 94514; Phone 634-6644. Also national senators and representatives at the Capitol switchboard: (202) 224-3121. (Addresses, courtesy Central Christian Observer, Wichita, Kansas).

Unfortunately, there doesn't seem to be any limit to what the liberals are willing to inflict on American children, in the name of "diversity," or "tolerance," or whatever. If there ever was a time when parents needed school vouchers, it is now. No matter how the story is spun, schools in New York are on a drive to bring as many kids as possible into homosexuality, and so we should be looking at all options to put these peddlers of moral degradation out of business. At one time private management of public schools was being considered as a viable option, but that idea seems to have fallen by the wayside. During the Clinton Administration, Senator Joe Lieberman, (D.) of Connecticut, and Rep. Dave Weldon, (R.) of Florida, advocated a nationwide pilot program for school choice, to be reviewed by Congress in three years so parents would have the option of choosing what is best for their child. But since teacher's unions wanted to keep the status quo, and in order to maintain their vast voting block, Clinton promised to veto it. These proposals were not for the purpose of eliminating the public school system, as the National Education Association would have us believe, but were for the purpose of creating competition as a means to bring about better education for all children.

A LIBERAL CONVERTS!

Nothing makes a conservative's case more than when a liberal finally sees the "light."Such a person is historian Ronald Radosh, a former left-wing activist and member of the Communist Party. He joined the party in the 1950's, so one might surmise that he was once a died-in-the-wool-radical leftist, since that time period was the scene of the McCarthy congressional trials that ruined the reputations of many people, and even some who were innocent of the communist label. Today, Radosh is a changed man. In an interview by a senior writer for *Insight* magazine, Stephen Goode, the former communist described himself as a moderate conservative ("Historian Takes a Political U-Turn," December 17, 2001).

When queried: "Then there is the left on American campuses? Radosh responded: "Yes, and it's the worst, most ridiculous example of what the left has become. It's always the elite colleges that are the worst. Brown University in Providence, Rhode Island, Wesleyan in Connecticut, Vassar in Poughkeepsie [N.Y.]. It's those schools—their bodies, their administrations, their faculties—that are the most politically correct and the most offensive when it comes to curtailing the speech of anybody who has a position that they consider conservative. It's at these schools that administrators prevent people who favor the war [presently, terrorist war] from speaking out even as they allow anti-war actions."

Mr. Radosh's theory as to why the elite schools always indulge in anti-Americanism is basically because they come from rich families and do not have to work and "can afford to be full-time radicals and revolutionaries." He goes on: "Also I think the faculties of these colleges, particularly the humanities faculties, have been taken over by the left. They target English faculties. The history departments are filled with lefties. And look at the courses that are taught—the kooky, far-out courses in the college catalogues that are geared in a very narrow way toward gender, class and race…The departments are politicized, and they're all politicized in the same way."

Explaining how the trend of communism expansion has changed in the universities since he was a college student, Radosh says: "Both the American Historical Association and Organization of American Historians now have presidents who are pro-communist Marxists, who gave politicized, left-wing speeches [upon assuming their presidencies]. Thirty years ago many leftist were traditional in the sense we believed that history was a very serious, scholarly undertaking with standards. Now you have whole fields of history which are totally politicized in the craziest ways."

Asked for an example of these ways, Radosh responded with the case of the Jewish merchant, Leo Frank, who was lynched in Atlanta in the 1920's. An article had been written up in the *Journal of American History* by a female historian. "At the end of the article there were three paragraphs attacking Ronald Reagan and the Reagan presidency. This was the lead article in the journal…What did Reagan have to do with the Frank lynching? Nothing! But there it was, confirming that anything is possible if you're on the left." Radosh went on to say that a conservative could not get away with this kind of "history."

"SITUATIONAL ETHICS" IN HIGH PLACES

Another consequence of replacing absolutes with the so-called new freedoms is the apparent lack of responsibility and accountability seen everywhere in our society today. Although there is enough guilt to go around, it has, indeed, been discouraging to see how commonplace it is for so many to ignore doing what they ought to do, and nowhere has it been more evident than in the highest offices of our country—Washington D.C., for instance. While it is essential to have strong debate when people have honest ("honest,"the key word here) disagreement on issues, this business of continually running for re-election instead of governing is downright disgusting and counterproductive. One would think that having honored positions of authority and privilege would be enough to fulfill the desires of both the members of the White House administration and Congress, but that doesn't seem to be the case—nor does the special perks and lavish pension funds from which they retire in grand style seem to satisfy many of them. Instead, the public is subjected to their constant celebrity-image building and their poll watching to see what will make them even more powerful. Moreover, much of what they do, or do not do, is done with great exaggeration, if not outright lies, and with the dramatics of ham actors.

The truth is our leaders' behavior have often correlated very well with the humanists' definition of "ethics." Tenet Three of *Manifesto II* reads: "We affirm that moral values derive their source from human experience. Ethics is autonomous and situational." (In other words, there are no absolutes.) How many of our leaders have abused their power, with the aid of the mainstream media, is one of the important subjects of this book.

We have seen the impact of "situational ethics" and how it works to protect the guilty. Throughout the '90's, whatever the misdeed, it soon became evident that "saving" the perpetrator was the only thing that mattered, that is if he or she was of the correct party.

A good example of the double standard was played out by former Speaker of the House, Tom Foley, who successfully squelched information on the Post Office scandal (headed by his wife). And there were Foley's "sweetheart deals" made with special interests that had landed him hundreds of thousands of dollars, but because of his position and power, these misdeeds were largely swept under the rug. But that's not the end of situational ethics in Foley's case. His character spoke for itself, and we should not have been too surprised at his power as a squelcher of the truth, given his penchant for wheeling and dealing to ensure a one-party government in which his opponents were locked out of the political process almost completely—that is, kicked off committees unless they were in total agreement with the ruling party at that time in order to prevent their bills and amendments coming to vote.

Ironically, his party can't seem to call for enough bipartisanship when they are not in the driver's seat.

Despite Foley's power to manipulate events where it suited his needs, he strongly recommended accountability for those he opposed. He thought there should be an investigation on former President Bush who was accused of delaying hostage release from Iran—supposedly done to aid Ronald Reagan's 1984 re-election chances—even though, as Foley admitted, there wasn't any evidence to warrant an investigation. His reasoning: "It would clear the air about this situation." But when the tables turned, those Foley supporters did not want an honest investigation to take place with a member of their own party, despite a mountain of evidence that suggested something was very wrong in the Clinton administration.

The 90's was a classic period of deception in high places, a time when we witnessed again and again the machinations of the a few who abused their power under media eyes that refused to be outraged. Those in the position of responsibility and power put their brand of "ethical" control buttons on at will, thus stifling unanswered questions regarding the Vincent Foster suicide and anything related to Whitewater, or to Travelgate, Filegate, Campaign Financegate, and all the other gates.

SOME END RESULTS

With society either desensitized, indoctrinated, or intimidated by labels like fanatic, meanspirited, racist, etc., liberals were able to confuse the voters and easily able to stack the offices of power with radical far-left-wingers during Bill Clinton's first term. This explains how former ACLU lawyer, Ruth Bader Ginsburg, was confirmed for the U.S. Supreme Court; how the 'priestess of politically correctness," Donna Shalala, was appointed to the Department of Health and Human Service; how a doctor from Arkansas, whose sex education programs not only failed in that state but also increased the misery it supposedly was to alleviate, became the new surgeon general for the United States (and then Congress came close to confirming her clone); and how a militant feminist, who went against the Boy Scouts because they were "morally straight," and who, along with her live-in, brought her 7-year old son to the 1993 San Francisco Gay Pride parade where he watched his mother publically smooch her female lover as they edged their way through the street, flanked on either side by cheering crowds, and where he was also allowed to witness the disgusting portrayal of "God" and "Uncle Sam" having anal intercourse, became the assistant secretary for the Department of Housing and Urban Development—and the public didn't even bat an eye.

Do these people see themselves as "self-actualized"? Is this the change Americans had in mind when they voted in the Clinton Administration? I think not. Sounds more like Americans wore blinders and stuck their heads in the sand and were led by the nose down the path of deception.

3

Contributions of the Feminist Movement?

"Who can find a virtuous woman? for her price is far above rubies...Her children rise up, and call her lessed; her husband also, and he praises her."—Proverbs 31:10,28

Another by-product of the 60's was the ugly turn the feminist move-ment took. While initially, the revolution started out as a noble endeavor to secure equality for women, particularly in the workplace, it was destined to breed havoc and divisiveness on the American family, Nevertheless, we certainly do applaud those in the movement who worked for and attained some positive things for women. But the problem lies in the fact that from the very beginning, the feminist agenda was under the supreme leadership of jealous women who deluded themselves into believing that because they were dissatisfied with their lot that all women suffered victimization at the hands of men, especially if they were white men. Had the feminist goals been merely to attain more respect and equality for women, so many of our cultural values which were needlessly trampled on and discarded, would have stood the test that comes with changing times, but that was not to be the case. These ladies were hard-core-militant types, who were not after fairness, but total domination of the sexes. Once again, the influence of secular humanistic thought was making inroads through America in the name of equality.

The help women were to receive in achieving fulfillment, more than not, backfired, inflicting unlimited damage to the traditional culture of Americans. Beside the flip-side of machoism, which women say they abhor, we got an even more arrogant tyranny, "femochoism," causing a lot of women, as well as a lot of men and children, the loss of their identities. The pluses to society have often been overshadowed by the ensuing family break-ups and all the dreadful fallout that entails.

It appears that many of the militant-feminist leaders, consciously or subconsciously, do not like being women, as they cannot even accept the differences in physical attributes between the sexes, let alone the innate emotional and spiritual differences, without which there would be little attraction for the opposite sex.

Columnist Debra J. Saunders doesn't mince words on this subject. She spoke out against the militant haranguing of the feminist in one of her syndicated columns, "NOW a shrillness became embarrassment to feminists," in which she stated the aberrations of the feminist movement perfectly, describing to a "T" many of the gung-ho females heading the *National Organization of Women* (*NOW*) who sound like, as she said, "nagging, overreacting, whining, fishwives."

If this indictment of militant feminist leaders sounds exaggerated and too harsh, lets' refresh our memories by revisiting their convention where they drew up their constitution, a document that clearly shows how far they have moved from traditional beliefs of the Bible (which states that "God hates divorce"), and how they have moved so deeply into the secular humanistic mold of thought.

Most of us would agree that there are legitimate reasons for divorce —I certainly do not advocate getting rid of it, but these gals are radical. For instance, at their Houston, Texas convention (1971), "The Declaration of Feminism," with crude bluntness, blasted marriage: "Marriage has existed for the benefit of man; and has been a legally sanctioned method of control over women...we must work to destroy it. The end of the institution of marriage is a necessary condition for the liberation of women to leave their husbands….All of history must be written in terms of the oppression of women." That women bought into this insanity is one thing, but that some men actually took the side of the feminist agenda, which in essence tells them to "get lost," is even more amazing.

And set out to dissolve marriages, they did. Pat Robertson states the effects of broken families in his book *The New Millennium*: "Every sociological test that has been taken for years has indicated that prolonged absence of either parent is damaging to children. Prolonged absence of the father or of the mother leads to dependency, lack of assertiveness, submission to peer pressure, susceptibility to drugs, inferior performance in school."

Another tenet of the feminist Declaration says "We must go back to ancient female religions like witchcraft." Commenting on this idea, Robertson talks about Bible times and the admiration Roman men had for Christian women whom they described as 'extraordinary.' "There was something about those Christians. They weren't like the ordinary heathen women. They had a poise and a dignity, and a stability and radiance about them that was different.

THE ENTERTAINMENT INDUSTRY

These hard-core militant feminists are generally an unhappy, bitter lot —always complaining, embracing lifestyles conducive to dissolving marriage and destroying family life, and, apparently, want very little to do with their inborn-feminine natures. Even so, it isn't so amazing that such a destructive philosophy caught on and spread like wildfire throughout the country when one considers the various sources these radical feminist had at their disposal. The entertainment industry is a major culprit. Instead, of supporting positive elements of the feminist movement, it lent its full support to everything that was destructive about the movement. For instance, themes in movies and television shows, for the most part, have been in direct dispute to traditional family values—replaced by single moms, promiscuity, and alternate lifestyles, all of which the media calls "tolerance"in order to support their own agenda—so that intact families virtually disappeared from the screen for several years. As a result, much of the feminist agenda has done a lot of harm to our male population. The sorry plight of too many boys can no longer be denied. They are behind girls academically, but ahead of girls in dropping out of school, getting on drugs, becoming alcoholics, joining gangs, committing crimes, etc. Boys top girls in every area if the news is bad, and yet the big push is to elevate girls. I am for elevating girls, but not at the expense of creating low self-esteem and self-destructive behaviors in boys, and that is exactly what has happened. Despite all I have said in defense of boys, and what documentation shows to be true, the sexual revolution is backfiring on girls too, which we will see later in this chapter.

The following is one of my letters that *The Wichita Eagle* published in June of 2001, which was a response to an anonymous caller to the paper's Opinion Line, which I think pretty much explains an ongoing-smear campaign against men.

The "Fool" in the House

Let me see, we've had three decades of television shows and an overabundance of movies that denigrate men, denouncing them as nitwits, or some kind of uncaring jerks, while their wives and kids (the latter adultlike beyond their years) have it all together. They, of course, are always busy saving the day from the "fool" in the their house.

Never mind that society has literally been screaming from the top of its collective lungs, via schools, courts, social services, etc., that the effects of making fathers irrelevant and worthless to the family unit has devastating repercussions. Yet we have people like the person who called in to the Opinion Line, May 29, in regard to ABC's cartoon "Lloyd in Space," which "made all men look like wimps and all women seem capable of doing anything," responding that "turn about is fair play." The caller made it clear that she had a bitter childhood situation, and therefore, apparently thinks it is okay that all men suffer humiliation in her desire for revenge.

The unhappy results of what is happening to the male population are occasionally showing up in TV documentaries which show just how vicious this mindset gets. Even judges are swayed by the feminist rhetoric. Granted there are many male devils, but the deck is usually stacked against all men, even before a hearing takes place. We are seeing too many documentaries where some ex-wives can't be cruel enough. They find ways to make their children hate their fathers, and ways to circumvent court orders to prevent fathers from seeing their own children.

MURPHY BROWN

I've always thought it odd that these militant feminists who were so outraged by former Vice President Dan Quayles' comment about the *Murphy Brown* show when he expressed concern over single mothers and the difficult job they have in raising their children in the ghetto—worrying about drive-by shootings, drugs, gangs, etc.—and yet couldn't see the blight under their own noses. He said: "It doesn't help matters when prime time TV has Murphy Brown—a character who supposedly epitomizes today's intelligent, highly paid, professional woman—mocking the importance of fathers, by bearing a child alone, and calling it just another lifestyle choice." Feminists went berserk, and media harassment of Quayle went on and on until his original intent was totally twisted into something mean.

But isn't it amazing how quickly we forget the liberal mindset on a particular issue? What Dan Quayle said in his speech was pooh-poohed and criticized beyond belief, but now is accepted as insightful and wise counsel. Basically, the theme of Quayle's speech on this issue said: "When families fail, society fails." He emphasized the fact that the government is really not the solution to the welfare state, that "marriage is probably the best anti-poverty program of all....For the government, transforming underclass culture means that our policies and programs must create a different incentive system. Our policies must be premised on, and must reinforce values such as family, hard work, integrity, and personal responsibility....Children need love and discipline. They need mothers and fathers....A welfare check is not a husband. The state is not a father. It is from parents that children learn how to behave in society; it is from parents above all that children come to understand values and themselves as men and women, mothers and fathers....Even though our cultural leaders in Hollywood, network TV, and the national newspapers routinely jeer at [these ideas], I think that most of us in this room know that some things are good, and other things are wrong. Now it's time to make the discussion public. It's time to talk again about family, hard work, integrity, and personal responsibility."

Apparently, after reading the polls, Mr. Clinton decided he was no longer "sick and tired of hearing about family values," and that Dan Quayle was right after all. As the pattern went at that time, the major media took its cue from what came out of the White House, and it soon became fashionable to talk about family values.

Considering how outraged women were over Quayle's Murphy Brown comment, I wondered why the same outraged women rarely, if ever, showed any concern over the stereotyping of "intelligent, highly paid, professional female" actresses on TV and in movies who are portrayed much like dogs in heat. Female characters, more often than not, sexually stampeded heir male acquaintances (usually unmarried, at least to one another), invite them to their bedrooms where they, in a state of uncontrolled frenzy, rip off their clothes as they enter into what looks like a lip-chewing contest, etc., etc. And this scenario includes their most casual acquaintances, and sometimes those of only a few minutes. The only difference between these women and prostitutes is that no money is involved. This is classic "femachoism," and sadly, girls are learning this behavior by what has become commonplace in movies and on TV. It is my understanding that teenage girls are now the carriers of condoms, as well as the initiators of procuring a date. Actually, men have nothing to brag about—they are not innocent. They are no different than the "Johns," either. The double standard is that they get off the hook.

CHARGING THE GATES OF ADULTHOOD

While I sympathize the plight of boys, I also sympathize the plight of girls. My complaints are not directed to females, per se, but against the militant feminist who have been successful in confusing and distorting the innate physical and emotional natures of males and females. While the sexual revolution has not been the friend to woman as many of them have believed, there has been for the past several years a gradual awakening and rethinking of this kind of "freedom," and the ensuing grave consequences that often follow.

We have read and heard a lot about the distressed condition of so many women who put their trust in the new morality—unwanted pregnancies, single motherhood, divorce, poverty, etc.—but little has been brought to our attention about the little grade-school girls who are already entering this same path of disillusionment. These children are suffering the consequences of the feminist movement, but in different ways than their male counterparts.

Carol Lynn Mithers raises some disturbing "red flags" in her article, "Teens too soon," for the *Ladies' Home Journal*, March, 2002 issue. She begins with a birthday party for an eleven-year-old girl: "When the cake comes out, slowly, smiles dim and heads begin to shake. 'None for me,' say several guests. 'I'm on a diet. I really need to lose some weight.'" Does this sound like children?

Ms. Mithers moves on to an elementary school where girls are talking about having sex and dating. But why not? The onslaught of sexual content is everywhere, so that. children are literally being fast forwarded into a quasi-adulthood. A report put out by the Girl Scouts

Research Institute, acquired from interviews conducted with several hundred girls, ages 8–12, found that most girls in this age group felt "pressured to behave like teenagers." Many experience what is called "developmental compression," meaning to grow more sophisticated at younger ages. These children are preoccupied with their appearance. One ten-year-old said: "Girls aren't supposed to do strenuous stuff. Girls draw flowers. Girls play with their nails or brush their hair." Another ten-year old offered her views: "You start worrying about your looks by the fifth grade. Whether your clothes are fashionable. Whether you are pretty."

Mither's research also showed that children are encouraged to think beyond their age levels. For instance, even kindergarten kids today have homework; 6 year olds "face the rigors of standardized tests; teachers are talking to them about college; and television pushes sex and beauty at them from commercials, to cartoons, to sitcoms." She says further: "While premature worldliness effects both sexes, parents and developmental experts worry more about the early preoccupation with gender and sex among girls. Speaking of girls between ages 8 and 12, Catherine Weigel Foy, M.S.W., an associate director at the Family Institute at Northwestern University, in Evanston, Illinois, and a therapist for middle school girls and their mothers, says: 'Girls should be children who feel they can do anything. This should be time to discover who you are—to be active and courageous and to revel in achievement. Being a girl should be secondary to being, say, an athlete or a computer wizard.'"

Mithers goes on to say: "Whether or not they are physically mature, girls under 12 increasingly see themselves as sexual beings. Preteen dress is often provocative…and tight mini skirts have become standard issue in stores catering to young girls." One mother complained: "What's out there is too grown-up. Does she understand these clothes are sexy as opposed to just fashionable or popular? Yes."

As anyone might guess, business takes advantage of the situation, knowing full well that there is money to be made from these eager kids to "fit in." "With this come-hither dressing comes other adult behavior —romantic interests in boys, awareness of sex, and dating that begins as early as fourth and fifth grades....Eight to 12 year olds spend more than $50 billion a year of their own money and influence another $250 billion in family spending. Hence the marketing of overly sophisticated clothes and preteen cosmetics. Magazines aimed at young girls are rife with sex and sexual imagery; read through one and you'll find an ad with a model in an open blouse (revealing a hint of naked breasts) clutching her inner thighs, and a feature on young male singers that shows them half naked. "

Another ten-year-old unwittingly pretty much sums up the curse on American children: "By fourth grade, you have worries about grades, boys, and your body. By fifth grade, everything's changed—the way you feel, the way you act and look. You're not a kid anymore."

INSTITUTIONALIZED SUPPORT

Another inroad the feminist movement made to demolish the traditional family was the push for women's studies in universities. These studies equate motherhood with the annihilation of women, and were, and are, not much more than organized hate-training sessions against men. Buttressed by giant political lobbyist such as the National Education Association (NOW) and Planned Parenthood, they were able to expand the idea of "there are no absolutes' philosophy (secular humanism in progress), and take control of the curriculum agenda. But with the polls indicating people were interested in restoring family values, President Clinton and the media jumped on the bandwagon in a big hurry. NOW was then forced to tone down its rhetoric considerably. They soon became less vocal about blathering in the background, never missing a chance to present their views as the answer to everything for women, continually lumping all of us together as though we were robots, droning on and on, saying "women think...women want..."

A plus for the women's movement is that it has helped women careerwise. A minus is it has done a lot to instill anger and a desire for revenge against male abuses. Admittedly some abuse is all too real and should be brought to light and action taken against it, but thanks to organizations like NOW, a good deal of abuse and sexual harassment has been blown out of proportion—in fact, manufactured and pressure cooked to the point of absurdity. The fact that radical feminist think men should think and act exactly as women do has caused some of the most extreme and abnormal situations. For instance, especially in the workplace, men became fearful of complimenting a woman; careful of how they asked for a date; cautious of the age-old flirtations between one single person to another—it might be sexual harassment! Even little boys, as shown in an earlier chapter, were punished for playing tag—again, sexual harassment! Women's organizations literally put men in straight jackets, with women overseeing the lunacy to make sure everything was politically correct.

There is still another divisive tactic the feminist movement used to gain power and control over its subjects. Beginning in the 60's, leaders of the cultural war continuously and methodically brainwashed the average young woman into believing that somehow she was really a nobody if she stayed home with her children and took care of the household chores. The feminist leadership made these women feel that their sense of fulfillment could only be attained if they put their ambitions above family and competed with men—not that there is anything wrong with a woman having a career, but no woman should be made to feel guilty if she chooses to be a homemaker. Any of us who have daughters, friends, or relatives of baby-boomer age know definitely that these women felt themselves inadequate and were ashamed to admit they were "only" housewives. We heard it all too often, first hand from their lips.

POLITICALLY CORRECT

Retired columnist of *The Wichita Eagle*, Myrne Roe, is a good example of someone who bought lock stock and barrel the ideas that came out of the '60's. One can imagine she has a handbook put out by NOW that "prescribes her essential nature" for her, to which she can refer to make sure she is always politically correct.

During the heat of the '92 presidential campaign, in her column "Essential nature can't be prescribed" (September 17), she attacked one of her favorite enemies, Marilyn Quayle, with such bitterness and gross exaggerations, I found myself questioning how secure Roe was in her own identity as a woman. I wondered, too, how she could justify her accusations that Marilyn Quayle thinks a woman's essential nature is to stay home and perform the tasks of cooking, grocery shopping, dusting, teaching her girls to wear pink, pleasing the man of the house while getting her identity through him, laughing at mother-in-law jokes, and speaking when her hubby says it's okay. Really!

Having said women's essential nature can't be prescribed, Roe then ended up prescribing the experiences that are "okay" for women: wives, mothers, cooks, authors, workers, universities, divorcees, single parents, book readers, and travelers (what a relief this varied list must have been to many women who wanted to be sure they fit the politically correct prescribed mold). Ironically, Roe seemed to be oblivious to the fact that many things on her "okay" list applied to Marilyn Quayle.

Contrary to what Myrne Roe said, I think it is safe to say that most women saw Marilyn Quayle as a woman who knew who she was/is—a woman with high moral standards, a role model for her children, a supportive wife mutually supported by her husband, and an intelligent, educated, articulate person who appears to be able to balance married life, raising kids, attending church (and maybe baking cookies too) with getting an education and achieving a professional career.

Planned Parenthood

Although Planned Parenthood has softened its rhetoric considerably, I think they have done teenage girls a disservice. The truth is this organization has promoted sexual activity among the teen population for years. Oh, yes, now they let everyone know they talk to the girls about abstinence, but that subject was forced on them because of complaints by churches and other conservative organizations. And since these alternative sources were having very good success with their programs, Planned Parenthood decided to get some unwarranted recognition by convincing the public they are doing the same thing. The truth is the leaders of Planned Parenthood brag boldly, thoughtlessly and irresponsibly, stating their objective, which is to serve teens with information on condoms and ways to keep parents in the dark. The subject of abstinence takes up very little of their time and gets mere lip service.

The 700 Club sent two girls in to get Planned Parenthood literature, and they were encouraged by the counselors to experiment sex in different ways. If their parents did not understand that they wanted to be sexually active, the advice was "don't tell them." If that isn't encouragement for these girls to have sex, I don't know what it. Anyone who may feel inclined not to trust *The 700 Club* as a source of information on this issue might check its assertions out through another source.

The truth of the matter is kids already know what to do to keep from getting pregnant. They know more about sex and contraceptives than any past generation in history. So far, most sex education has helped to alert kids to be ready for sex, makes others want to get ready, and makes others feel something is wrong with them if they don't get ready. In the meantime, maybe Planned Parenthood ought to consider changing its name to something that fits their services more appropriately, like "Sex Information for Kids and How to Keep Parents in the Dark." Ed says, "To sum it up Planned Parenthood tells teenage girls that there is nothing wrong with having premarital sex, and there is nothing wrong with having an abortion."

THE ELITIST CLIQUE CLUB

Despite the constant drill we have been subjected to over the years, there is reason for optimism, as more conservative women have decided they have been silent long enough, and are speaking out against the propaganda and the fallibility of the feminist leaders. Michelle Malkin of the *Los Angeles Daily News* says that the success of the feminist so-called push for equality has caused another big problem. She says there are not enough role models for young girls in the mainstream culture today, and furthermore "white men are no longer the blame, but the women themselves." Malkin describes these militant feminists as a "clique of Virtuous Female Role Models" who are "as clannish, privileged and fiercely self-preserving as any private men's-only golf club still standing."

She supports her description of the ladies with a brief critique of (D.Calif.) Barbara Boxer's book, *Strangers in the Senate: Politics and the New Revolution of Women in America*, which Malkin says "reads like an open love letter to herself and her close female friends. She [Boxer, the ham] writes glowingly of female colleagues who are among the most left-wing, anti-military, pro-spending representatives in Congress." Who are the famous "role models" that Malkin says "belong to the clique of virtuous females?" They are 1) the author of the forward, Hillary Rodham Clinton, whom Boxer "praises as a role model and pioneer;" 2) the "Fawning reviewers on the back cover, Congresswoman Pat Schroeder, D-Col. (now retired), and Hollywood actress-singer Barbara Streisand;" and 3) "the first photograph in *Strangers*, a beaming Boxer sandwiched between Streisand the feminist icon Anita Hill."

Malkin goes on to say, "I'm tired of watching women receive acclaim for exploiting their emotions and their sex. And the double standards are wearing thin. Streisand is famous for complaining about such differential treatment in the entertainment industry; A man is commanding—a woman is demanding. 'A man is forceful—a woman is pushy. He's assertive—she's aggressive. He strategizes—she manipulates.'" The point I think Malkin makes is that Miss Streisand can't see past her nose and recognize these femacho traits in the female characters in movies and also in her militant sisters.?

As if to say, "Give me a break," Malkin writes: "But let's be honest about the double standards between men and women. Liberal women who criticize the welfare system are champions of the poor. Conservative women who do so are racist. Liberal women who talk about family values are enlightened pillars of the community. Conservative women who do so are self-righteous. Liberal women who tackle policy issues on Capitol Hill are brilliant. Conservative women who do so are—well, you know about their uteruses." (The uterus comment refers to a nasty crack made by feminist Naomi Wolf against conservative former U.N. Ambassador Jeane Kirkpatrick.)

I find what Malkin says about liberal women applies just as well to liberal men. Evidently, the press and the talking heads on TV thought it was okay after Clinton was elected to mention such things as family values, illegal immigrants, tougher laws for criminals, or welfare reform, and they heaped positive upon positive accolades upon him, both verbally and in print in regard to these issues; whereas conservatives who tried to talk about the same issues, years before the Clinton reign, were routinely branded as meanspirited radicals, and right-wing fringe element by both Democrats and the established media—the latter giving full coverage and negative editorials in support of Democrats who compared their opponents, at that time, to some of the meanest people in history.

MORE ON THE ELITIST FEMINIST VIEW

It seems to me that even a died-in-the-wool feminist must at times have to feel their leader's motives are suspect. Consider the treatment of their '90's idol, Anita Hill, who really had no evidence against Clarence Thomas except her word that of Paula Jones, who did have significantly more evidence of what she charged Bill Clinton than pubic hair on a Coke bottle and few other remarks. At that time, columnist Linda Bowles of *Creators Syndicate* wrote in defense of Paula Jones.

"They [feminist] watched Jones getting mauled and trashed but did nothing and said nothing....Jones fought against overwhelming odds to get her day in court. She fought her way through the phalanx of political hoods, White House hit squads, legal leeches, and paid political assassins with which Clinton has surrounded himself....Clinton thought he could intimidate her into withdrawing from the battle. He saw himself as the most powerful man in the world, and he saw her as a nobody. He would browbeat and bully her into submission. He made a mistake. She grew stronger with each malicious attack....It is clear that elitist, radical feminists are not that impressed with the true grit of Paula Jones. They fancy a different kind of woman—say, a woman such as Hillary Clinton."

R. Emmett Tyrrell, Jr., editor of *The American Spectator*, spoke of the dubious stand the feminist had taken on the Lewinsky/Clinton affair—siding with the President: "The geniuses [feminist leaders] who have brought us such legal monstrosities as sexual harassment argue that the relationship between Monica Lewinsky and her boss in the Oval Office was 'consensual.' These are the same geniuses who took one woman's long-delayed word against Clarence Thomas' appointment by George Bush to serve on the Supreme Court. They also argue that a man's loose language, choice of clothing and office art can create a 'climate of fear,' which gives women vast legal claims.

Yet, when a man of Bill Clinton's charms, power and seniority seduces, uses and abandons a 21-year old member of his intern program, they protest that the relationship is consensual."

So why the double standard? Tyrrell wrote: "It is because their [feminist leaders] primary goal is not the advancement of women but the advancement of the left-wing of the Democratic Party. Most feminist spokeswomen are simply left-wing Democrats. For over a decade, that species of Democrat has been unpopular. Thus, the lady left-wingers hide behind a mask—the mask of feminism....She [Lewinsky} has served more than one great purpose."

A RETURN TO SANITY

After dominating women's issues for more than 30 years, finally the time was ripe fornew leadership, one that would be more feminine-masculine-family friendly. That answer came in the late '90's with the rise of Concerned Women for America (CWA), whose membership quickly surpassed NOW's membership by a 3–1 margin. Also, with the wisdom of Kate O'Beirne, vice president of government relations at the *Heritage Foundation*, who is a great spokesperson for the changing of the guard, things began to move in the right direction. In an interview with reporter Barbara Woener, O'Beirne said: "Women on Capitol Hill fit the feminist stereotype....Radical feminism is profoundly anti-child and anti-family because it is radically individualistic, and that's just irreconcilable with the responsibilities and duties of a wife and mother. That's why we saw in the 60's and 70's such hostility to marriage and to the detriment of children." She went on to talk about how the feminists try to soften their image, "aligning themselveswith a whole class of family issues and defining them their way. The ultimate goals of expanding government and interfering in family autonomy have not changed. It's a very clever tactic."

According to O'Beirne, the feminist have had an easier time to get their agenda across, because the media, being basically liberal, are their sympathetic listeners. "I've even detected a double standard on the part of the media. Their women correspondents are not expected to be as unbiased as their male counterparts...women in the media get away with a certain point of view because often the men they work with won't rein them in."

Thankfully, NOW does not enjoy the hold they once had on women, a fact that is upsetting to president of the organization, Patricia Ireland. At one point she became so desperate she tried to pick a fight with the Christian organization for men, *PromiseKeepers*, whose primary goal is to get men to face up to their responsibility to their wives and children—and we thought that is what these feminist leaders wanted?? Also it was interesting to watch Ms. Ireland on the TV show, *Crossfire*, as she ignored the question put to her three different times: "What has NOW done for families? She could not answer it because she knew its leaders had not helped families, but instead they had done a lot to promote dissension and division in the family.

I found Judy Smith's letter to *The Wichita Eagle* interesting and informative on the issues just mentioned. Ms. Smith is the State Director of CWA in Kansas (2/19/02). She talks about a panel discussion she participated in at *Friends University* to explore the national women's movements in the 1960's. She writes: "Everyone except for me identified themselves as "feminists" and spoke of the '60's as a time for justice and empowerment, but I heard anger and fear of not being able to keep this empowerment.

"Empowerment is not something that can be legislated. Empowerment becomes a power play; my empowerment comes at the expense of someone else.

"Women at the turn of the last century understood this concept. Christian women's clubs, suffragettes and temperance ladies worked together to make a better place for themselves and their children. They saw that alcohol was destroying families and worked to pass child-labor laws and to eliminate prostitution. Setting aside their differences, they worked together."

She goes on to say that there is a lot more to be done where rape, child abuse, poverty of divorced women, etc. exist, but "It is time for women to leave our victim mentality behind and work for the good of all. We need to get beyond ourselves and get busy. Do it for the children."

PART II

Drawing a Counterfeit Portrait/Charting the Course

4

Who are the Mean spirited?

*"Woe unto them that call evil good, and good evil: that put dark-
ness for light, and light for darkness; that put bitter for sweet,
and sweet for bitter"! (Isaiah 5:20)*

There are probably as many Christian Democrats as there are Christian
Republicans, but that is a matter of no import because God is not
interested in political parties. He is interested in our hearts and our
souls. Nevertheless, this fact does not obscure another fact that the
majority of Democrats lean to the left, thus aligning themselves, unwittingly,much closer to secular humanistic views than they would probably care to think. It stands to reason that the further they lean to the
left, the more liberal they become, and should they lean too far, then
they have become one with the secular-humanistic views mentioned in
Chapter One. Republicans are not immune to fanaticism either; lean-
ing too far to the right, they become stiff-necked and case-hardened
extremists. Extremists on either side do not make wholesome contributions to their families or to society at large.

Well, it is not just in movies, TV, music, art, and education that the
big liberals work their strategies to manipulate and shape public thinking in order to achieve their own selfish desires for power and control.
The impact of secular humanism leaves no area of our lives untouched.
Despite the fact that liberals continue to repeat the same mistakes of

the past, they have been able to maintain their stranglehold on the American public. The political scene is no different. Many elected officials go to Washington inspired and idealistic in their dreams of making the world a better place to live. Unfortunately, not enough of them are successful in remaining true to their principles

MISLEADING TERMS

The strategies to mold thinking is ever on the minds of politicians. The Clinton/Gore Administration loved to piously call the 1980's "the era of greed." But even if this misconception were true, they missed the pile of logs in their own eyes, as the 1990's could accurately be called "the era of immorality and hypocrisy ." Much of this book zeros in on the 90's because that period in our history epitomizes all forms of deceitful and corruptive strategies practiced in politics, while, at the same time, the pretense of virtue was practiced as well.

Once we understand that the liberal strategy is based in deception, all pieces of the puzzle fall in place as a clear picture. The process begins with politicians creating a desired image for themselves through word power. In order to disguise the truth, it is necessary that they use misleading terms, euphorisms and that cloak the unpalatable in homey words and high sounding phrases; and the mainstream media gods, primarily liberal, either presents the misrepresentation as fact, or half-heartedly challenges it or ignores it. Liberals and the mainstream media work their strategies in much the same way, but not as co-conspirators through national network hookups. However, this does not mean they are entirely independent of one another, as we shall see later on.

In my opinion, political correctness is a symptom of liberalism. It shuns absolutes; it shames and controls through chastisement; it gives the politically correct a false sense of pride and saintliness. If the public is confused about what is truth, it is understandable, at least to some extent. For instance, we were bashed with an onslaught of new taxes in 1993 because we paid no attention to their new name, "investments."

We got hoodwinked again all the while "bean counting" was being described as "fairness" or "diversity" or "looking like America," and ended up getting all those unethical (some actual criminal) characters in the White House. Still, we listened to the flowery speech of those who were far out of the mainstream, as they classified themselves as "centrists" or "moderates." The ultimate scam was/is proscribed, stifled speech to enforce "politically correctness" into unpassed law by "righteous" power heads (thought police), for the sole purpose of personal power and control. Has anyone read *Animal Farm*?

Orlando Sentinel columnist, Kathleen Parker, pulls no punches in her definition of political correctness: "camouflaging truth to protect the psyches of the silly." In her column, "Memorialize accuracy, not just symbolism" (1/18/02), she talks about the three New York City firefighters who lost their lives raising the flag at ground zero. Her complaint is that the 19-foot statue being erected in their honor is politically correct, that is, because the three firefighters were white, but the statue of them is not. Parker writes: "Now they're of various ethnicities and hues—white, black and Hispanic—to better reflect the ethnic content of the department....Many New York City firefighters and their families are upset by the falsification of real events. It's not about race, they say; it's about reality."

Also, the fact that blacks and Hispanics make up approximately three percent (or 345) of the New York City fire departments, the rest are white (or 11,155) is not a good reason to distort the symbol honoring these men. Parker goes on to say "Once you start slicing and dicing truth, there's no end to it. And once you become comfortable with little adjustments to truth, a tweak here and a tweak there, you begin not to notice when truth disappears altogether. Where truth is absent, tyranny reigns. Such, ultimately, is the loathsome promise of political correctness." She ends saying, "But honoring those people [blacks and Hispanics] shouldn't require appropriating the glory of others."

Name Callers

The next step to gain power and control is to back up the "good" image liberals falsely create for themselves with name-calling that will brand the opposition as meanspirited, radical, fanatic, fringe element, extremist, and whatever else comes across as undesirable. This strategy also includes using children and/or college students as their priority recipients of the "good" they have to offer, thus making themselves appear noble and caring, while their opponents are cast as noncompassionate dregs of society. To make sure this strategy sinks deep into the psyches of the public, they repeat it ad infinitum, and in a chorus in which all liberals sing, they repeat and repeat for as long as it takes to burn the brand in.

For several months after the bombing of the federal building in Oklahoma City on April 19, 1995, there was a lot of accusations directed against the right wing of the Republican Party, claiming they were responsible for the tragedy. In fact, the President, himself, credited the terrible event with his political recovery. Even though there was absolutely no supporting evidence to validate these claims, he and other Democrats spread the lie for weeks that the tragedy was the result of Republican rhetoric. Supposedly, it was their "hateful" language that pushed someone over the brink into lunacy. Quite an accusation! Hate language had been around for a long time, but the intensity and viciousness of the name-callers reached new limits for weeks on end. There can be no doubt that Timothy McVeigh was an extremist on the right, but the right wing of the Republican Party was not responsible for his actions. It gets real interesting when you take a close look and see who are the guiltiest name callers and what viciousness passes their lips. Who are the meanspirited?

Besides Jessie Jackson's hateful description of the members of the Christian Coalition—Nazi types, KKK, etc.—the portrayal of men of the cloth by Hollywood, ranging from low-lives to downright vile and evil, demonic creatures, and the blasphemous "art" already mentioned, there has been a flood of hateful name-calling from the left, directed at right "wingers" on an almost daily basis since the famous 1994 election when Republicans were voted into majority status in the House of Representatives.

After Democrats lost their majority status, some of them went so far as to make a career of finding ways to bad mouth conservatives. Syndicated columnist Robert Novak talked about one of the sources called "The Project," in his column. "The Project," he wrote, "is a coordinated, calculated effort that would culminate in the destruction of Newt Gingrich." He says it operates as "a day by day plan to 'investigate' the House speaker and drive him from office. 'We meet once a week to cover what he's done through the week,' said Rep. Johnston, promising that 'we're going to stay on his back.'"

According to Novak, then House Minority Whip David Bonior and Minority Leader Richard Gephardt were represented at those meetings, and the White House was kept informed. Also, to keep nasty attitudes going, hateful language ever expressed, and anger erupting, the Democratic National Committee published a weekly NewtGram, trashing the speaker. Members of The Project Newt vented their anger over losing out to the Republicans, and Newt Gingrich taking over leadership was their chosen victim to bash. By constantly ripping him to pieces, they thought they could win back majority status in 1996. However, to date (2002), that has not happened. Let us remember that "The Contract for America," authored by Newt Gingrich is what helped the Republicans win the majority in the House. Bill Clinton ended up signing a good portion of the "Contract" into law and also took unearned credit for it.

Members of The Project consisted of some of the loud mouths, screechers and whiners who never missed a chance to bellyache about an imagined "something." Who were (and probably still are) the unhappy Democrats in Congress who get hysterical about anything that might diminish their power over the public. The most infamous are Patsy Schroeder (now retired), Charles Rangel, Christopher Dodd,

Carol Moseley-Braun (later voted out), David Bonier, Barbara Boxer, Maxine Waters, Dick Gephardt, and Barney Frank, and others. Apparently, these people and others had given up on trying to solve problems, and had nothing better to do than spew out an endless stream of venomous language: "The Republicans are going to starve the kids to death;" "they're going to take the food out of children's mouths," (some even interviewed little grade school kids and wanted to know their opinion of the starvation they are about to face (how irresponsible can one get?); "they're balancing the budget on the backs of the elderly and the disabled;" "they're giving all the money to the rich," "…the rich," "…the rich," "…the rich," "…are radical," "…are extremists," "…are racists," "blah," "blah," "blah."

However, after having taken a survey among Americans and finding out the "rich" theme wasn't accomplishing what they had hoped, Democrats changed "rich" to the "wealthiest Americans." In a two-minute informal speech to introduce the new mantra, Vice President Al Gore repeated the new mantra ten times, and three other Democrats in their spot before the microphone carried on and on how the Republicans were giving it all to the wealthiest Americans. And years later, the tiresome mantra is on-going.

But what insult could be worse than being characterized as a Hitler type? Rep. John Lewis made the comparison of Republicans to the holocaust, saying, "They're coming for our children, they're coming for the poor, they're coming for the sick, the elderly and the disabled." (Again, I ask, how irresponsible can one get?) We can only imagine what the major networks would have done had these outrageous statements been made by any Republican against any Democrat. Evidently, they feel it is okay to make Republicans and conservatives synonymous with the meanest people in the history of the world.

And the poison language goes on. Rep. Charles Rangel picked right up on the Nazi theme and accused Republicans of being just that, Nazis. Juan Williams, columnist and talk show panelist, called the bombing in Oklahoma City "the essence of the Anglo white man taken to some extreme, and I will grant you that. But it's the same kind of ideas that have fueled so much of the right-wing triumph over the agenda here in Washington." And Carl Rowan said he was "absolutely certain the harshest rhetoric of the Gingriches and Doles creates a climate of violence in America." (Again, I ask, how irresponsible can one get?)

And where was the media when these outrageous accusations were made against conservatives or Republicans?—nowhere! Besides that, they thought it was funny. In 1988 John Kerry thought himself a comedian saying that the Secret Service had orders to kill Dan Quayle if George Bush died. Thank God, no crack like this ever came out of the Bush White House. The media would have the "comedian's" head on a platter. It gets worse when the president and the vice president chime in with their version of hate language. Al Gore, speaking at a Democrat social gathering, referred to Newt Gingrich and Bob Dole as a two-headed monster. You'll never hear a Republican representative or senator using this kind of language against a Democrat. Even if they wanted to, the media would not stand for it. Read on to see typical media attitude if the hate is directed toward the "right" party.

I made a list of the hate language used against Senator Dole, which was an anonymously written editorial by one of the staff members of *The Wichita Eagle*—"Again the two Mr. Doles are considering running for the presidency in 1996" (August 8,1994).The writer of the piece pretty much illustrated the attitude of the media and their use of hate terms as "acceptable discourse" if directed at a Republican. Descriptive terms referring to Dole were "cranky," "Smart remark," "scathing look," "mean-spirited," "nasty," "gridlock(er)," "short-tempered," "blatant partisanship," "hypocritical." (It appeared as though the writer was in need of help, not the Senator.)

If the name-calling had been omitted, the very short article of only a few inches would shrink to teeny weeny; an omission of Dole's name would result in most of us thinking that the writer was talking about then Majority Leader of the Senate, George Mitchell. No one could top him in blatant partisanship, unless it was Rep. Henry Gonzales. Remember the Bush years how Mitchell was the big gridlocker, and how in the first two years of Clinton's presidency, he was one of the most blatant hypocrites in pointing his guilty finger everywhere but where it belonged, and continually whining because he thought others were exercising the power he felt belonged only to him and his buddies. Chapter 6 gives an account of the capers Mitchell pulled.

Owing to the fact that the '90's was an era of unbridled deception and hypocrisy, it has become the most classic example of partisanship practiced for the sake of power and control, as well as a classic example of hate language. Speaking of hate language, Jeff Jacoby, reporter for *The Boston Globe*, writes: "In 1997, I am sorry to report, little has changed. Hate speech was usually ignored when it came from the left. But when it came from the right, it was deemed intolerable. Even mild insults flung by conservatives were pounced on. When Trent Lott, the Senate majority leader, said on television last June that President Clinton 'acts like a spoiled brat,' network news shows jumped to scold him. When Rev. Jerry Falwell referred to Ellen DeGeneres, the came-out-lesbian TV star, 'Ellen Degenerate,' he was excoriated even by the right-wing radio hosts.

"But there is no objection when Senator Jesse Helms was compared to 'old South…slave owners' by *CNN* pundit William Schneider and called 'a terrorist' by Clinton's close friend George Stephanopoulos. Ugly name-calling is okay when you're mocking a conservative. We notice that Senator Robert Byrd (D-W.Va.) was actually a member of the Ku Klux Klan at one time, but no one brings that fact up.

"Left-wing journalist Robert Scheer was not chided for describing Republicans as cold-hearted creatures who 'would rather kill people than raise taxes.' Nor was *ABC*'s Sam Donaldson, when he analogized Newt Gingrich to the bloody Soviet dictator Lenin: 'They both make a revolution by shooting people.' Nor Jesse Jackson, for suggesting that California Governor Pete Wilson is a hardened racist: 'Just as [Gov.

George] Wallace once blocked school doors, now Wilson blocks school doors.'"

Jacoby's other examples of hate language are comparisons of Republicans to Nazis. "Tim Fleck, a Houston Press columnist, warned readers that Gary Polland, the conservative Republican chairman of Harris County, Texas, had probably been 'reading too much *Mein Kampf* for his own good.' Why the Hitler comparison? Because Polland had rated candidates for local office based on their answers to a questionnaire. Fleck's piece was titled, 'Look Out for the GOPstapo!'

"When Al Gore denounced a GOP welfare proposal as 'un-American, simply un-American,' that was simply an example of the vigorous, often obnoxious rhetoric that is part and parcel of democratic politics. But not Interior Secretary Bruce Babbitt's charge that critics of the administration's global warming policies are 'murderers of small children...it is to leave children and grandchildren locked in a car on a hot day with the windows sealed tight'....nobody called him on it....Left playwright Tony Kushner wished for 'Bob Dole, Newt, and Trent Lott (to) join hands and jump off the top of the Washington monument.' Then he called NEA opponents 'neo-barbarians,' 'certifiable madmen,' 'bigots,' 'racists,' and 'homophobic.' A notable conservative who said such things would be abominated. Kushner was applauded."

These hate mongers had so few examples of hate language coming from the right from which to draw attention away from themselves, and so they accused Republicans of the things they were most guilty, and the media would aid and abet whomever the left chose to harass. However, one who deserved the criticism he got was Republican J. Gordon Liddy, whose remark to shoot feds in the head or the groin because they wear bullet-proof vests, was certainly a good example of hate language, and was in very bad taste. In reality, though, most of us knew in advance that the media would give Liddy a thorough tongue lashing, and they did. The truth is had he been a Democrat, they would have ignored the remark, as they have all the vicious and uncalled for ones made by the left.

Another example liberals used against the right was Newt Gingrich's accusation that the left was responsible for Susan Smith murdering her two children—admittedly he went too far with this accusation. And one more example the left relied on trying to make themselves look above name-calling was when Dick Armey called Barney Frank, Barney "Fag" (which Armey called a "mis-speak"). Not much for the pious, righteous left to try to elevate themselves above such talk and appear innocent of their own tawdry behavior, but that did not stop them.

The idea behind name-calling is to intimidate the opposition into backing off a course that is perceived to be a successful one. The Democrats knew that the major media would ignore their venomous language; they understood so-called acceptable discourse was/is in their favor, no matter what its flavor. But as obnoxious and tiresome as it is, there are those who see hate language as characteristic of the struggle to survive: in this case, the dying, gasping, death rattle of the liberal secular humanists who insisted on reinventing America after the mode of Sodom and Gohomora. However, I believe Sodom and Gohomora's hold on America is so strong, it is wishful thinking to believe it will become irrelevant. I cannot sympathize with the liberals if they lose ground, but, at least on some level, I think I know how they must feel. In the 60's when almost everything conservatives believed in was being turned upside down, it was an extremely disturbing experience, like all hell had broken loose.

GOVERNMENT DEPENDENCY

If liberals are to maintain their job security and assure their re-election chances, government dependency is essential to them; it is the glue that holds their plots together, the insurance that promises power and control. In my opinion liberals are not nearly as saintly and compassionate as they would have us believe. The more people who depend on the government, the more powerful an incumbent becomes. That was why the Democrats made the big pitch for the Motor Voter bill—to get the vote of everyone otherwise too lazy to register; that is what was behind the last-minute-naturalization drive in 1996, when 75,000 immigrants were rushed through into citizenship. Never mind that ordinary procedures were not followed and that many of the new citizens had police records. The fact that these new arrivals were potential Democratic voters is what really counted with the Clinton Administration. Also, by-passing laws is one of the reason the term "illegal", when it refers to foreigners, means nothing today.

I don't know how California bears up under the financial strain of all the illegal aliens pouring over its borders, especially into the hospitals, many of whom do so to give birth so that their child will automatically be an American citizen. Schools are hard hit too. Since it takes time to assimilate the children of both legal and illegal aliens into the language and culture, overall grade-point averages are brought down, not to speak of the great need for social services that have hindered the economy of that state. Controls need to be set and enforced. New Mexico, Arizona, and Texas are feeling the burden placed on their school systems as well as the financial strain for the same reasons.

So why do Democrats like the present system? Because it benefits the Democrat Party. Think about it: Al Gore won all states in the last election in which there is a heavy Mexican population, with the exception of Texas, and President Bush won all the rest.

Republicans are after the vote too, but since they are losing out, they better do something about the border, or in not too many years, they will be an irrelevant political party. Right now they are boxed in and may be in a no-win position on this issue. Chances are if they try to alter this situation with stricter border control, liberals will quickly brand them as racists. However, one would think President Bush could see what the political ramifications are for his party on this issue, but instead he appeared to be on the side of Democrats when he went out of his way to try to claim legal status for the illegal Mexican population in the states. His stand on this issue raised an understandable controversy about all ethnic groups who might be here illegally. Perhaps Bush thought he would get the Mexican vote next time around, but unless he is willing to grow welfare handouts considerably on their behalf, it is a lost cause.

Politicians love to use the "crisis" angle as a way to increase government dependency, and Democrats know this game all too well. The idea is to create as much anxiety and guilt as possible by calling their favored issues a "crisis"—an often used tactic by the Clinton Administration. The list of crises convenient to liberal causes is long and well-known, but probably the infamous 1992 crisis is the best example of distortion indicative of these special "crises." It supposedly was "the worst economy in 50 years. A lot was said about a job crisis. People were "only a pink slip away from losing their jobs," and many were asking the question: "Will I have a job tomorrow?" At that time, we heard that real wages were down, and bankruptcies were up, and furthermore, "everything that was down should be up," and what was "up, should be down." This was the time when all that name-calling just mention above was going on fast and furiously. Behind this "crisis" were the guilty culprits—you know, those Hitler and KKK types—the dreaded Republicans. I'm not sure how we made it through that particular crisis, but somehow we did—WHEW!

I read a letter in the "Reader Views" section of *The Wichita Eagle*, "Using workers," by Galen Barnes (3/2/02) that gives a good explanation as to why government dependency is so popular. Mr. Barnes, a former Democrat and union worker, tells us he knows that "Democrats have no intention of helping the poor or working class. They only want to use them." Referring to a 1996 study, he says: "the welfare system created by the Democrats was easy to get on; hard to get off (you were punished for going to school, getting training, etc.); kept two-thirds of recipients on welfare for eight years or longer; and kept the poor and minorities in small crowded ghettos in large cities. This was intentional!"

Barnes goes on to say: "Democrats know that if you create another welfare or unemployment recipient, you've created another Democratic vote. The reason the Democrats and the media want the extension of unemployment benefits—but not the job incentives—is to keep as many people as possible on unemployment right up to the elections this fall."

THE LEGACY OF LIBERALISM

Much has already been said about the destruction liberalism leaves in its wake, but seeing it through the eyes of creditable professionals whose job necessitates study and research of political issues drives the point home much better than I can do. I like columnist Walter Williams analysis of the mess liberal Democrats got us in with all their "heartfelt" concern for the American people. He is one of a growing number of black journalists who is conservative. But thankfully we are seeing more black people turning from the party that "helped and cared so much for them, and to some degree, has kept them enslaved and dependent." Williams writes for the *Conservative Chronicle*, spring 1994:

"List our most serious social problems. You'll find liberal instigation or advocacy at their core. Take AIDS and other sexually transmitted diseases. What philosophy criticized traditional values and advocated free sex? It wasn't conservatives. Look at the plague of illegitimacy, particularly among blacks (66 percent). Again, liberals work, demeaning and attacking traditional values. What about our drug plague? It was liberals who celebrated drug usage....

"How about educational decline? Who advocated the watering down of standards, condemnation of academic achievement tests, social promotion and substitution of multiculturalism, miseducation and condoms for math and science? Who fights educational reform and supports incompetent teachers? It is not conservatives.

"There is no question that liberal visions have turned day into night, hope into despair, and triumph into defeat. The $64,000 question is why do we continue to heed the corrupt liberal agenda?" My answer to that question is people like The Reverends (whom as far as I can see do not pastor a church anywhere) Jesse Jackson and Al Sharpton.

Another black journalist, Thomas Sowell, shares the same sentiments as Williams. In his commentary, December 15, 1994, *Conservative Chronicle*, he wrote:

"Those who still cling to the 1960's liberal vision not only do not trouble themselves with history, but even make up phoney history to justify their own failed policies. Everything that goes wrong in the ghetto today is called 'legacy of slavery' by those who ignore the fact that the same kinds of patterns existed among various European immigrant groups when they lived in the slums.

"The excuse-mongers also ignore the fact that black communities did not have anywhere near today's levels of crime, family breakdown, and other social problems half a century ago when they were a half a century closer to the era of slavery. What the ghettoes are suffering from today is much more a legacy of 1960 liberalism."

He goes on to say "A hundred years ago, the marriage rate among blacks was higher than among whites—and remained so in every census from 1890 to 1940. Slavery had separated people, but it could not destroy the family feelings they had for each other. Liberal social programs have done that, often by preventing a family from being formed in the first place. Husband Ed makes the point that President Johnson's "Great Society" did more to damage black families than the depression did, and in some respects even slavery, since it tore them apart.

"The painful question now is whether we can escape the legacy of liberalism." A report on *CBN's Newswatch* on February 24, 1995, said: "Black conservatives are emerging as one of the fastest growing political and social forces in the nation." The National Association for the Advancement of Colored People (NAACP) conducted a survey which found that 40% of its members called themselves conservatives; and a report in *National Minority Politics* magazine said that 75% of its new subscribers—10,000 since November's election—belong to the Republican party. But in answer to these surveys, Jesse Jackson calls the black conservative movement "irrelevant," while other black leaders say it is just a "fad." Nevertheless, these changes have not translated into Republican votes. Why? Could the all-out-intensive drive during election years by the *NAACP* and people like Jesse Jackson and Al Sharpton who effectively know how to play the race card and keep blacks captive in the mindset of victimhood be the reason?

To these assertions a staff member of Reagan's State Department and presidential contender in 1996, Dr. Alan Keyes says: "These people [liberals] have been following a fad for the last 30 years....It has not worked—theirs was the fad!" He says further that the human experience of a thousand years cannot be substituted for answers some "godless social scientists come up with—theirs is the trendy little models of how families could be, and how society could be reconstructed."

Nationally syndicated columnist, Paul Craig Roberts, to my knowledge, is the first in his field to write about race politics as victimizing both black and white people—*Human Events,* "Shelby Steele for President of Harvard" (week of Jan. 21, 2002).

He talks about Harvard's current president, Larry Summers, who after only a few weeks "has been emasculated by Jesse Jackson, Al Sharpton and the Afro-American Studies Department. The problem: If President Summers doesn't see things the way the aforementioned do, they will play the race card.

Mr. Roberts writes: "Harvard needs a new president. My candidate is Shelby Steele....The aptly named Steele, a scholar at Stanford, has the backbone needed for the Harvard presidency. As he is black himself, so race cards won't work on him." The gravity of the situation is best stated by Mr. Steele, himself: "Whites lack the authority to say what they see. Facts have to be denied if the facts can be accused of 'insensitivity' to blacks. Consequently, whites cannot enforce standards and have become silent throughout the educational system as mediocrity destroys excellence.

"The outcome is disastrous: The public schools are all but devastated, universities are stunted by ideology, corporations are more unctuous than churches, the media are more unctuous yet and American politicians—of left and right—speak barren cliches."

Steele goes on to say "The vacuum in white authority," is 'cancerous.' Mediocrity rules. Victimology replaces fact-based learning, as muted whites fear to prod blacks to serious achievement. The universities and public schools have become extensions of the welfare system, where blacks learn to 'live off the largesse of white guilt.'"

Mr. Roberts says he has black candidates for two more Ivy League universities where academic standards are drowning in white guilt: Thomas Sowell for president of Princeton and Walter Williams for president of Yale....With blacks as president, these three universities could dispense with their fraudulent Afro-American Studies departments. These departments teach blacks to hate whites and whites to hate themselves, and spend the remainder of their efforts agitating for slavery reparations....There are a lot of victims in a country, and they are not all black. We could do something about the black and white victims of shoddy education. All we need is Shelby Steele as president of Harvard to lead the way."

This article can be found in its entirety in the paper *Human Events*, dated "week of January 21, 2002. It is worth the effort to look it up in your local library.

5

Orchestrating Political Campaigns

○ ○
"The wise in heart will receive commandments; but the prating fool shall fall."—Proverbs 10:8

MEDIA CAMPAIGN MANAGERS

To have lasting results and maintain the power liberals crave, deception has to be internalized, and much of the media see this as their job. Of course, it is the special bonding liberals have with major liberal TV news networks and the press (both forums operating under the politics of bias and omission of facts). Instead of reporting the news objectively, they have set themselves up as campaign managers, upholding and advancing left-wing policies by being too soft on liberals and too hard on conservatives.

Under the heading, "media campaign managers," is the all important diversionary/damage control tactics the media has routinely used to shift attention away from a particular member of their political party when they are in trouble. A major trick is to replace big news stories with trivia. Brent Bozell of *Creators Syndicate, Inc.* illustrates the problem very well in his commentary entitled, "Fluff over substance rules at the networks." His first example is an interview ABC's *Prime Time Live* had with Ron Brown's lover, Noland Hill (June '97), in which Miss Hill claimed Brown had used his position in the Commerce Depart-

81

ment "as a personal monetary printing press"—(also it was discovered after his death that he was to collect a $700,000 payoff from Vietnam for his work to normalize the country's relations with the U.S.). Bozell writes: "No evening or morning news network has yet to follow up or even mention the allegations." According to Bozell, the story was replaced with a total of 20 stories on UFO's.

The story of Webster Hubbell falsifying his consulting work for Los Angeles, which made it possible for him to cheat that city out of $25,000, was largely ignored by the media. They swapped it for something more important—an interview with a Georgia man who caught a 7-foot alligator.

Another story that received little media attention was the $500,000 Clinton raised for his campaign through calls from the Oval Office. Even though Clinton was caught in a lie when he claimed he could not remember, the media had very little interest in pursuing this news story. How did they respond? Bozell reports: "The next day *Good Morning America* devoted a few minutes to the story, but all other news shows took a pass. Over on NBC, Katie Couric did spend a whole interview segment on a more important development: Disco-era platform shoes making a fashion comeback."

Well, the media did sweat it out for a short while during the revelation of Al Gores' infamous Buddhist Temple fund-raiser, but the pressure didn't last too long. They lucked out with a new diversion cropping up just in time, which enabled them to speedily control the potential damage the new information would cause to the administration: the bipartisan Senate Governmental Affairs Committee offer of immunity to two Buddhist nuns who attended the affair. "This key development," writes Bozell, "received no coverage. The networks were too immersed in Mike Tyson's eating habits."

Probably the story that "takes the cake" was the gloss-over the media did in regard to the 37 briefings John Huang had gathering secret CIA intelligence on China. Bozell writes: "This startling development was passed over during the next few days so all three networks could cover a story that was over 200 years old: A Ship Revolutionary War traitor Benedict Arnold commanded had been located in Lake Champlain."

Notice how often Tim Russett, host of Sunday morning's *Meet the Press*, has Senator Tom Daschle on his show, and how he always lets him have a lot of air time. Daschle uses each question asked of him to give a long, long speech. This does not bother Russett at all. He sits patiently and lets him spiel on. If Daschle evades answering a hard question, Russett does not persist as he does when the guest is a Republican. The same thing can be said of Hillary Clinton, who really doesn't bother to answer questions at all. She treats these sessions as photo-ops. She uses every question as an opportunity to say that she is "working so hard," "trying so hard," she is "so committed to" whatever, and of course, "the children," "the children." I have yet to see a TV talking-head treat Hillary as they do other politicians.

Then we have Katie Couric (NBC), who shamelessly suggested on national television, without any regard to the fact that terrorist were operating throughout the Clinton Administration and little was done about it, that the September 11th attacks on America could have been averted "if we had a President with more foreign policy experience." The bottom line is that in today's established media, liberals generally have their "cake and can eat it too." And reporters and newscaster were upset when Rep. Susan Molanari took the position as anchor for CBS because she might not be objective—"as they are."

MEDIA FRAUD

There is plenty of documented proof that the mainstream media favors the left's agenda, and there is no better place to start than the 1992 presidential campaign and its aftermath, simply because the incidents that happened then were the most blatant deceptive practices in recent history. Result studies by *Freedom Forum* and *Times Mirror Center*, which researched bias in the media during that time, show that Democrat reporters outnumbered Republican reporters 4–1. Given that fact, it should come as no surprise that their findings also indicated the press coverage for the same time period was unfair and hurt Bush. For example, now we know for sure George Stephanopoulos' call to President Bush on the *Larry King Live* show was not a random call, but a political manoeuver to embarrass him, and that Larry King publically lied about the call; that Rick Kaplan, executive producer of *Prime Time,* did a lot of plotting and manipulating behind the scenes during the campaign to aid Clinton. He attended Clinton's campaign staff meetings, helped set up his campaign press office, helped him with his presentation at the New Hampshire primary, edited interviews made with Clinton, and arranged some public appearances for him. (And many thought staffers at *Prime Time* spent their time objectively gathering factual information.)

We also know that Don Hewit, *60 Minutes"* executive producer, stooped to sensationalism, one day before the election, by airing the ridiculous story Ross Perot cooked up about Bush savaging his daughter's wedding. What Perot was seeking revenge for was an event that occurred during the Reagan presidency. Then Vice-president Bush under the direction of President Reagan relayed a message to Perot he didn't like, and so Perot decided to "kill the messenger" when the occasion presented itself. The 1988 presidential election was the perfect time to carry out his sick scheme. As so often is the case, the media, more than happy to act as campaign managers, opted to protect their own and presented little to no information to show up the farce for what it was.

We also heard nothing from the media regarding Kaplan's sly manipulations, and next to nothing about the 8,000 letters to *Prime Time,* 90% of which gave examples and outrage of media bias against Bush. Add to these findings, Hollywood's support, 90% of which goes to the liberal party, and you can see how one party managed to control the legislative branch of the government for 40 years. However, this is only one more breakdown in the press's duty to give factual information to American citizens so that they might vote intelligently.

ROMANCING THE CLINTONS

We cannot deny the cleverness of the cross-country bus tours during the 1992 campaign, which made for good public relations and gave the Clintons the appearance of being one of us—in touch with the common folk. The bus tours literally enthralled the media to the point of romanticism, and lusting for a liberal president, they bent over backwards to showcase him in the most positive way. For instance, do you recall ever having heard such heart-rending narration by a reporter on any candidate in the past: "Something is happening out there. A feeling...call it hope." Against inspiring music played in the background, the narrator went on to talk about the absence of fear, about change, about the new direction the country was headed. Then picturing Clinton and Gore he ended his drama; speaking in reverential and religious tones, he said, "We are not alone."

And what about the nauseating, gushy love-in productions that many journalists created? What an interesting poll this question would have made: Who slobbered more over the Clintons—Dan Rostenskowski, acting more like a man in love than a congressman "debating" the health care issue with Hillary Clinton, or Dan Rather when he poured out libations via satellite with the president (summer of '93)? "If we could be one-hundredth as great as you and Hillary Rodham Clinton have been in the White House, we'd take it right now and walk away winners..." Rather ended his worship service thus: "Thank you very much and tell Mrs. Clinton we respect her and we're pulling for her.

Nevertheless, even though the first couple were the recipients of such favorable media attention, which also protectively held back as much as possible all information harmful to them, and viciously attacked anyone who dared to shed any light on what might have, or did happen, Mr. Clinton complained from time to time about the negative press he got. While conservative magazines and newspapers filled up pages of the deceptive practices of the media where this administration was concerned, the mainstream media dodged these issues as though they were the bubonic plague.

Author, lecturer, and TV and radio guest commentator, Cal Thomas, gave examples of some Clinton love-ins by various reporters and media people in his column in *The Conservative Chronicle*. One was about Lance Morrow's "Man of the Year" cover story on January 4, 1993, in which he told his readers that Clinton's conduct during the campaign "served to rehabilitate and restore the legitimacy of American politics, and thus, prospectively, of government itself." Another was an article published in the December 24, 1993, issue of the *Washington Post* emoting about the touchy-feely Clintons: "He [Clinton] borrowed from the cotton industry the touch, the feel, the fabric of our lives..." Also, Tom Foreman of *ABC* following Clinton's appearance with children on network TV (Feb. 20), Thomas wrote that he had "elevated him [Clinton] to Hans Christian Andersen status." And never to be excelled, much less excluded, on a Clinton love-in is Eleanor Clift, reporter for *Newsweek*. According to Thomas she has been "conducting a journalistic love affair with both Clintons and enjoying access to the president because of it." Where the Clintons are concerned, never do we hear an objective thought come out of her mouth. In fact, she doesn't have to think very much about any issue; whatever Clinton says and does is always exactly her opinion. Actually, pretty much the same thing can be said of columnist Margaret Carlson.

Considering all the scandals surrounding the Clinton administration, one would expect that the love-ins would come to a sudden halt, now and forever. But, no! Cal Thomas writes(Jan. '98): "With the exception of the ever-vigilant *Washington Times* and some reporting by the *Los Angeles Times*, the writing, commentary and broadcasting, masquerading as reporting in the mainstream press, has been downright worshipful." Thomas quotes Howard Rosenberg of *The Los Angeles Times* after Clinton's second inaugural address: "His sturdy jaw precedes him. He smiles from sea to shining sea....Is this president a candidate for Mt. Rushmore or what? In fact, when it comes to influencing the public, a single medley of expressions from Clinton may be worth much more, to much of America, than every ugly accusation Paula Jones can muster."

Also, Tony Snow, reporter for *Detroit News,* thinks the Clintons, and liberals in general, have had a free ride with the press. He said: "Although the president often complains about his press clippings, most reporters handed in their teeth the day he took office. Irregularities that would have inspired congressional investigations during the Reagan-Bush years now get dismissed with a shrug, and reporters pelt the President with such marshmallows as: "Do you really run eight-minute miles? Finalists in the Miss America pageant face harsher interrogations."

Summing up this point on media bias, he wrote: "The real threat to the First Amendment comes from journalists who gladly serve as megaphones for the prestigious and powerful and hiss at colleagues, who ask impolitic questions."

Columnist Kathleen Parker of the *Orlando Sentinel* writes about the emotion and drama at the 2000 Democrat National Convention, which she renamed "Human Emotion Project"(Democrats manufactured emotions, 8/22/2000). Apparently, believing we would have another liberal Democrat president in the White House, she writes: "Four more years of victims and survivors."

Ms. Parker quoted Harvey Robinson, who wrote "The Human Comedy," in 1937, saying that he "must have had the DNC 2000 in mind when he said that political campaigns are 'emotional orgies which endeavor to distract attention from the real issues involved, and…actually paralyze what slight powers of cerebration man can normally muster.'"

But Ms. Parker agrees that "The Democrats' strategy is nothing less than staggering genius—bringing out a victim from behind every curtain. The genius," she says, "lies in the fact that even to acknowledge the strategy is to reveal oneself as heartless. To suggest that this well-orchestrated circus of emotion-choking, hard-luck stories designed to numb minds and swell hearts is to be mean, cynical and callous." And I say, "we just witnessed another example of how politically correctness is becoming an unwritten national law."

Ms. Parker ends her piece, saying "There was Al Gore, stifling emotion as he promised to pray for John [Kennedy]. Maybe his concern was sincere, but how would we know? That's the problem with manufactured emotion. After a while, it's all suspect."

DENIALS AND DOUBLE STANDARDS

Despite blatant media bias, especially throughout the campaign and for nearly two years after the new administration was installed, we saw the news media in total denial, rating themselves as fair and unbiased. Without realizing it, columnist Bill Thompson illustrated the bias very well in his article, "Liberal media not soft on Clinton," in *The Wichita Eagle* (Feb. 1994), claiming that the theory which says "the media pulverized George Bush and anointed Clinton as president is ridiculous." But instead, of making his intended point indicated in the title, Thompson proved his theory wrong himself. By his own writing, he illustrated a perfect example of how far the press can go in their denial of the truth, which is always at the detriment of society.

Thompson began referring to some of the problems Clinton had early on in the campaign and implied that since these problems had been reported, the press had been fair. He wrote: "If the new guy messes up during his first few days or weeks in office, he ought to face the same criticism that the previous president encountered when he made mistakes." However, when one considers the stumbling, back-pedaling, promise breaking, etc. of President Clinton were unprecedented, and at times almost unbelievable, continuing for months on end, the media were very soft. Bill Clinton can thank his lucky stars he was not a Republican, or the press would have filled their pens with venom for some unrelenting attacks. Thompson ignored the obvious and plunged further into denial, saying that the media "didn't care whether the candidate was Republican or Democrat." But the fact is what Clinton got was far softer than what Bush got, and for far less.

To get more specific, consider the broken promises of raising taxes by both Bush and Clinton. One difference is that Bush waited two years after taking office before he raised taxes, which he did as a compromise with Congress. The deal was that Congress would cut spending by two dollars for every one dollar of increased taxes. Bush made this deal because he could get no legislation through without the democratic controlled Congress tacking on a lot of "pork"—done, of course, so that the president would be forced to veto the bill. It was a perfect strategy, used especially by guys like George Mitchell and Tom Foley to embarrass and brand him as a do-nothing president. Once Bush took the bait, they reneged on their part of the bargain. And did this irresponsible behavior get the media's attention? No, nary a word, but Bush's mistake was played to the hilt even after he admitted it was a mistake. However, considering his many years dealing with conniving politicians, Bush should have known better. Anyway, considering the outcome of the 1994 congressional election, no doubt many voters began to realize the best thing that could happen in the next election was as President Bush advised: "Sweep the House," for that is exactly what happened two years later.

Now for the rest of the story: Candidate Clinton began in January of 1992, promising a tax cut for the middle class because he said they had "paid through the nose," and he kept that promise going month after month throughout the year. As late as September, he said, "We should cut middle-class taxes immediately by 10 percent." And in another speech that same month, he said, "The only people who will pay more income taxes are the wealthiest two percent. Then one month before the election, he said: "We want to give modest middle-class tax relief to restore some fairness, especially to middle-class people with families with incomes of under $60,000 per year." And again in the same month, he was adamant in his promise, saying, "I'm not going to raise taxes on the middle-class Americans to pay for the programs I've recommended. If the money isn't available, I will cut the programs." But in less than two weeks before inauguration day, Clinton changed his tune: "From New Hampshire forward, for reasons that absolutely mystify me, the press thought the most important issue in the race was the middle-class tax cut. I never did meet any voter who thought that."

It soon became apparent that he never intended to keep his promise, but that it had served as a means to rack up votes. After being in office only a few months, Clinton totally reversed himself on the promised tax cut. At one point he "backed up" his reasoning, saying that he didn't believe the citizens could be trusted to spend their money wisely. Evidently, he thought the government knew what was best; everything was put on the table for tax increases, including the value added tax, which, if passed, would have broken the backs of just about everyone. Lucky for Americans, the issue caused such an uproar he was forced to back down with the pretense that he really never intended to do it anyway. Nevertheless, in the end, he gave Americans the highest tax increase in history—$250 billion; George Bush raised taxes $165 billion. And where was the media? No where in sight.

Furthermore, the Office of Management Budgets (OMB), which was Clinton's source of information regarding the deficit, put out the adjusted figures in August of 1992, and Clinton knew at that time what they were. His shock and dismay after taking office were feigned reactions, based on a false justification which he had planned months before in order to raise everyone's taxes. The scam was to make taxing the middle class appear as something beyond his control, and that he was forced to renege on his promise. He felt pretty safe in his deceitfulness as far as the media were concerned, and apparently banked on them not to expose the con, and right he was. There were virtually no hard questions asked of President Clinton for breaking his pledge, no flack, nothing. Compare the bashing President Bush took over raising taxes from the media with the near silence on Clinton for the same offense, and for an amount that was considerably higher than the Bush tax increase.

The drama continues: "It's the economy, stupid." (By the way, I saw absolutely no response from the media—wasn't "stupid" directed at his opponent, President Bush?)It was interesting to note that only a matter of days after the election, we suddenly heard the report that the economy was "doing better than the media had expected." Did this mean George Bush did not "cook the books" after all? And might we also assume he was correct in saying "The figures don't add up?" But was the media embarrassed or apologetic for having supported the Clinton team on this issue? No! Can we really believe Mr. Clinton's excuse, "We just found out." I think not.

The truth is President Bush was right when he questioned the figures. They didn't add up because the economy had begun its upward swing more than one and half years before Clinton was elected. In fact, the turn-around began in March of 1991. But please note that the announcement informing the public that the country was coming out of the recession came 19 months after the fact!

Thankfully, there were enough people at that time who did not buy into the "situational ethics" garbage, and somewhere well into Clinton's second year in office, his credibility sank in the polls, but even his poor image was not due to sound reporting by the major media. It was that the electorate couldn't square what came out of his mouth with his actions. However, media backing for Clinton had gone much further than ignoring facts. They supported the false figures he gave out and dredged up as many people as they could find who were out of work, or who would complain sufficiently to support the trumped up cataclysmic-sky-is-falling views the Clinton team wanted to come across to the voters.

To add insult to injury, Clinton was never too proud to take credit for himself whether or not it was warranted—like the economic recovery that was well underway before he took office, or for his so-called budget bill, which was vigorously reworked and changed in Congress by the Senate Finance Committee until it barely resembled the Clinton version. I guess he felt he deserved to claim the finished product, as he had worked hard twisting arms—dishing out reprisals for those who would not vote for it, and porking those who would vote against their consciences. When the bill finally passed by only one vote, it did not seem to bother him that literally no one was in favor of the original mess, either in Congress or the nation as a whole. Clinton pridefully claimed victory. William Rusher, columnist for *Newspaper Enterprise Association,* writes: "Presumably Dave Gergen has taught him that claiming a victory can be as good as actually winning one."

The fact is at no time in recent history were so many misled by a leader who is a vacillator by nature, a man who talks out of both sides of his mouth, and then goes before the public in denial, trying to get his foot out of it. The media were always consistent, though. They did report and debate Clinton's erring ways, but when their heart wasn't in it, they used their favorite line: "The public isn't interested," or "they just want the president to govern." They also packed the airways with Clinton operatives who would literally lay down their own reputations, if not their lives, in order to defend him. No spin was too ridiculous or absurd. They dodged questions, pointed to President Nixon, or they would dig up a negative on anyone willing to tell the truth, and trash him or her (Hillary was the head honchoette in the trashing department). Amid smiles and a show of adoration, it wasn't long until the media would proudly claim Mr. Clinton as "The Comeback Kid." They zeroed in on his oratorical skills, and all was forgiven.

As for President Bush, the media presented a different story, a never-ending harassment. Besides the unreliable arm-chair-character analysis, we forever heard things like "Bush trying to defend himself," or "Bush trying to look presidential," or "Bush trying to cover for," or "Bush avoiding such and such," or "The Administration nervous about," etc. Bush was even criticized for his R & R breaks, but Clinton was said to be "refreshed," "renewed," "ready to tackle the job."

Examples of Bush harassment are numerous, but two stories serve to make the point and illustrate perfectly the media abuse that most reporters inflicted on him. During the heat of the campaign, both of the following stories appeared in *The Wichita Eagle* on June 5, 1991.

One reporter, Andrew Rosenthal, relied heavily on his knowledge of connotative power of words in an effort to paint President Bush as uncooperative and defensive, instead of what really was going on—Bush not succumbing to Rosenthal's level of interrogation. The title of his commentary was "Bush trying to focus on his agenda."

Rosenthal began his bash of the president by telling his readers what went on in his mind, but the author's intention to sway his readers to his way of thinking backfired and merely exemplified the harassment to which Bush was subjected, as Rosenthal tried over and over to force him to talk about Ross Perot. He wrote: "Seeking to regain the political offensive...President Bush found himself repeatedly on the defensive." (Repeatedly" is the key word here, as the subject each time was Perot.) In the next paragraph Rosenthal said, "Bush appeared intent on avoiding any questions about Perot...." Again in the following paragraph, Rosenthal said, "Bush refused to discuss Perot...." Further on, as though he had not convinced his reader, he repeated himself again: "From the onset Bush avoided answering questions about Perot."

Rosenthal also saw himself as the interpreter of Bush's chosen setting "...surrounded by the trappings of power." (But we have to wonder had the president been at Kennebunkport, would it have been that he was trying to look like a family man? Or that he was shirking his duty? Or was he trying to look outdoorsman like? Or what?)

Then winding down his psycho-analysis, Rosenthall unwittingly reaffirmed for his readers the fact that Bush was not allowed to speak his mind but was continually badgered to talk about Perot. Once again (and by this time we hoped for the last time) he complained that the President "refused to say much about Perot," thus repeating himself to the point of redundancy. Being the omniscient speaker in this tale, Rosenthal ended his personal point-of-view, telling us "the White

House was clearly rattled," which, of course, was Rosenthal's aim and hope.

Another reporter, James Flanigan, whose column appeared in the same issue of the paper, gave some hope to the reader (at least it helps to make my point). Flanigan merely went back to the basics of good journalism and reported the news by telling us what Perot said. There was no badgering to get him to talk about Bush. Also, the writer made no putdowns on Perot; neither did he attempt to read his mind. He left the reader to draw his or her own conclusions from the information he gave—what a novel idea. "As husband Ed, speaking of the Rosenthal article, said, "Years ago, a lot of this kind of "reporting" would belong on the Op Ed page."

Though Rosenthal did not cover all the bases for poor journalism, he did use the same tactics a fiction writer uses to develop a character—judging from the Public Forum page of some newspapers and magazines, this is something the public is tired of. The public do not want fictional reporting. They want reporters who do not continually try to program their thought processes with images and impressions they themselves create. This kind of reporter-story-telling strategy —suppressing, distorting, omitting factual information—may have been at least one reason why the public did some long overdue overhauling of the government process on November 8, 1994.

The odd thing is that Clinton never appreciated the fact that the media was always on his side (or maybe it was intimidation or sympathy he was after)—we often heard him cry about the "adverse press," and how hard they were on him. Maybe more people would have arrived at the truth if they had mentally role played with all the colossal screwups we saw, especially the first year and a half in the Clinton administration, by inserting George Bush or Ronald Reagan in each one. The outcome for either of them would have been disastrous.

6

Pulling the Wool Over the Public's Eyes

○ ○

"His mouth is full of cursing and deceit and fraud: under his tongue is mischief and vanity."—Psalm 20:17

CRYING THE BLUES

The media were not the only source that make deception easy for Mr. Clinton. Friends in high places did too, but it would be hard to top former Senate Majority Leader George Mitchell's whining and carrying on about the Republican filibuster that would prevent passage of Clinton's "economic" bill. He cried "They won't give the President's programs a chance; they want to embarrass the President; they want to defeat the President and cause his programs to fail."

Columnist Donald Lambro wrote that Mitchell was "singing a different tune four years ago." Back then "he prevented an up or down vote on Bush's capital gains tax cut bill to unlock new venture capital for business expansion and jobs...that was the year when Mitchell ruthlessly carried out a one-man filibuster in the democratic-controlled Senate against Bush's capgain tax cut, the year of his economic growth program." It is also odd that Senate Finance Committee Chairman, Lloyd Bentsen, who spoke so highly of Clinton's economic stimulus bill, opposed the Bush economic bill, saying "it was bad economic policy, bad savings policy, bad tax policy and bad fiscal policy."

Well, we might agree with Bentsen if the Republican filibuster had been a game of revenge, a "tit for tat," but that was not the case. According to Lambro, there were significant differences between the Republican and Mitchell filibusters. About Mitchell, he wrote: "…the cold-blooded partisan Mitchell was interested in only one thing in 1989: preventing a proven economic stimulus proposal from becoming law. Had the capital gains tax rate been cut in half, as many Republicans proposed, the economy would have been given a strong booster shot that would have avoided the recession. Mitchell used the rules to prevent enactment of a bipartisan jobs bill that would have strengthened the economy and lowered the deficit; then Senate Minority Leader, Robert Dole, to whom Mitchell railed against, used the rates to block a partisan political payoff to the nations' mayors and other special interests that would have added $16 billion to the worst deficit in U.S. history."

If Lambro's report of the two incidents sounds one-sided, the important thing to remember is that the Clinton bill was killed in the Senate because it had too much pork attached to it, too much spending, too much waste, and would have created too few real jobs. Though the Republicans were instrumental in killing this bill, being in the minority, they could not have done it alone. The truth is that many Democrats saw the true worth of the bill, and fearing revenge at the polls, voted against it. On the other hand, Bush's economic bill had wide bipartisan support in both Houses of Congress, but was vigorously fought down by Mitchell who was determined that the administration would not get credit for anything that would benefit the economy. Besides commenting on the many Democrats who opposed Clinton's bill, Lambro summarized a *Wall Street Journal* editorial which was far more critical of the Clinton economic bill than he. The editorial, Lambro said "blamed Mitchell for letting the economy drift into a prolonged recession—the key factor that helped the Democrats recapture the White House. The purpose of the Bush economic bill was to release a wave of new business investments in the economy.

Mitchell had more to do with the 1990/91 recession than any other lawmaker in Congress."

Another of the many hypocritical statements Mitchell made during George Bush's presidency was that "the middle class has been soaked too long and too hard...we Democrats want to give them a tax break, etc., etc." Unfortunately, the media chose not to question why Mitchell had a complete change of heart when the new president arrived, and why he suddenly felt it was okay to soak the middle class, as nearly everything was on the table for a tax increase.

LOSERS HAVE MEANSPIRITED REACTIONS

Democrats went into overdrive singing the blues after they lost control of Congress in 1994. They had nearly forty years in their progression toward being power tyrants. Scarcely ever did the word "bipartisanship" pass their lips up to that time, but it soon became their favorite whine and wail once they got knocked off the "catbird seat," and they never grew weary of crying out for bipartisanship—that is until Senator Jim Jeffords switched parties and put them back in the majority. Now they are not interested in bipartisanship at all.

Before Jeffords, the Democrats found two targets on which to vent their grief and anger over losing their power hold on Congress. Number One was Newt Gingrich—their rationalization, his book deal. But the real reason was because of his and the Republicans' outstanding record of accomplishments in the first 100 days of their leadership. This was one bitter pill for Democrats to swallow.

Brent Bozell wrote in his column in *The Conservative Chronicle*, February 3, 1995, "The Gingrich and Wright book deals are two very different stories. The royalty arrangement for Jim Wright's book was highly unusual: Wright got 55% of book sales—four times the industrial standard—from his publisher, a former campaign worker." His special deal with labor unions to buy large quantities of his speeches, stapled together as books, ended up netting him 69 counts of ethics violations, which forced him into resignation to avoid being indicted.

On the other hand, the Democrats, rightly or not, went after Gingrich because his publisher had interests pending before Congress. Bozell wrote that virtually everyone in business in this regulatory age have interests in Congress. He went on to say that when Gingrich's contract is finalized, he will do as "congressmen-turned authors," and submit it to the Ethics Committee.

Bozell said that if the two deals are considered equal scandals, "it's only fair to expect equal coverage." But that was not the case. The attacks on Gingrich were hot and heavy for weeks, but on Wright, Bozell reported: "The networks did not run a single story on Wright's ethical problems."

Conservative talk-show host and author, Rush Limbaugh('s), findings seemed to indicate the same pattern of imbalance Bozell talked about whenever a Democrat and Republican are involved. Limbaugh gave a report on his television show (first week of June, 1995) from the research he found on *Nexus*. His discovery was that the major media did 901 stories on Newt Gingrich and his book deal in the period of one month, while in a period of one and a half years, they did only 82 stories on Secretary of Commerce, Ron Brown, regarding bribery and conflicts of interest allegations—so, who is the media after?

The fact is that from the beginning, Newt Gingrich was doomed to extreme ridicule from the Democrats (and the media) because they could not handle not being in charge—forty years had spoiled them, and they acted like brats. To top it off, Gingrich had so many good ideas (and many got passed and signed by Clinton), it was like pouring salt into their wounds. So the Democrats and the media were not able to bash Gingrich enough. Their strategy to hold him down was to constantly tell the American people that he was the most disliked and unpopular politician in America. It worked!

It is important to note that the Gingrich book deal consisted of $3 million advance. He settled for one dollar. Hillary Clinton got an

advance of $8 million and the howl was quickly squelched, and she set-
tled for $8 million.

The second target Democrats decided to pounce on at that time was
Senator Bob Dole. However, it took them several months to "get
something" on him. The sin: Dole had the courage to tell it how it is
with Hollywood sleaze, and one of the left's big complaints was that his
motives were suspect because he did not take on the sleaze factor earlier—as if the suddenly-pious media did.

I imagine Senator Dole waited for what he thought was the right
time to speak out against Hollywood's sleazy "entertainment". Surely,
he must have considered what the media did to Vice President Dan
Quayle for this "offense"; and surely, the time must have seemed ripe
to him—after all a Democrat, Senator Lieberman, was already on
record of criticizing the film industry for producing sleaze. Therefore,
the media could not go berserk and accuse him of censorship, of violat-
ing the First Amendment, of trying to force his brand of morality
down the collective throats of all the rest of us, etc.

Well, if that is what was on Dole's mind, he was right on all counts.
However, liberals can always create a negative out of a positive when is
comes to their opponent, and they did just that. Some Democrats and
talking heads in the media registered the complaint that Dole failed to
catalogue every movie, TV show, producer, and actor that used violence, foul language, or sex to entertain—as did the *New York Times*
columnist Jay Carr. Of course, in my opinion, that is what the media
wished Dole had done; then they could brand him as some kind of
extremist nut, and maybe even a McCarthyite type.

A typical media rationalization by an anonymous staff member of
The Wichita Eagle (June 3, 2000) defended the entertainment industry,
saying it did not create a "blood-and-sex drenched culture," and that
we would not see much of it if it had not been in demand. Nonsense!
Hollywood is known for pushing the envelop. As soon as they feel they
have sufficiently bathed the public in one bit of garbage, they move on
to the next, and then the next. If you bombard people long enough

with sleaze—two generations, at least—many will become desensitized or even addicted to it. Even so, people do have a responsibility in this matter, as *The Eagle* writer indicated, but Hollywood has made smut commonplace, and some can no longer distinguish between it and what is normal. Of course, that is the intention of its creators.

Apparently a liberal, and feeling somewhat left out of the debate, *The Eagle* writer complained that "conservatives do not have a corner on the nation's moral health"—something we probably all agree on, but we wonder why the media and other liberals don't get on board and quit pulling in the ACLU to fight for obscenity and the things they say they abhor—makes their motives suspect."

CREDIT FOR A GOOD ECONOMY

We hear an awful lot of boasting about Clinton's wonderful record on the economy by himself, the Democrats, and the talking heads on television. Remember the jubilant claim of victory he made for his first budget bill back in 1993? But what were the facts then? Columnist Jeffrey Hart of *Creators Syndicate, Inc.*, writes: "This bad legislation passed by embarrassingly small margins."

However, the idea of spending cuts proved to be just another manipulative strategy for votes, as were so many other things proposed by Clinton, for they, too, pretty much fell by the wayside. Meanwhile, Tim Penny (D) and John Kasick (R) took the president at his word and drafted bills that would significantly cut the deficit over a period of five years (Kasick's with 160 cuts), but the administration threatened congressmen with all kinds of reprisals if they voted for it. Several Democrats were disgusted with the White House performance on this matter and spoke out against the president. In fact, Penny was so disgusted with Clinton's misrepresentation of his intentions that he put in for retirement. The former democratic presidential candidate, Paul Tsongas, called the administration and those in Congress who opposed the bill "hypocrites." Lambro reported the furor over the president's actions: "The administration used every lobbying trick it could muster, alleging that the cuts would hurt the economy and would endanger funding for Clinton's health-care plan(Hillary's health-care plan turned out to be a big flop, anyway). In fact, the original $103 billion plan, which was trimmed back to win more support, would have cut only one cent out of every dollar spent over the next five years. The bill received the endorsement of dozens of Democrats and Republicans in the House and Senate, and more than a dozen deficit-fighting organizations around the country—including Tsongas' bipartisan Concord Coalition.

"But the raw power of the presidency and appropriations committee barons to withhold important projects from lawmakers won out in the end, and the bold deficit-cutting plan lost by only a handful of votes— 219-213....An opportunity to take a real whack at the deficit was lost, and the hand that held back the ax was Bill Clinton's."

Next on the agenda, looking to soothe the ruffled feathers in Congress, the administration offered a substitute bill to cancel $5.9 billion in spending. However, when Clinton talked about reinventing government, the savings he said then were $108 billion. But even the $5.9 billion projection "spending cut," according to the Congressional Budget Office (CBO) was greatly exaggerated, which reported the real amount more in the neighborhood of $305 million over five years. The CBO also said the same of Gore's waste-cutting plan, that the figures did not add up, that some 21 bureaucracies would be created, and at best save only one-third of its projected savings.

You might ask, "Why was the economy so great during the '90's if it were not for Bill Clinton? Cal Thomas gives some interesting reasons for deficit reduction (with little to no credit to Clinton) in his syndicated column: "A new study by the congressional Joint Economic Committee (JEC) shows that the bulk of the $126 billion decline is due to economic and accounting changes mostly unrelated to policy. According to the JEC study, $71 billion of the decline is accounted for by a continuation of the business cycle upswing underway since 1991,

$21 billion by swings in deposit insurance outlays and $8 billion in auctions of radio bands.

"When those effects are set aside, the decline in the deficit is a much less impressive $26 billion, thanks to a single policy change—a reduction in discretionary defense spending. Tax increases have not reduced the deficit."

James Glassman of American Enterprise Institute gives a good deal of credit to Ronald Reagan for the economy, which he says began in 1982 after Reagan's marginal tax cuts and restraints on the regulatory side began to take effect. He calls it the "Reagan boom"—"the longest expansion and strongest in American history, with the brief exception, a mild recession in 1990," [and that could have been brought under control quickly, as explained earlier in this chapter, except for then Senate Majority Leader George Mitchell]. One hundred and forty one CEO's and CFO's of top performing businesses participated in a survey on this issue. The results showed that they generally agreed with Glassman's assessment of the '90's economy. Three times as many business executives gave credit to Reagan as did to Clinton. However, most all of these executives rated increased productivity, federal reserve policies, and information technologies high on the list of reasons for the economic boom. Glassman says the 90's economic boom is merely a continuation of the 80's and attributes much of this success to Reagan's victory over the Cold War and the subsequent smaller government that followed.

Drew Parkhill, CBN Senior Editor of Finance, also believes the number one reason for the '90's economy is the free market, but he attributes much of it to Reagan's policies, which he claims strengthened the free market. "Reagan's tax cuts put more money into the hands of baby boomers, and everybody really—it made a strong stock market stronger, made a strong economy.

Glassman says that the '90's had access to the "peace dividend" that was talked about in the "80's. It came about as "the result of what Reagan did, because Congress would not cut domestic spending and

Reagan forced defense spending through." Glassman says the peace dividend resulted in more than a 50% cut in defense spending, and "a savings of $250 billion, or $2,500 per family, per year."

Parkhill adds another reason for the good economy: the bond market was so high that it killed off inflation, and Reagan let Paul Voelker do the same thing with short-term interest rates at the Federal Reserve. Parkhill goes on to say that Reagan did not get credit because the media detested him when he ran for president, and detested him after he was president. "Remember *Newsweek's* 1982 cover, 'Reagan's America: The poor get poorer,' but in 1984 when we had the strongest economy in 33 years, you didn't see any 'Reagan's America: Everyone gets richer' cover. So they're not about to give Reagan any credit."

Other world leaders agreed with Glassman and Parkhill's assessment of the economy, claiming Ronald Reagan as "the chief architect of economic strength of the 80's and 90's." Former Prime Minister of England, Margaret Thatcher writes: "Today's American prosperity is the result, above all, of the fundamental shift of direction President Reagan promoted in the 80's."

And what about the balanced budget and the surplus of revenue during the Clinton Administration? Parkhill claims there was no balanced budget and no surplus because of the many years of looting the Social Security fund to cover the deficit and the rest of government; there are only a lot of IOU's left in that fund. And besides that, he says, "The national debt is scheduled to go up $1 trillion in the next 5–6 years. It is a bipartisan fiction—there really is not a surplus."

Journalist Jeffrey Hart came to the same conclusion. He wrote (1/14/98): "The so-called balanced-budget agreement is fiction. That the government has shrunk is fiction. That the government has shrunk is due to the recent economic boom, which enhances government revenue. (The real cuts are scheduled to be made after Clinton leaves office.) Yet even that charade was unacceptable to most Democrats in office."

So, what about the largest deficit in history coming out of the 80's? Many Republicans are now saying that it was necessary. They feel the deficit was an investment that resulted in the end of the Cold War and the downfall of communism in the Soviet Union, along with its rippling effect, which assured the ultimate payoff—our present robust economy. Also, the S &L's were paid off in the '80's.

Due to his many screwups, early in President Clinton's first term in office, there was speculation as to whether he was really relevant in the scheme of things. At one point, thinks looked so bleak for him, he actually came before the cameras and declared that he was still relevant. Later, as his polls numbers climbed, he regained his confidence and reverted back to his original agenda of socialism, especially in his "State of the Union" addresses. There he was a virtual Santa Claus promising handouts and entitlements to everyone. The public with its short memory were apparently contented and happy with all the "gifts," even if they had to pay for them with higher taxes. But one thing they did reject was Hillary's expensive socialized health-care program, which would have eventually broken the backs of the middle class. Even though Republicans often did a disappointing job of holding the reins on this man (and Hillary too, for that matter), they definitely were a deterring force to stop the Clinton dream of an American socialist society, at least to some extent.

THE 2000 RECESSION

There probably will always be disagreements on the subject of the 1990's economic boom and who should get credit for it. While Bill Clinton never missed a chance to pat himself on the back (and Democrats too) for the money flow of those years, many economic analysts gave the majority of the credit to the policies of Ronald Reagan, as noted in the previous section. In his article "Recession Shock," *Insight* (12/31/01), Columnist John Berlau writes: "From 1982 to 2000, save only for two quarters in the early 1990's, the United States experienced such economic growth and prosperity as she never before had seen.... Suddenly, a few months before George W. Bush took office, it all seemed to come to an end. What happened?"

At first the decline was attributed solely to the "bubble" created by the Internet and technology stocks and the unsound and over speculation bids. Berlau writes: "But some observers noticed that something else was going on at the time the markets started to fall: "The Clinton Securities and Exchange Commission (SEC), led by Chairman Arthur Levitt, was busy dismantling reforms from the Reagan administration that had made it easier for small businesses to raise money from the stock market." Levitt's SEC, in search of fraud, punished legitimate businesses, which they later had to admit was almost non-existent.

According to Economist Lawrence Kudlow this breakdown of regulatory reform coincides with the fall of the NASDAQ high-tech market in March, 2000. Dean Devine, senior scholar of the American Conservative Union's Task Force on Regulatory Reform agrees that the timing "is almost precisely when, through a series of administrative rules, Levitt's SEC blocked small entrepreneurial firms from the access to capital markets that they enjoyed since the early 1980's....Unlike most of the times in the past, it looks like this was a stock-market led recession....Levitt and Clinton disrupted the markets and then the market led to the weakening of the economy."

Evidently facts do not matter. Some believe that the Democrats, and especially Senate Majority leader Tom Daschle, is hopeful that the economy will not recover before the 2002 congressional elections so he and his party can use the "Bush recession" as their "ace-in-the-hole" to win majorities in both houses of Congress. Berlau goes on to say: "Devine, who is reputed to be as politically savvy as they come, thinks Republicans should set the record straight about what he calls the 'Clinton-Levitt recession.'" But no one should hold their breath that this will happen. One thing the Republicans have made clear is that they do not stand up for themselves very well. Most of the time it appears that they "just want to get along"—probably why they are often called "the stupid party."

According to Brian Wesbury, chief economist at the brokerage firm of Griffin, Kubik, Stephens & Thompson in Chicago, recessions are caused mostly by "policy mistakes." "He attributes the current slump to Federal Reserve Chairman Alan Greenspan's tightening of interest rates beginning in May, 2000, to taxes being at a record-high share of gross domestic product (GDP) and to the chilling effect on technology sector of the government's pursuit of Microsoft Corp. He adds that the SEC regulations could have easily contributed heavily to this....Anything that inhibits the free flow of capital is a negative for economic growth in the long run or even in the short run."

Since the Bush administration has their own man, Harvey Pitt, chairing the SEC, "small-business people have noticed a change in environment." Greg Halpern, CEO of Circle Group Internet, says the "business people he knows are getting their offerings approved in 60 to 90 days, in contrast to the 14 months in which his company's paperwork was hung out to linger...Pitt recently told a group of accountants that, from now on [in contrast to the Clinton-Levitt era] 'The commission will make sound decisions in a respectful, affirmative way, not in a demeaning, demanding or demonizing way.'

"But Devine says Pitt will have to do more than that. He will have to reverse Levitt's policies as well as push further deregulation, both to stimulate the economy and to place the blame where it belongs."

FUNDING THE LEFT

Pat Robertson illustrates how the liberal, humanistic view dominates media coverage of the news in his book, *The Turning Tide*. He lists several major and minor networks and gives percentages of the liberal producers and anchor men and women on them, along with their comments of support for the left-wing agenda. What he found in his research was that they have contributed not only vocally to the left, but also with vast monetary support to their favored liberal candidates. Quoting former president of CBS, Van Gordon Sauter, on this subject, Robertson writes that the media has become a "tremendous advocacy group. Look at *Newsweek Magazine*. Look at *Time* magazine. The subjectivity that just runs through them I find absolutely stunning. If you look at the *New York Time,* the *Boston Globe*, the *Washington Post*...the liberalism of these papers manifests itself in their news columns, not just on their editorial pages."

Likewise, Brent Bozell of the Media Research Center reports much the same thing going on in regard to philanthropy giving patterns of the entertainment industry. During the 1991–92 election period this industry gave a ratio of 73 to 27 percent more to Democrats than to Republicans. The same thing happened the following two years with PAC money given by *Disney, MCA, Paramount, Sony Pictures, Time Warner,* and *Viacom,* totaling 74 percent to the Democrats and 26 percent to the Republicans. Producer Aaron Spelling, Bozell says, "is the most generous donor," since 1966, giving $44,500 to Democrats, plus another $24,000 to the Democrat Party, compared to only $2,500 to Republicans. Some of the recipients of the big bucks were "Dianne Feinstein (D.Calif.); Ted Kennedy (D.Mass.); and John Kerry (D.Mass.); former Sen. Alan Cranston (D.Calif.); and Rep. Pat Schroeder (D.Col.); and former Rep. Mel Levine (D.Calif.)."

Also, during the Bush administration, "Four media foundations— the Boston Globe Foundation, General Electric Foundation (GE owns NBC), New York Times Company Foundation, and *The Washington Post*-related Philip L. Graham Fund—gave nearly $3.5 million in donations to identifiably liberal or conservative groups. Of that total, $2.85 million (or 82 percent) was earmarked for the liberal groups.

LARGE CORPORATIONS BUCKLE TO LIBERAL CAUSES

While it is well-known that Republicans generally get larger donations from big business than do Democrats, some things are not exactly what they seem to be. In early January of 1994 CBN's *Newswatch* gave a surprising report on corporate philanthropy. In essence the report said that ordinarily we would not expect large corporations to support liberal causes, simply because these organizations are "anti-free market capitalism," but research shows just the opposite. Many large corporations contribute huge sums of money to left-wing organizations.

Why is this true? Fred Smith of Competitive Enterprise Institute says it has to do with a very important commodity to business—public opinion. He says: "If there is a conflict like animal rights or the fur movement or the abortion issue, business cannot afford the bad publicity." With left-wing groups breathing down business' back, many of them end up trying to pay them off in hopes they will not harass them further. Smith says: "Business tries to placate powerful liberal groups. If they don't, they will lobby against them. They think maybe it [money] will give us a few friends, but they get sued anyway—corporate philanthropy is almost extortion."

Another agency, Capital Research Center, studies corporate giving patterns. Stu Nolan of the Center and co-author of the *Politics of Corporate Philanthropy Hypocrisy*, says, "They [corporations] favor the left in a dramatic way." Last year the center studied the financial gift patterns of hundreds of corporations which had contributed at least $25,000 to both left and right of center groups. The irony was that left of center groups were favored 3–2. However one would expect the opposite results since "right of center groups are more for free market, private enterprise, and free solution, while left of center groups tend to be anti-private sector and advocate raising personal and corporate taxes."

Ironically, the groups receiving most of the money are actually anti-private sector; some advocate raising personal and corporate tax rates. Fred Smith used the analogy of a crocodile not satisfied with a man's leg to describe the situation. "It [the crocodile] goes after the rest of him." Grover Norquist of Americans for Tax Reform explained that the problem continues to a large extent because corporations, while they "do have to state their contributions to campaigns, do not have to reveal their corporate budgets."

THE JACKSON SHAKEDOWN

Senior reporter for *Insight*, Kenneth R. Timmerman, writes an article that raises a lot of questions about Jesse Jackson and the way he operates through Rainbow/PUSH Coalition International Trade Bureau ("Jackson Continues Wall Street Waltz" (1/28/02). The subtitle of Timmerman's article reads: "Critics claim the reverend's annual shakedown of corporate America does little more than line the pockets of select cronies and his "nonprofit" empire." The question Timmerman asks is "Will corporate America ever learn?"

Later, speaking of a man whom he describes as "a self-styled reverend without a church," he continues: "The question critics are asking is why—what do Jackson and his racial brokerage have to offer corporate America, let alone Main Street or the inner city? What's going on here?" Jackson's defense is, of course, slavery: "Without the slave trade, there couldn't have been a Wall Street....We bring to Wall Street as shareholders, not sharecroppers, a key to Wall Street's growth: market, money, talent and location." He claims further that "minorities couldn't make it in America on talent alone" (evidently he hasn't checked that idea out with Secretary of State Colon Powel, National Security Advisor Condoleeza Rice, former presidential candidate and talk show host, Alan Keyes, Rep. Rep. J.C. Watts, (R-Ok.); Supreme Court Justice Clarence Thomas, talk show hostess Oprah Winfrey, and numerous other people of color who have made it to the top without threatening anyone or practicing bloodsucking tactics upon them).

Also, Jackson's critics question his work to support minorities, as they feel he hasn't done very much to bring improvement to impoverished communities. It appears to them he is more interested in enriching himself and his cronies and those at the top of the corporate ladder and pinning "honorary" titles on them, that is, people "such as bond broker 'Silver' sponsor Ron Blaylock—who in turn made substantial contributions to Jackson's nonprofit empire after reaping the benefits of his racial-brokerage service."

Rainbow/PUSH "allows" it participants to "earn" titles of "Gold" or "Silver" or "platinum," depending on the amount of their donation. But, of course, the pressure is great to do so, as Jackson and his team have methods to make any corporation that does not comply with the *boss'* wishes, sorry—very sorry. Coca-Cola is one of those companies Timmerman says who is "grateful to have survived Jackson's latest shakedown, secured with the expert assistance of race-baiting legal eagles such as Johnnie Cochran and Willie Gary." So, too, is "Verizon Communication Inc. after paying Jackson's group $800,000 in 1999, in recognition for his efforts of racial 'healing'".

Timmerman lists the honoraries: "'Gold' sponsors include AOL Time Warner and Prudential Financial—the 'silver' friends are Pepsi, Daimler-Chrysler and AT&T, whose chairman…has been a staunch Jackson ally and major contributor to the Democratic Party."

Once Jackson places his weighty thumb on a corporation, whether the allegations he makes are true or not, it seems a costly financial transaction takes place. Toyota's "conversion" is a good example: The charge was that Toyota had "a print ad he [Jackson] claimed was racially offensive." An immediate threat ensued of a black boycott against the company. Timmerman writes: "Toyota's '21st Century Diversity Strategy' was a direct outgrowth of the Jackson's threat."

But, apparently, the pressure did not end there. On January 15, 2002, the Jackson team held a three-day celebration in New York City with their corporate friends attending. The "privilege" of hosting the big party and picking up the tab were "Platinum" sponsors Citigroup and Goldman Sachs (one can only guess what their crime against Rainbow/PUSH might have been). Also in attendance was a representative of Toyota. Vice President of the company's motor sales, Irv Miller, "unveiled Toyota's plan to dole out $700 million in contracts to minority businesses." This might be a noble gesture on the part of Toyota, but the big question becomes—whose pockets are being lined?

Surprise! Surprise! Politics are involved! Timmerman writes: "Jackson launched his Wall Street gambit in 1997, with the benediction of Bill Clinton, Federal Reserve Chairman Alan Greenspan and corporate bigwigs such as Citigroup Chairman Sanford Weill....Revenues for Jackson's non-profit empire sky-rocketed from $4 million in 1997, to more than $14 million just two years later."

And another big surprise! At the big "celebration" party, Jackson claims victimhood—"economic terrorism" at the hands of the Bush Administration—"I have been on the 'red-squad list' by [Attorney General John] Ashcroft and others; they're after us. They're using [Osma] bin Laden as an excuse to come after us."

Well, the party did not end on a good note, at least for "conservative black activist Rev. Jesse Lee Peterson, who is also "a talk-show host, author and founder of the Brotherhood Organization of a New Destiny (BOND)." He made the mistake of asking Toyota's Irv Miller the wrong question: "As the president of a non profit conservative organization, BOND, I'm concerned that our young people will be locked out of any training programs offered by Toyota because of our conservative beliefs. How are you going to make sure that organizations like ours are not discriminated against by Rainbow/PUSH and its members?"

Understandably, this question did not sit well with the Jackson crowd which responded with shouts and jeers. Peterson said, "To put it simply, all hell broke loose. Eventually, Jackson turned to his son, Jonathan, and shouted: 'Get his ass our of here!'" Timmerman goes on:

"Later the burly, younger Jackson spotted Peterson returning to the room to hand literature on his organization to Miller. Jonathan made a beeline for us from the other side of the room, slamming into Rev. Peterson with a forearm shiv[ver] and nearly knocking him to the ground."

In the meantime, Jackson's "occupation" has allowed him to enjoy the best money can buy, life in luxurious hotels, multi-million dollar homes, limousine service, mistresses, etc. Despite Jackson's lack of credentials as a member of the clergy, an obsequious media have never questioned "The Reverend's" motives, but neither has the Internal Revenue Service—the latter giving him a pass on obscure bookkeeping practices and undeclared revenues, that is until recently. Thanks to Bill O'Reilly of *Fox News*, who hammered away on Jackson's operations for weeks, and Timmerman's book, *SHAKEDOWN Exposing the Real Jesse Jackson*, which is even a heavier hammer.

Timmerman smashes Jackson's image as a man who is a guardian for the poor, a protector of the downtrodden, and a great defender of civil rights. But the question is whether we will ever see justice applied to Mr. Jackson as it should be. My guess is that since he does so much for the Democrat Party, and for the fact that the IRS Commissioner, Charles O. Rossetti is a Clinton holdover who only goes after conservatives and suspected Clinton adversaries, Jackson will get a limp slap on the wrist. But no matter what happens, his credibility has been severely damaged. We will still have someone more interested in race-baiting than truth to take his place—Al Sharpton.

7

Setting the Roadblocks

o o o o o o o o o o o o o o o o o o o o o o o o o o o o o o o o o o

He is a merchant, the balances of deceit are in his hand: he loveth to oppress. Hosea 12:7

We have seen the political barriers that hinder honest and sincere debate that keep any sane resolutions for society's needs from being realized. The deterrents stem from inflated egos whose unquenchable desire for power and control insists that they must always have the last word. Absolutes and principles take second place to rationalizations and lies and coverups, while accountability and responsibility are systematically diminished. "Situational ethics" and political correctness become synonymous with truth. Forget authenticity, the goal is to outwit one's opponent with demagoguery. Truth doesn't matter; it is whoever can speak the most often before the cameras with an oily, glib tongue—the slick, oily, smooth, sleight-of-hand type.

CAMPAIGN 2000

Given the finance campaign scandals of the Clinton Administration and all the other scandals it had been involved in recent years, one would think that Democrats, above all people, would want to elevate their image and take the "high road" when possible, but instead, they tried to hijack the GOP nomination process in Election 2000—the religious/political fiasco in the Michigan primary. This unfortunate scene involved some harsh phone calls from Pat Robertson, Christian leader on CBN's *The 700 Club*, who . strongly opposed Senator John McCain as a presidential candidate for president: one reason being the McCain/Feingold reform bill, which, if passed, would hurt Republicans and help Democrats; another, a hateful quote against Christians made by a McCain supporter, Senator Warren Rudman (R).

In the meantime, Bush made the statement that Robertson had acted apart from his campaign. The McCain side went into immediate production of what they called the "Catholic Alert" (a non-existent organization), portraying Bush as a bigoted Catholic hater. The charge against Bush was, of course, untrue, but it was played to the hilt for some time as possibly having some merit. The main reason the lie lasted as long as it did was that the media "loved" John McCain. My contention is that the media not so much loved McCain as they used him to weaken Bush's chances in the election. Regardless of the seriousness of their affections, the main stream electronic media described their own behavior in terms of their "love affair with McCain," "a crush on McCain, "in the tank for McCain," "the media darling."

And what does all this have to do with hijacking the GOP nomination process? Of course, Democrats saw an immediate advantage for themselves in the wrangling between the McCain and Bush teams. Congressman John Conyers (D) led the pack to further weaken George Bush's chances of victory by putting together fifty people to work the phones in an effort to get Democrats out to cast a revenge vote against the Michigan Governor who supported George Bush. So, you might ask: "What is wrong with that"? The answer is nothing, if that was all there was to it, but the scheme was to tell Democrats they could vote for McCain and then switch back in the general election and vote for Al Gore. McCain was informed of what was taking place, but since the scheme tilted the election outcome in his favor, he did not follow his pledge to take the high road. He later lied about his knowledge of the plot, but got caught in a trap of his own making when one day after his denial, one of his aides let the "cat out of the bag" and told the truth. Yet, we saw no media clamor as what would certainly would have happened if this scenario had been perpetrated on, at that time, media-darling John McCain.

Well, the outcome of this deception, as we know, worked and won McCain the Michigan primary—the reason being that Democrats and Independents outnumbered Republicans in their own primary. However, what it finally boiled down to is that Democrats, voting 80% for McCain, made the difference. Contrast that fact with George Bush's win of the Republican vote by a large majority. I think all of us could agree that both Democrats and Republicans want the privilege of nominating their own candidate for president, but that fact did not faze Democrats as they pulled similar tactics to the Michigan primary in other states as well, knowing full well, the media would not show them up for their unethical behavior.

ELECTION 2000

Well, it is hard to find a word that accurately describes Election 2000—phenomenal, astonishing, uncanny, what? One would think that all the curves, twists and bends rendered in that long and tedious ordeal to arrive at a final decision may have been necessary, but Thomas Sowell disagrees: "Nothing had happened in the Florida election that does not happen in other elections…The Florida Supreme Court rushed in to solve a non-problem—and its 'solution' created a mess that threatened a constitutional crisis…The real issue was not whether Bush would have won yet again in the latest in a series of recounts. The real issue was whether this kind of perversion of the law was to be allowed to continue—and to provide a precedent for chaos after every future close election".

What a shame that it took a year after Election 2000 for the media to declare George W. Bush the official winner for president. In my opinion three primary reasons created the standoff that led to this problem.

First of all, there was a predetermined decision to call for recounts in highly democratic counties if Al Gore did not win Florida—thus, the 50 lawyer brigade dispatched immediately to that state (which quickly mounted to nearly 70) to prod and poke disgruntled voters on and on into a state of frenzy. Thanks to the likes of Jessie Jackson and MSNBC. Sowell says, "After George W. Bush won the election in Florida and then the official recount, Gore had to come up with something to cause a re-count under different rules."

Voila! the second reason: the idea that the infamous "butterfly ballots" were so complicated the average person could not figure them out. Common sense tells me that since these squabbling senior citizens in Florida—for the most part educated, fairly affluent people, and likely voters all their lives—did not pay careful attention to what they were doing. Given the amount of howling and whining they did before the camera, I can't imagine that any of them were too intimidated to ask for another ballot if they misvoted, much less, help if they needed it, as the media suggested. The responsibility of the voter is to follow the arrow next to the candidate's name to the circle designated—not that difficult. It appears these people were a part of a Jewish community which traditionally vote Democrat. It is also important to note that they did not complain until after they found out that Gore did not win the electoral vote. To try to drum up sympathy for these people, the media even suggested special training for the volunteers who work the primaries—supposedly they did not know how to help voters—and classes for voters so they would know how to vote—since when?? Ridiculous, but nevertheless, it wasn't long until the Florida Supreme Court mandated recounts in Democrat counties, where Gore hoped to gain more votes. Columnist Hans S. Nichols said that the numbers never did add up for Gore, not even after the Gore camp managed to disqualify some 1,420 military votes, knowing full well that the majority of these votes would go for Bush.

The third reason resulted from the fact that the judges of the Florida Supreme Court, who were Democrats, would not order a uniform standard by which the votes were to be counted—thus, the U.S. Supreme Court finally stepped in and overruled them.

At the time all this was going on, I thought the Gore team was extremely lucky. They kept the counting and recounting going for quite some time, which, in the first place, according to Florida election laws was illegal since the candidate had already won in those counties.

Sowell writes: "What Gore wanted—and got—was a manual recount in a few Democratic strongholds, based on local Democrat officials' guesses as to what dimpled chads meant, while the vast majority of the counties in the state counted only clear perforations of the ballot as votes." And here is the very important point Sowell makes: "That meant freezing Bush's slim majority vote totals in the rest of Florida, while allowing local Democrats in these few counties to go prospecting for more Gore 'votes' by counting dents on the ballots as votes." Ed says (with tongue in cheek): "Of all the absurdities in the post-election recount, the one thing the Democrats omitted was the claim that of the people who did not vote, a vast majority would have voted for Gore, and he would have won. In fact, they did everything but assassinate Bush."

It seemed there would be no end of trials to gain the crown for Al Gore. When all attempts had failed to scrounge up the desired number of votes that would push him over the top, Democrats asked Secretary of State Katherine Harris to extend the deadline. Even Texas recounts were thrown out to the public as an excuse to keep this farce ongoing, but, of course, it had no bearing to the Florida situation at all. In Texas only one count of the ballots thrown out by the machine is allowed, and that is done by an unchanging uniform standard throughout. Many believe that Gore actually gained more "votes" than was his due with two recounts, and in some places, as many as three.

"Even though the Supreme Court halted the official recounts on Dec. 12, the tabulating of votes was far from over. On the contrary, the media formed their own alliances, grouping off into consortiums to determine voter intent under a variety of different circumstances....In April, the *Miami Herald* and *USA Today* completed the first comprehensive study of undervotes. They concluded that Bush would have widened his 537 vote victory to a 1,665-vote margin if the recount mandated by the Florida Supreme Court had continued. Bush would have won even using standards that Gore favored, namely counting faintly dimpled undervotes....Having spent more than $900,000 on its study, National Opinion Research Center (NORC) aimed to 'provide a historical record for one of the most remarkable presidential elections in U. S. history'....despite NORC misgivings," the New York Times conceded that "George W. Bush would have won even if the United States Supreme Court had allowed the statewide manual recount of the votes that the Florida Supreme Court had ordered to go forward." *The Wall Street Journal* also noted, "the outcome proves the point we and others were making all along, which is that you can't change the election rules after the votes have been cast."

Human Events, week of Feb. 4, 2002—Mark R. Levin, President of Landmark Legal Foundation. "Bush would have undoubtedly been president had the U.S. Supreme Court not intervened at all....If there's a challenge to any of the certified Electoral College votes by at least one member of the Senate and House, the House then determines the President by a majority vote of the state delegations. There were more Republican state delegates in the House, meaning that George Bush would have been elected President even had the Supreme Court not reversed the unconstitutional actions of the Florida Supreme Court."

Levin also brings up the "self-serving, extra-constitutional straw man," former Congressman and White House counsel to Bill Clinton, Abner Mikva, whose argument is that since Bush did not receive "the mandate of national *plurality*" he should not be president. Levin goes on to say: "Of course, Mikva dares not complain that Bush lacked a *majority* of the popular vote, for that would have disqualified his beloved Bill Clinton from making any Supreme Court nominations. Neither in 1992 nor 1996 did Clinton receive a majority vote. In fact, in 1992, Clinton received 43% of the popular vote. In 2000, Bush received 48%. Consequently, Bush received a larger number of votes than Clinton did in 1992."

McCain Impudence

The fact that John McCain was a war hero, and rightly praised for such, should not be viewed as reason or cover to praise him for his bad conduct after the election. In my opinion his impudence runs long and deep. From childhood forward, McCain seems to have enjoyed bucking his superiors, and most of the time it appeared as though it was only for the sake of just being obstinate.

After the election, McCain held such bitter feelings toward the new president that he proceeded immediately into his "critical-right-now agenda." His campaign-reform bill was presented as a crisis that could not wait. The content of the proposed bill is also another example of McCain's obstinate behavior, as he knew from the beginning the good reason why almost all Democrats loved the bill: simply because it was detrimental to Republicans as it was to beneficial to Democrats. The weak alteration applied to the bill in regard to union dues did not go far enough, and could very well have moved the Republicans into a future state of irrelevancy. What many people do not realize about soft money is that it buys for Republicans what the media and the unions give to the Democrat Party. The media is approximately 80% liberal Democrat, and there is no doubt, they have been known to either make or break a person.

Having a president of his own party, one would think McCain would have shown him some deference, at least for his first 100 days, but that was not the case. He also set up his agenda for tax cuts, an energy program, and whatever else he could come up with to upstage

President Bush. In fact, the media were touting him as the most powerful man in the Senate.

However, McCain's in-your-face attitude soon backfired. Arizona citizens were considering a recall of his senate seat and threatening to run someone else in his place. It wasn't long until McCain went before the cameras and praised the president for doing the right thing on various issues. Actually, he has become a good spokesman for President Bush, and probably endeared himself to his constituency. I, personally, have come to like him much better, but I will agree with McCain on one point of contention he held against candidate Bush. I thought Bush went too far with his accusation that McCain did not support cancer research for women. In my opinion that really hit below the belt, and I can understand McCain's bitterness on this issue. After all his sister died of breast cancer.

THE DASCHLE FACTOR

Senator Tom Daschle owes his present status as Senate majority leader to Senator Jim Jeffords (I-Vt.), whom he persuaded to disavow his Republican affiliation." Given the fact that Daschle did not earn the position, makes no difference to him whatever. He sees himself pretty much as a supreme ruler.

Syndicated Columnist Cal Thomas says that President Bush faces the reincarnation of the former Senate Majority Leader George Mitchell, D-Maine—namely, the new Majority Leader Tom Daschle, D-S.D. ("Time for Bush to take on Daschle," *Tribune Media Services*, Jan. 9, 2002). Thomas writes: "The elder Bush mistakenly believed that he could get along with Mitchell and that his "kinder-gentler" approach would bring Mitchell around. Mitchell tied up every meaningful piece of legislation Bush tried to enact, then blamed Bush for the lack of results. Surely this President Bush can see an instant replay coming."

Well, if the President doesn't see an instant replay, he better wake up and soon. The handwriting showed up on the wall when leader Daschle put his first roadblock in place to stop the Bush agenda, his "legislative order" to allow votes only when there is a "supermajority" of 60 votes, and then he falsely passes it off as an historical precedent. Of course, it is not. Thomas' advice to the President is to quote Franklin D. Roosevelt, James Madison, and Thomas Jefferson, all of whom opposed supermajority because the result is minority rule. Thomas goes on to say that "President Bush's adversaries are not Democrats, per se. Some moderate Democrats have joined with him on some issues. His opponent is 'liberalism'"—surprise, surprise, liberalism!

Brent Bozell of Media Research Center comes to very much the same conclusion as Cal Thomas. He says Daschle just "smiles through breakfast meetings with Bush as he strangles the nation's business," which includes "a tax-cut package to stimulate the war-damaged economy and recession," and a bill "to promote greater energy independence." Furthermore, he says the Democrats complain about military tribunals while holding up the federal courts of any new judges. "Bozell asks: "So where are the media, those haters of obstructionism? You can find them in Daschle's pocket…Unlike Clinton, Bush can't count on a sympathetic media to shame his opposition or make them unpopular for blocking his agenda."

And so in his quest to rule uninhibited, it is apparent that Tom Daschle has appointed himself leader of his own personal *triumvirate*. According to reporter Hans S. Nichols, "Daschle seems to be trying to coexist on two different ideological planes." For instance, on the one hand, he supports "$20 billion in unauthorized year-end spending even as he protests deficits…he publically supported an economic-stimulus package while privately doing everything possible to ensure that no such package would come to the Senate floor." Nichols goes on to quote a conservative operative: "Contrasting his [Daschle] 'heart-land talk in South Dakota and his liberal talk in Washington' will be illuminating to all." The illuminating factor is about the referendum to abolish the "death tax" in South Dakota, which passed by 80% of the vote, but back in Washington, Daschle blocked its repeal.

So what effect does Daschle's increasingly partisan tone have on Republicans? Nichols writes: "Republican operatives are cheered by Daschle's noisy leftward march, which they are convinced the public finds annoying, and because the Senate majority leader is finally showing his true colors." And surely Republicans were also pleased over one of Daschle's biggest blunders—blaming President Bush's tax cut "as the biggest reason the surplus is nearly gone." This remark prompted twelve members of his own party, who had voted for the president's $1.35 trillion tax cut, to immediately speak out against him on this issue. These Democrat senators include Diane Feinstein (Cal.); Max Cleland (Ga.); Ben Nelson (Neb.); John Thune (S. D.); Jean Carnahan (Mo.); Tim Johnson (S.D.); Blanche Lincoln (Ark.); Robert Torricelli (N.J.); Mary L. Landrieu (La.); Zell Miller (Ga.). Sen. Miller spoke out against Daschle's stand, and said: "How do you have as one of your highest priorities to re-elect the moderate Democrats from South Dakota, Montana, and Missouri on one hand, then on the other hand blame them for voting for a tax cut that he [Daschle] maintains has created this recession?"

In my opinion, President Bush relies too much on extending the "olive branch" to Daschle and the Democrats who have no intention of working in a bipartisan manner. They have their own priorities, which do not include anything that might help Republicans or this president get anything of much significance passed into law.

THE JUDICIAL TIE-UP

Now that Democrats are in control of the Senate, due to Jefford's revenge switch, they are once again singing a different tune on procedural methods, and changing them so that they benefit their party— what is all this talk about "bipartisanship? When they were not in control, they loved to quote Chief Justice William Rehnquist, that is until the Florida electoral vote that elected George W. Bush President. Justice Rehnquist warned in 1997, that judicial "vacancies cannot remain at such high levels indefinitely without eroding the quality of justice [that] traditionally has been associated with the federal judiciary" (columnist Hans S. Nichols, Dec. 3, 2001 issue of *Insight*). As recent as January, 2002, the Chief Justice reprimanded the Democratically controlled Senate for holding up scores of judicial nominations, saying, "The rate of obstructionism is well in excess of the openly partisan days when Republicans controlled the upper chamber while Clinton was in office."

Hans S. Nichols' column "Democrats Refuse to Act Judiciously, Dec. 3, 2001 issue of *Insight* writes: "One of the dogged critics of the Republican handling of President Bill Clinton's judicial nominees was Sen. Patrick Leahy (D-Vt.), now chairman of the Senate Judiciary Committee." Standing before the Senate, Leahy declared: "Any week in which the Senate does not confirm three judges is a week in which the Senate is failing to address the vacancy crisis. Any fortnight in which we have gone without a judicial-confirmation hearing marks two weeks in which the Senate is falling further behind." But now that Democrats have the upper hand, Leahy shows no interest in confirming judges. Nichols writes: "On his watch, more than 37 judicial nominees have yet to receive so much as the courtesy of a hearing."

Nichols claims that the Democrat's stonewall of President Bush's federal-judge nominees have "created a crisis in U. S. Law enforcement." Many are beginning to speak out against these deliberate and unreasonable delays. John Nowacki of Freedom Congress Foundation gives us another example of the hypocrisy of Leahy's words. To candidate Bush, Leahy announced: "Although we are [from] different parties, I have agreed with Gov. George Bush who has said that in the Senate a nominee ought to get a vote up or down, within 60 day."

But that was then, and now is now—Mr. Leahy has never once backed up his words with deeds. In fact, he has done a complete 180 degree turn-around since George W. Bush became president. One need only look at the disparity between the confirmations made in the last three administrations and the present one to see what is going on. For instance, President Reagan got "91 percent confirmation rate for federal judges his first year in office...President George H.W. Bush got 62 percent...Bill Clinton, 58 percent" (both Reagan and Clinton had their own party in control of Senate); but President George W. Bush got a mere 20 percent in his first year, amounting to 12 confirmations, and these were either "Clinton holdovers, or from a state with two Democratic senators."

Actually, with Mr. Leahy heading the confirmation committee, it appears we have a one-man operation to decide "yea" or "nay" on federal judges. Leahy is the second member of the *triumvirate*, and of course, he and Daschle and the third member, Senator Ted Kennedy, have great influence on each other—all three acting more like children in the game of "gotcha" than United State senators out to do the people's business. These men think alike. In March 2000, when there were only 75 vacancies, Daschle worried that "there is a dire shortage—we have a judicial emergency right now, throughout the country. And it's important for us to respond to that emergency and confirm the many, many judges whose nominations are still languishing either in committee or on the floor". Of course, the "dire shortage" issue is not applicable to the situation in the Bush administration as far as either Daschle or Leahy are concerned. Today, there are more than 100 vacancies languishing it looks like for the duration.

Nichols goes on to explain one of the Democrat's strategies to obstruct confirmation hearing: "Leahy has proposed changing the confidentiality rules regarding the raw file the FBI compiles on all nominees. 'Essentially, Leahy wants to leak embarrassing history from a nominee's file, from messy divorces to college pranks,' says an aide familiar with the proposal. 'Here's a guy who's already been kicked off a committee for leaking, and now he's chairman of committee on privacy. It's ridiculous." The truth is that if Leahy were a Republican, he would have been forced out of the Senate back in the '80's for publicly exposing U.S. secret agents, which the FBI confirmed at that time caused the assassination of a least one agent.

But that is a major point I am trying to make in this book—Democrats get to have it both ways. Whether or not the majority of Democrats call themselves "secular humanist"or not, is not important. The fact that they talk and behave after that mode of thinking is the important issue, and definitely shows the impact this "religion" has had on American society.

Columnist R. Levin (Inside Washington, week of Feb, 4, 2002) talks about former White House counsel to Bill Clinton, Abner Mikva, and his argument that "fundamental issues" before the high court should be decided by a super-majority of justices, not a 5–4 majority" because he doesn't like the outcome of some of the U.S. Supreme Court decisions. Levin writes: "His solution: The Senate should pack the Supreme Court through the backdoor by refusing to give its advise and consent to potential Bush nominees. For instance, if Chief Justice William Rehnquist and Justice Sandra Day O'Connor were to step down, and the Senate were not to act to replace them, the liberal side of the court would hold a 4–3 majority." But this is exactly what Leahy and the Democrats are after, holding up the confirmations until they have a Democrat in the White House. They do not work for the good of the country, but for personal power and control.

Former White House counsel C. Boyden Gray warns that the "delayed resolution of regulatory disputes in the federal courts will affect the economy…This is the tip of a huge regulatory iceberg, and over time it has the potential to snowball, and that could be disastrous." Nichols concludes his column with a quote from a senior Republican: "At the end of the day, Republican senators can push as hard as they want, but if the White House doesn't back them up, it doesn't matter."

"BORKING"
PICKERING

And the "propaganda war" continued. Never has a confirmation hearing been so vicious and meanspirited as the one for Charles Pickering, a federal district judge in Mississippi, not even the one against Judge Robert Bork, nor Justice Clarence Thomas. One GOP staffer called it "the mother of all confirmation battles." So what was all this malicious behavior about. On *Fox News Sunday* (3/3/02), Senate Minority Leader Trent Lott (R-Miss.) said: "This is really about the Supreme Court. This is a shot at the President saying, 'If you come up with a basically conservative Republican who is pro-life, we're going to take him down.'"

Columnist for *Human Events*, David Freddoso echoed the Senators sentiments: "Senate Democrats…have seized on the U.S. Circuit Court nomination of Charles Pickering, Sr. as a chance to practice the vicious techniques they used to stop Robert Bork's nomination to the Supreme Court in 1987, and also to send a message of intimidation to the White House."

The leader behind the obstruction, of course, was none other than the second member of the triumvirate, Senate Judiciary Chairman Patrick Leahy, who wasted no time in stalling the Pickering nomination so that he could collect hundreds of documents on his opinions, in hopes of finding something the committee could use against him. In the meantime, several liberal groups like NOW, The American Way, and NAACP came out with their loud mouths to defeat Pickering's confirmation. The "big dig" for dirt was intense and passionate, even though nothing they came up with "held water." In fact, all that surfaced on the judge's life, work, and character was positive. For instance, President Marie-Jose Ragab of the Dulles, Virginia branch of the NAACP received calls from various organizations asking her and her people to speak out against Pickering, but she said: "The people who called didn't really have any arguments against him…It was just a matter of 'sticking together' with other liberal groups." The Dulles branch should be commended for holding firmly to their principles, as it can't be easy to break with the view of the national NAACP. Dulles-NOW also sent a press release in favor of Pickering.

No one should be surprised that Democrats played the race card to smear Pickering, but, instead, many of us had come to expect it. However, they didn't quite have the nerve to call him a racist, since his record shows exactly the opposite is true. So they had to soften their rhetoric to something more politically correct—his "insensitivity toward civil right." Freddoso goes on to say that proving the Judge a racist "would be difficult to do, since Pickering's letters of recommendation feature glowing tributes from former three-term Mississippi NAACP President Nathan Jordan, numerous black public officials in Mississippi, and the brother of slain civil rights leader Medgar Evers." He also had letters from a black man he defended in "a racially charged 1981 robbery case," who wrote that "Pickering is a fair and just man who impartiality is always obvious." The fact is that both black and white people, who have had dealings with the Judge, talk about him in terms of being a "trailblazer for racial reconciliation,"and his service on the board of the University of Mississippi's Institute for Racial Reconciliation only enhances that image.

Also, a spokeswoman for the American Bar Association (ABA) told *Human Events* the criteria they use in rating a nominee are "compassion, "freedom from bias" and "commitment to equal justice under the law." The ABA gave Judge Pickering its highest rating, "well qualified." But it soon became apparent that nothing would stop these Democrat leaders in their attempt to smear his name. Senate Majority Leader Tom Daschle told CNN's Wolf Blitzer that he would oppose Pickering if the vote, which he was complicate in preventing, comes to the Senate floor. "It's been a tradition that a leader does not oppose a leader's nominee," is his excuse. My question is "where is the media outrage at such blatant lies to assassinate a good American's character"?

IN SEARCH OF A BUSH SCANDAL

With all the polls showing how popular President Bush is with the American people, and how high he rates on all issues, ranging from the war on terrorism, to the domestic scene, to the trust he has earned, Democrats are running scared. A *Washington Post*-ABC news poll (Feb. 2002), which cuts across all demographic groups, indicated that Democrats are losing on all grounds, even on key issues that they have for years claimed ownership.

Of course, Democrats are alarmed, and especially since they have no clear-cut policies of their own on which to campaign in the November election, 2002. Theirs is to blame and search for something, a "gotcha," so to speak, on the president—anything to stop their downward spiral in the polls. Democrats learned years ago if they harped on an issue long enough, it would become "truth" to the American people, and so Senator Ted Kennedy, the third member of the triumvirate, put a good deal of his energy into the party's cause and led the "sting" attack on the Bush tax cuts, asking that part of the enacted law be repealed, including also bringing back the death tax.

But Kennedy's plan quickly backfired on him, as one quarter of his own party in the Senate had voted for Bush's tax cut. Since details of the fallout are recorded earlier in this chapter, suffice to say that Senator Zell Miller of Georgia was one of several Democrats who spoke out against Kennedy on this matter: "How can a family or a business make any long-range plans with a here-today, maybe-gone tomorrow tax cut, a tax policy that has a perishable date on it, like a quart of milk?" Also, the IRS published its schedule for 2001, which did not help to prove the Democrat's cause; accordingly, if Kennedy was able to repeal the tax cut, it would not be the "wealthiest" Americans that would be hurt. It would hurt those making more than $65,550 and married couples making more than $100,250 in taxable income. Senator Chuck Grassley (R-Iowa) said: "If the Democrats succeed in raising taxes, they'll cost even more Americans their jobs. I believe the American people will oppose Senator Kennedy's bad idea, and it won't gain traction in the Senate"—and it did not.

The next attempted "sting" operation was the recession, which, of course, "Bush had caused," but that, too, turned out to be another dud that didn't fire (as noted above in "The Daschle Factor"). Nationally syndicated columnist Donald Lambro says that "running deficits in a time of war and a recession is perfectly understandable to most voters"—and evidently the voters do understand the uniqueness of this time in our history.

So what's a political party to do when it is sinking in the polls, and every sting operation fails. Well, there's the shrinking-budget surpluses—yes, that is it! The salivating Tom Daschle and Ted Kennedy and their minions must have thought they had a sure bet this time. But columnists Stephen Moore and Phil Kerpen, speaking of the Democrat charges, said that "…these recriminations about the return of federal deficit spending would be encouraging except that they lack even a seed of sincerity" (*Human Events*, "Who Lost the Budget Surplus?" Jan. 28, 2002). They go on to say, "One year ago, the Congressional Budget Office predicted that the budget surplus for 2002 would be $313 billion. Now Congress is forecasting a $21 billion deficit for the year. That's a lot of fiscal slippage in just one year. What in the world happened? Who lost the surplus?

Of course, Daschle and Kennedy said it was the Bush Tax cut, but Moore and Kerpen gave a more complete answer. They see four factors involved in the surplus shrinkage, which are as follows:

1.) The Bush tax cut, which accounts for less than $40 billion in tax revenue the government will extract from workers and businesses (amounting to 2% out of every dollar paid). "A crumb of a tax cut are what the Democrats are all hot and bothered about?"

2.) The recession accounts for about 2/3 of the surplus's disappearance—"We've lost about $160 billion in expected revenues for 2002, because 1.5 million fewer people are working and because fewer businesses are making profits for Uncle Sam to tax."

3.) A government spending spree, which is the most controllable factor behind the deterioration of the budget outlook and accounts for 18% of the lost surplus. "The Congress is spending money at a faster pace than any Congress since 1970's.

4.) Military and home security expenditures required to fight the war on terrorism. Beyond the 4% federal-spending hike Congress had originally predicted, about half of the increased spending went for matters required to fight this war.

Of the four factors that have caused the surplus to shrink, Moore and Kerpen say the recession and increased federal spending are by far the biggest contributing factors. They said: "In fact, if this year Congress would just hold spending growth level to the growth of inflation, there would be at least a $50 billion surplus." But that doesn't seem to likely to happen, as they tell us that the spending addiction has its hold on both parties: "Since 1995, when Republicans first took control of the House and Senate, spending discipline has eroded with every passing year." Also, according to the National Taxpapers Union in 1995, "there were some 500 members of the House and Senate who wanted to cut spending more than they wanted to increase it…in 2000, there were exactly two advocates of smaller government"—Rep. Ron Paul (R-Tex.) and Jim Sensenbrenner (R-Wis.) voted for less overall spending.

Moore and Kerpen name Kennedy and Daschle as "two of the biggest spenders in the history of the United States Senate. No single American is probably more responsible for the $4 trillion national debt than Ted Kennedy. Both Daschle and Kennedy have been "long-term opponents of the balanced budget amendment that would permanently outlaw deficit spending. The Daschle's and Kennedys of the world need to be hog-tied, before their latest spending spree creates another trillion in debt for our children to pay off."

Just as the tax cut issue was getting Kennedy and Daschle nowhere, word came that the economy was reviving and the recession gradually coming to an end. Although Republicans did not do a good job in placing the shrinking surplus at the feet of the big spenders, luck was with them, for the issue had not caught on with the public. So what would the next "sting" be?

Well, just in the nick of time came the collapse of the giant corporation ENRON, and several of the Democrat leaders could scarcely hide their delight, especially Henry Waxman (D-CA.) and Democrat National Committee chairman, Terry McAuliffe. I'm sure Daschle, Kennedy, Leahy, Gephardt, Schummer, etc., thought, "We've got him! At last, we've got him! But after several months, Democrats have not found the coveted "smoking gun" they so wanted to see.

Since President Bush wasted no time after inauguration day to cancel the Kyoto Protocol, thus saving ENRON's competitor, the U.S. coal industry, it does not seem likely that Democrats would be stupid enough to try to "put Bush in bed with ENRON, but that "red flag" did not stop some of them, especially Rep. Henry Waxman, who, like many Democrats salivated at the thought of a Bush scandal.

When media analyst Rich Noyes (Media Research Center) said that the ENRON situation is "a scandal without wrongdoing," it is evident that he was talking about the Bush administration. Alluding to the association between the President and Key Lay, Noyes went on to say: "The media are saying you are responsible for what your friends are doing outside of government, which is the opposite of the standard during the Clinton years."

At first the searching-for-a-Bush scandal Democrats criticized the president for having done too much for ENRON—even though Ken Lay had pinned high hopes on the Kyoto treaty to indirectly start the flow of cash his way, and Bush had canceled it. According to Robert Novak, the reason Lay had pushed the Clinton Administration so hard to ratify the treaty was so that ENRON could get control of energy emissions. As a part of seeing his dream come true, Lay had already laid some serious groundwork with the most radical environmentalists. Novak wrote: "...Lay wanted restrictions on carbon dioxide emissions under the Kyoto agreement to artificially create a market for CO_2

'credits' to be purchased to burn coal. ENRON would enjoy the profits from buying and selling emission credits to other energy sources."

When the Democrats failed to nail President Bush for "doing too much for ENRON," they reversed themselves, saying he didn't do enough to help the failing industry, which, in turn, would help its employees. But that was wishful thinking on the part of Waxman and his cohorts—if only the President had helped, then they would have him boxed in a corner for looking out for "his and ENRON's interests."

Has anyone noticed how the media likes to stress the friendship between ENRON's chairman, Ken Lay, and President Bush while they purposely down-played the friendship between former President Clinton and Lay. Mr. Lay, who was a big advocate of Kyoto global warming treaty, often turned to Bill Clinton for help. He was also one of the Clinton's golf buddies, as well as a member of the Clinton-25-membership on Council on Sustainable Government. Furthermore, it appears that the ENRON executives were more interested in Al Gore winning the White House than they were George Bush. Otherwise, why did so many of them watch the 2000 election returns with Al Gore? I guess maybe someone upstairs was looking out for President Bush.

One would think that since the president went against Kyoto Protocol, Attorney General John Ashcroft recusing himself from the ENRON investigation, Bush and the GOP launching an investigation to redeem ENRON worker's pension losses, plus no evidence of any kind to show the existence of a *quid pro quo*, that these facts would stifle the accusations against the President and ENRON involvement. But no! Senator Fritz Hollings (D-W. Va.), his face red with anger made the most scathing and bitter tirade against President Bush, accusing him of collaboration with ENRON's Ken Lay in order to line his own pockets.

So what's the next "sting"? As a guest on *Fox News, Bill O'Reilly* of the Fox network prophesied what was already in play—the administration was too secretive. He was right. Senator Daschle had been whining on television that the president did not tell anyone about the administration's shadow government. Much to his chagrin, some Democrats went public and announced that they had been informed of it. Then the next night, Chris Matthews of the television show, *Hardball*, put forth his agenda, which was a list of the Bush Administration's "secrets," and he too railed on how this "administration needs to be more open." However he ended up with "egg" on his face when he complained about Congressional leaders not knowing anything about the shadow government created by the Bush administration, and there was no correction of his error the next night. It is doubtful that anything will stop these desperados in their mad search for something that will work against the President.

But isn't it odd how Democrats get attention off their own problems? Take GLOBAL CROSSING, which is the fourth largest bankruptcy in history, that gets literally no media attention whatever, but for that matter where are the Republicans and the Justice Department? DNC Chairman Terry McAuliffe, with the help of "GLOBAL CROSSING's chairman Gary Winnick, who is a big donor to the Democrats, turned an investment of $100,000 into $18 million. He and Hillary Clinton ought to get together and show us all how it is done. What does McAuliffe have to say about it—nothing. But he has plenty of time to mouth off and point his finger at ENRON.

THE ENVIRONMENTAL EXTREMISTS

The late Barbara Olson, who was killed in the hijacked airplane that was flown into the pentagon on September 11, 2001, writes about the massive land grabs Bill Clinton made in his last few days in office in her book *The Final Days*, which bears the subtitle, *The Last, Desperate Abuses of Power by the Clinton White House*. On the jacket of her book reads: "Barbara served as a prosecutor for the Department of Justice and as counsel to a congressional committee before going into private practice. She was a much sought-after legal analyst and commentator on television and radio. Barbara will be missed by the many who enjoyed her spirit, her wit, and her commitment to principle." To this last statement I can only say a heartfelt, "Amen."

In regard to the Clinton land grabs, Mrs. Olson writes: "When it came to national monuments, however, Clinton's regal style soared into the reaches of pharaoic megalomania. He launched a vast land grab that made a mockery of limited powers that had been granted to the president under the Antiquities Act of 1906....The most controversial of his additions...came on September 18,1996, when Bill Clinton, with virtually no public warning, congressional consultation, or concern for either due process or the rights of those directly affected, established the Grand Staircase-Escalante National Monument in Utah. At a whopping 1.7 million acres...It was a blatant reelection campaign stunt. Clinton knew the environmentalists in the east would applaud his action. The sparsely populated areas in Utah hurt by his decision were not going to support him anyway."

Some of the other huge land grabs Ms. Olson lists are The Grand Canyon-Parashant National Monument, consisting of 1,104,000 acres; Agua Fria in Arizona, consisting of 71,000 acres; the entire California coast, 840 miles. Ms. Olson writes: "This coastline already comes under the protection of the state of California, fifteen county governments, and the California Coastal Commission. But Clinton wanted his name associated with the preservation of this glorious area." It is important to note that these three land grabs were signed into law by Clinton on Jan. 11, 2001, just days before he left the White House.

But that is not all. The glut of Clinton-land grabs, is astounding, to say the least: Grand Sequoia Monument in California, 327,769 acres; 164,000 acres in Colorado set aside for the Canyons of the Ancients; 52,000 acres Cascade Siskiyou and 195,000 acre Hanford Reach; and 128,917 acres, the Ironwood Forest. The lists goes on and ends after a grand total of 5,868,767 acres taken under federal control.

Ms. Olson goes on: "It is difficult to assess the impact Clinton's actions will ultimately have. So much of the West is controlled by the federal government that these states have come to resent the immense federal presence and influence exercised from thousands of miles away. There was no effort to balance the interests and economies of the areas most directly concerned. The raw exercise of single-minded authority without hearings or public notice, did not leave any room or time for careful planning or balanced deliberations. The only certain effect of these actions was an immense personal legacy for Bill Clinton."

Writer for *Insight, Sister Daily,* and *The Washington Times,* Valerie Richardson's story in the Dec. 24 issue of *Insight,* "In Idaho, the Loggers Are Losing," pretty much bears out what Barbara Olson had concluded. Richardson tells us that the harvesting of timber in rural Idaho has been so drastically cut, due to the Clinton administration regulations, that it has caused a heavy price to the logging communities, not only that business, but to related businesses as well, and also to the school systems. "Cascade's neighborhoods were peppered with 'For Sale' signs as families sought jobs elsewhere…including some whose roots in the town of about 1,000 went back three generations." Schools were forced to fire teachers and cut back on elective courses, and nearly thirty thousand jobs were lost, creating "a lot of anger, dislocation and poverty."

Chairman George J. Harad of Boise Cascade Corp told Richardson: "Despite an adequate supply of timber, under the policies of the Clinton administration and pressure from environmental groups, the amount of timber offered for commercial harvest has declined more than 90 percent over the past five years."

I don't question the need for some restrictions and regulations, but I do question the need for such a sudden glut of land grabs, many of which appear as being done for the sake of Clinton's legacy. Richardson explains how the forestry business was regulated before Clinton messed with it: "Each year, the U.S. Forest Service offers stands of timber for sale as determined under the forest plan, then takes bids and awards the sale to the highest bidder. (The national forests are distinct from wilderness areas, where trees by law cannot be harvested; in Idaho, where 68 percent of the Gem State's 53 million acres is run by the federal government, 7.5 percent of the land is classified as wilderness.)

"Starting with the mid-1980's however, environmental groups began stepping up their opposition to timber sales in the national forests. Recently, they've managed to bring the process to a grinding halt by filing legal challenges, or appeals, to most timber sales. The appeals usually are based on perceived problems with the sale, such as a failure to take into account endangered species or sensitive wildlife habitat.... Even when the appeals fail, the process can drag on for years.—causing the small logging outfits to go out of business." Cascade Mayor Larry Walters says: As soon as you put a sale up, you get hit with appeals. By the time it's resolved, that wood is no good anymore. It's just a waste."

An important argument against the Clinton decrees is that logging companies and their related organizations took care of the forest, replanting and clearing deadwood and diseased trees on a consistent basis. But now the environmentalist rely on fires to remove deadwood. Richardson writes: "The recent rash of forest fires, which locals blame on the Forest Service's official reluctance to clear dead and diseased wood, has been another impediment...but environmentalists argue 'that fire clears the deadwood more naturally than chain saws.'" John McCarthy of the Idaho Conservative League responds: "I'd rather see us use fire as the tool of first choice than chain saws as the tool of first choice."

Also, Valley County commissioner and rancher, Phil Davis says that the "fires have been anything but natural, burning so hot and so long that the land takes decades to regenerate. He noted that 25 percent of the Payette National Forest has burned in the last few years, while the summer of 2000 fires left blackened an area the size of Rhode Island (1,052 square miles)." The dominant view in the logging industry is that the environmentalist, who had Clinton's ear on promoting their agenda, have actually caused unnecessary damage to the environment.

Even so, some are encouraged and hopeful that the mills will come back: One reason is that "Shortly after taking office, President George W. Bush put the brakes on the Clinton administrations' plan to rope off 40 million acres of forest as roadless areas, a move that would have cut off access to yet more timber. Another reason is the "demand for paper products and lumber hasn't abated." In the meantime, the Clinton regulations on U.S. timber production has been a gift to the Canadian timber business, which didn't waste time in taking advantage of the American situation. American companies could no longer compete with their neighbor. However, more hope came for the U.S. timber industry when "on Oct. 31, the Commerce Department agreed to impose tariffs of as much as 40 percent on Canadian lumber, citing trade practices that have given the Canadians an unfair advantage."

Nevertheless, pro and cons continue as to what is going to happen to the timber industry in Idaho. Some feel the Bush Administrations wants to help, but that he is "subject to the same push and pulls" in the political world as others have been. Gov. Kempthorne predicts a future in which most logging on national forests is tied to forest health. "It probably won't be cutting for the sake of cutting; it'll be for clearing the fuel load on the national forests, The facts now prove that if we don't reduce the fuel load, we'll continue to see the forests blackened." And former mill worker and union representative, Steve Bliss says, "The pendulum is probably going to swing back, but for a lot of these towns it's too late. There's never going to be another sawmill in Horseshoe Bend or Cascade—it would cost $50 million in today's dollars to build it."

Aside from the Clinton-legacy-land grabs is another issue that caused a lot of flack and economic headaches for the Bush Administration; that was arsenic in the water. But I did not worry about arsenic in the water or air pollution any more after George W. Bush became president than I did in the previous eight years. The changes Bill Clinton made in the last few days of his administration were not to go into effect for six years, anyway. For this reason, common sense told me that if our lives were suddenly in peril, they had been throughout the Clinton administration. If Mr. Clinton suddenly discovered the situation to be a true emergency, then it stands to reason that our lives were to remain in peril for the next six years, regardless of what President Bush decided to do once an evaluation on this matter had been completed.

If we take into account the unseemly behavior in which the Clintons left office, and with two thirds of the population believing Bush is more honest than he, we can understand why the new administration may not have felt secure in plunging headlong into any of Clinton's last-minute decisions.

My personal belief is that Bill Clinton wanted to throw serious roadblocks in the way of the new President in order to cause him a lot of "economic headaches. I believe the new regulations he issued were done in hopes of backing President Bush into a corner. For instance, if Bush left the new policies in tact, businesses might be financially damaged; if he put a hold on them so that the situation could be scientifically studied, he would suffer public ridicule, and that is exactly what happened—"Bush didn't care if our water supply was poison."

A rather negative opinion, I admit, but I have always thought of the former president as a con artist. And much to my surprise, I discovered that an active supporter of Bill Clinton over the years, now has the same opinion of him. Don Hewitt, producer of "*60 Minutes*," dubbed him as the ultimate "con man" who has been "able to get away with just about everything" (*The O'Reilly Factor*, April 18,2001). But isn't this just the same old typical honesty that comes after the fact that Democrat's practice to redeem themselves? Once Clinton was out of office, Democrats began to speak out against his character on the same things they previously had spun stories to protect him.

In regard to the arsenic issue, Barbara Olson writes: "Several days before he left office, Bill Clinton imposed a full 608 pages of "Ergonomic" rules, aimed at complaints of repetitive motion injuries that saddled business with compliance nightmares…The new rules went far beyond the scope of those proposed by federal safety agencies and discussed with the public. And they had little or no scientific or medical justification. Fortunately, Congress repealed the ergonomic rules soon after President Clinton moved out of the White House."

Olson goes on to say that the new environmental regulations on arsenic ("a naturally occurring substance, in drinking water") were the first in 60 years to be implemented with the intent to reduce "the standard from 50 parts per billion to 10 parts per billion. There is no scientific consensus about levels of arsenic, and neither the need for nor ultimate cost of the new rule was apparent….The only clear need for the rule was the need for Clintonistas to enact rules."

Further examination of the Clinton plan showed that it "would have required hundreds of towns to install new filtration systems on wells, doubling or even tripling water rates. Overall costs would run in the billions, and since water systems are almost entirely public, the taxpayers, not 'industry' would be stuck with the tab."

Even though the Bush Administration had rejected the ergonomic rules, the political damage was done. A literal storm of criticism hit the airways. Olson writes: "No matter how unnecessary the arsenic rule was, no matter how costly it would be to implement, revocation of the rule put President Bush in the untenable political position of being opposed to reducing the level of arsenic—a poison in the public's mind irrespective of amount—in water we drink. No amount of explanation could take away the image—or the opportunity for environmentalist demagoguery and cartoonist punditry."

Another example of how impossible it is to get straight, honest talk out of the media and their lackeys—the Democrats, the radical environmentalist, the liberals, etc.—is Seth Borenstein's column, "Bush promises to slash power plant pollutants (Knight Ridder Newspaper, 2/16/02). Mr. Borenstein writes: "President Bush vowed Thursday to slice by about 70 percent the levels of three of the four most important air pollutants that power plants emit, using strategies heavy on economic incentives and light on regulations…He also proposed voluntary goals to slow the increase in carbon dioxide, and other greenhouse gases."

But it doesn't make any difference to these liberals that Bush actually called for these reductions of air pollutants by 2018 that "would cut nitrogen oxides, which causes smog, by 67 percent; sulfur dioxide, which produces soot and acid rain, by 73 percent; and mercury, which taints fish, by 69 percent;" and also that Bush "would reduce the rate of growth of carbon dioxide emissions by 4.5 percent more than the present projected figure. The environmentalist call all these improvements for clean air "a backward step, a rollback of the Clean Air Act masquerading as step forward".

The Bush administration's theory says we need to"recognize that economic growth and environmental protection go hand in hand." But Democrats support their know-it-all gods, the environmentalist, and so long as they get that huge voting block, the fact that they may be pushing a sane or insane agenda is really not important to them. As for me, I am tired of a shallow press that protects some of the extreme measures taken by environmentalist groups, but is more than happy to present an image of them as only a protective and benevolent agency while they ignore any possibility their agenda might be political. Never do we see the other side of the issue when these agencies place rats and fleas above people, or when they call a farmer's property a "wetland" because a puddle appears on it once every two or three years.

PART III
A Quest for Power

8

The Hillary Persona, Which One?

o o o o o o o o o o o o o o o o o o o o o o o o o o o o o o o
*"Many seek the ruler's favor, but justice for man comes from the
Lord." (Proverbs 29:26)*

For two years, prior to the 1996 election, the public had not seen or
heard much about the first lady and her ambitious agenda. The image
portrayed on the screens of our minds then was anything but a political
activist busy shaping policy. Instead, during this time period Hillary
Clinton was cast in a passive role as loving wife and mother. The only
reason she played out the part in this particular setting was that she had
been forced to do so, since her personal ambition for power and control was exactly what got her into trouble. The psychological strategy
was the usual: Let time and a counterfeit persona gradually blot out the
true character from the public's perception of her. Couple the media's
ability to make or break a person with American's willingness to be
duped, and one can easily assume that a vast number of people have
already forgotten how driven she was to "raise our consciousness," a la
Hillary.

Unfortunately, both Clintons have successfully used the chameleon
act throughout their adult lives to get themselves out of trouble, only
to let their true colors show as soon as their necks were out of the

noose. The true character of Hillary is what we saw in the first few years of the Clinton administration. At first the public was charmed by her good looks and glib tongue, but when her actions spoke for themselves, exposing her quest for power, her attitude of self-righteousness, and her desire to control and direct events, she came across more as a greedy, militant feminist than one who would inspire us to higher levels of thinking—at least, some of us.

Martin Gross, author of *The Great Whitewater Fiasco*, gives some biological background on Hillary, starting with her college days at Wellesley in the 60's where she underwent a dramatic transformation, changing from a conservative Republican to a radical-left-wing liberal. Described by former classmates as an unattractive hippy-type with straight stringy hair, oversized granny glasses, clod-hopper shoes, baggy sweaters and skirts, and one who also was a regular in and out of the Black Panther headquarters, gives us some insight into her mental makeup and just how far left she really is.

Gross writes, she was "an agitator in the forefront of student campus protest, fighting for open dorm rights and student control of the curriculum," and an active protester of the Vietnam War. As for her support of the Black Panthers, Gross writes: "In the midst of the Panther trial, she helped organize students, who with her took turns monitoring the courtroom proceedings and reporting back to the American Civil Liberties Union. (In some ways, her actions are reminiscent of what happened to Patty Hearst's attempt to bring the establishment down—minus the guns).

R. Emmett Tyrrell, Jr., editor of *The American Specator* gives a similar background account of Hillary, and her husband as well, in regard to her accusations that it is a "right-wing conspiracy" behind all the scandals revolving around her and her husband. He writes: "As for her talk of being beset by 'extremists,' I invite the citizenry to take a look at the Clintons' personal history. In college days, they engaged in all the left-wing protests. Then, in adult life, they lied about it. Hillary even served, while at Yale Law School on a radical law review that depicted policemen as pigs deserving to be shot. She worked as an intern (oops, that word again) for a far-left law firm that defended the Black Panthers. In years prior to her tenure as first lady, she served on the boards of various left-wing organizations and labored ardently in left-wing causes.

"This is all a matter of historic record. It is not made up....That she denounces a moderate conservative such as independent counsel Kenneth Starr as "right-wing" and "extremist" speaks volumes about her own extremism and leaves one to wonder about her respect for civil liberties....

"Again, reviewing the Clintons' lives. While most young people were studying, socializing and developing well-rounded personalities, the Clintons were ceaseless politicians. They were constant candidates in student government. Upon entering adult life, they continued their full immersion in politics. They have no other lives than political lives. It is as perverse for them to cry 'politics' as it would be for a clergyman to scorn religion....And now the first lady is attempting to shift the nation's attention from her husband's infantile sex scandals to what she claims are the excesses of her perceived enemies."

Tyrrell goes on to say that today the Clintons are involved in the same scandals they have been for years. He adds: "...the Clintons have not been able to disprove any element in any story we have ever reported—not in our stories of adultery, financial corruption, obstruction of justice, abuse of power, conflicts of interest or any of the other ingredients of Clinton politics....It would take a miracle worker to keep such scandals alive if they lacked substance."

Upon her advent to the White House, we saw a more sophisticated Hillary. In an effort to maintain an element of mystery and a sense of superiority over her "subjects," Hillary has always talked in vague, pious generalities. Very little has been spelled out; thus leaving her audience hard pressed to decipher her political views. For instance, take the phrase we so often heard in her speeches—"politics of meaning." Columnist Don Feder's article, "Hillary chooses new left hack as her mentor," (*Conservative Chronicle*, June '93) sheds some light on where Hillary comes from. It turns out that the terms, "politics of meaning" was coined by her philosopher guru, Michael Lerner, whom Feder described as a radical leftist: "To encounter a Jew to the left of Michael Lerner, one would have to exhume the remains of Leon Trotsky [Russian revolutionist who helped Lenin come to power]. How revealing, then, that Hillary Clinton has chosen this new left hack in prophetic drag as her spiritual mentor."

Feder goes on to describe the first meeting between guru Lerner and his disciple Hillary which took place at the White House reception early in the new administration. "Am I your mouthpiece or what?" Hillary exclaimed. "There followed a schmoozing session in the First Lady's office, where she completed his sentences. (Lerner: "It's amazing how much we seem to be on the same wave-length.'")

If you have never heard of Michael Lerner, probably the dialogue doesn't mean much. Feder identifies his character traits in a question and answer quiz. "Who is Michael Lerner? 1) The former head of Berkeley SDS. 2) An ideologue described by a colleague as 'a little Marxist cell." 3) A militant who told the *Seattle Times* in 1970, 'I dig Marx,' and posed before a banner with a hammer and sickle. Answer: All of the above."

Then giving his readers an even clearer picture of how Lerner's mind works, Feder illustrated just how strong his "convictions" and his belief are in the need for "loving families and ethically and spiritually grounded communities," as Lerner likes to put it. The story goes that he, a declared pro-family advocate, "married one of his students (performing the ceremony himself)." The couple's "wedding cake was decorated with the slogan 'Smash Monogamy.'" However, the marriage was short-lived, and he married $1 million drugstore heiress Nan Fink and then divorced her three years later. "Fleetingly loving families," writes Feder.

Apparently, though, guru Lerner had a great deal of success in instilling his philosophy firmly in Hillary's mind, as we saw in her obsession with the "politics of meaning"—at least she seemed never to tire of asking questions like "What do our governmental institutions mean...our lives in today's world...to be a part of institutions...to be human? (etc.) And her answer: "We need a new politics of meaning...the great challenge of living is to redefine yourself in your moment...I would like to talk about reality sometimes, authentic reality, inauthentic reality and what we have to accept of what we see."

And what was the end result of that kind of blathering? The media celebrated Hillary's "enlightened" vision, even though no one knew what she meant. At that time, Peter Jennings of *ABC* exemplified the major media's "reporting" of the news where Hillary was concerned. He was quick to call her the "problem solver." During the height of the health care debate, he said: "This individual had come an awfully long way in the last year or so. And then we thought—no, maybe it's the country which has come a long way. Mrs. Clinton's passion for health care is undeniably deep." Jennings ended his "objective report" praising Hillary's contribution to the children of Arkansas.

HILLARY'S MEDICARE DEBACLE

Well, what about the health care plan? It was defeated because it was created in secrecy, because the medical industry was left out of the solution, because of its complexity, because of the mandated finance structure on business, because of no choice of doctors outside one's HMO without incurring financial penalties or prison terms or both, and because it required one-seventh of the economy to implement, plus a tremendous growth in bureaucracy to operate it. Nevertheless, when the plan went down, the Clinton's blamed their defeat on special interest groups and Republicans (even though Democrats were in the majority at the time), and the public's "misunderstanding" of what was in it.

If I may digress for a moment: The complaints of Hillary Clinton and Vice-president Dick Cheney's secrecy are not comparable, as a lot of people tried to make them. The difference is that Hillary was not an elected official; therefore, she was answerable to no one, and could not be fired.

Columnist Jeffrey Hart wrote: "She (Hillary) reportedly blamed everyone involved for the failure of the plan, except the two people most responsible for the whole thing: herself and her arrogant guru, Ira Magaziner." Later on "she claimed that the plan was merely a sort of opening bid, and that she expected the whole thing to be much modified—'deconstructed'—in Congress."

But judging from all that has been written about Hillary's character, if true, this woman would not expect anything she is a part of to be modified. Elizabeth Drew, in her book *On the Edge: The Clinton Presidency*, quotes a White House staff member who described Hillary as a person not to be crossed and a person who would not forget: "She's the only person around here people are afraid of." In fact, it seems anyone who has researched her background, from college, to Little Rock, to the White House would naturally perceive her to have expected the 1,400 page plan to sail through Congress simply because her fingerprints were on it. Arrogance aside, why wouldn't she have that expectation? After all, the media for most of the Clinton presidency gushed over her, giving glowing editorials and interviews on her behalf— hardly a week ever went by that we didn't hear about her superior intelligence—plus certain members of Congress too busy fawning over her and making fools of themselves to ask any intelligent questions on the "misunderstood project." Why wouldn't she figure her health plan was a done deal?

So what's the bottom line on health care? When Hillary's health care plan went down, Hart, along with several other reporters, said it wasn't over for Hillary. "She has her own agenda….She's going to give health care another shot, and is trying to keep Ira Magaziner in a top spot." According to Hart, there would be a larger focus on children in the next go-around—and as soon as the power shifted in Congress, we saw White House hysteria over Republicans "starving kids to death" and the Clinton's "suffer the little children" push at the UN Convention for the so-called "Rights of the Child."

Time proved Hart to be right, but it was the evidence of Hillary's involvement in some unsavory financial ventures that soon forced her to put a temporary hold on her ambitions. However, with Clinton's re-election, followed by a rapid favorable climb in the polls for both of them, it wasn't long until the administration was once again ready to go forward with a new strategy to force Hillary's original health care plan upon an electorate that had just a few years before rejected it. But this time their contrivance would inflict havoc on senior citizens by placing strict limitations on their health-care service. The Clinton plan would not allow senior citizens to see any doctor for any reason outside their "assigned doctor," even if they were willing to pay for the service themselves.

How would the president get Hillary's project through Congress?—by tacking one item at a time of her original plan onto other bills which have nothing to do with health care. The sad thing, it was not only the president's own party that goes along with this fraud, but also quite a few spineless Republicans who were scared out of their wits to stand up to the badgering they would get from Clinton and the media if they don't go along.

Well, this kind of slick dealing was nothing new with the Clintons. When Mrs. Clinton went before Congress back in 1993, running her health care plan as the way to go, she said there were to be no increases in Medicare: "We are thinking zero growth in costs." But even though the Republican plan had allowed for an increase of 5.5% in spending, the administration and congressional Democrats raved on and on that the Republican plan was too severe in its cuts, and a "terrible tragedy" that would bring "terrible consequences" and "devastate the medical program." At that time, Senator Ted Kennedy roared and growled loudly, addressing Republicans: "Keep your greedy-budget-cutting hands off our Medicare system." How is it possible for a media that claims they try very hard to be objective, let things as blatant as this lie go by without a challenging word on their part?

ON BEHALF OF THE CHILDREN

Hillary's fans do not like to hear their heroine referred to as a socialist, much less a socialist with Marxist leanings, but her actions are the proof of where she stands. One of her prime objectives as the governor's wife was to work on the fertile soil of children's minds.

Thomas Sowell's research on public school education produced some interesting facts regarding Hillary's agenda in this area. He writes: "In her celebrated 1979 article in the 'Harvard Educational Review,' Hillary Rodham challenged the idea of parents 'unilaterally' making decisions about the raising of their children, and questioned whether even courts could look out for the best interests of children in legal cases, but was wholly uncritical of organizations she called 'children's allies,' who wanted a bigger say."

Also, based on the same article, Martin Gross confirms Sowell's findings in this matter: "Hillary had gone overboard, comparing the inadequate legal rights of children today to those of blacks, women, and Native Americans historically, asking for more freedom for children in such areas as schooling, motherhood, abortion, etc."

In view of Hillary's later role as director of the Children's Defense Fund (whose main concern is to defend children against their parents), Sowell cites further evidence that her plan is to weaken the parent/child relationship. For instance, he says "much of the enthusiasm for Head Start is that it leads to various services being supplied to families." He goes on to say that her idea of getting the social worker inside the home is to tell parents how to "raise their children, and perhaps to give or withhold government goodies according to how well they accept such advice."

According to Sowell, the Clinton's special summer programs for "gifted" or "talented" children (called "Arkansas Governor's School") was just another avenue to indoctrinate radical left-wing theories in young malleable minds. The program he said did very little to achieve further intellectual development, but was primarily an ideological indoctrination of the liberal agenda. For instance, he said that teenagers were subjected "to a one-sided barrage of films, lectures, and readings favoring homosexuality, 'animal liberation,' 'pacifism,' and a whole string of other causes dear to the left and far left. One reading program challenged the idea of 'a male god and a male savior,' another pictured poverty being a result of conspiracy by the American establishment. (A little hypocrisy here, upbraiding the right for insisting we have too much government, huh?)

There would have been no point in holding onto the past, and all could have easily been forgiven and done with if it were not for the fact that the Clinton's ideology had not changed over the years, and with the White House as their official residence, their ideology was still very relevant. It soon became obvious that Mom and Pop Clinton's stepped-up attention on behalf of the children was well underway. In February of 1995, Hillary announced that the administration had signed the United Nations Convention on the Rights of the Child." The New World Nanny, as Don Feder called the organization, and its ten "experts," representing different governments, gave children the right to express themselves on all matters, including school curriculums, right to privacy (thus overruling parental teachings on the sexual conduct of their children), right to choose their own religion, or to object any religious training, and every other thing the Big Ten considered as adequate care for children—food, clothing and shelter.

Already the experts were on the job, keeping a watchful eye on the British government, lecturing its officials against some disciplinary actions of parents and teachers, as well as the "need" not to maintain detention centers for hardcore-juvenile offenders. There would be public advocates to intervene between parent and child on behalf of the child.

According to Feder, the new order placed the UN as the ultimate authority in the parenting of the child, while at the same time, making no allowance for parental supervision and guidance. Superseding the Tenth Amendment, the government would undertake financial and moral obligations of the child, as well as its development in self-esteem and health care services. Might this parenting by government mandate be what Hillary calls "ethos of caring"?

The outcome of the operation "masterminded" by Hillary Clinton went down a course similar to the one of her infamous healthcare plan. Doug Phillips, Director of Federal Relations at the National Center for Home Education gives a clear picture of the process in his article, "A Call to Action."

"During the 103rd Congress, both houses of Congress introduced resolutions requesting that the President sign the treaty. Due in part to the pressure generated from hundreds of thousands of letters and phone calls in opposition to the treaty, the President never formally signed the document. After the landslide Republican victory in November of 1994, many parents stopped writing and calling their senators. No sooner had the phone calls and letters dissipated then Hillary Clinton announced to the world that the treaty would be signed and submitted to the Senate. On February 16, 1995, President Clinton's Ambassador to the United Nations signed the treaty in preparation for sending it to the Senate for ratification. For the treaty to become the "supreme law of the land," two-thirds of the Senate must ratify it. This means over one-third (34 U.S. senators) can block it.

"As a result of a new wave of phone calls and letter in February 1995, 32 U.S. senators now publicly and in writing are on record as opposing the treaty! Furthermore, Senators Lott and Helms have introduced Senate Resolution 133 to specifically condemn the *U.N. Convention On the Rights of the Child* and ask Clinton not to send it to the Senate for ratification."

We can have the same assurance that the Clintons will come up with some unique ingenious plan to reinvent themselves as soon as their popularity wanes, as we do that the sun will rise in the east and set in the west, and the chief designer of these chameleon acts will, of course, be Hillary. Just before the election in 1996, the hard edge of Hillary's personality had become obvious to so many people that Hillary had to do something. The "mother" of all her schemes to change her stripes this time was the "leak" to journalist Walter Isaacson that she and the president had "talked about adopting a baby. The topic soon became news. They were "hoping to have another child," she said—aah, ooh, how sweet. But just as suddenly as the subject was aired, it was just as suddenly dropped as the promise of a second term in the White House became evident.

However, this fake adoption plan also drew attention away from Hillary's real agenda, an anti-traditional-family goal she had worked for her entire adult life (and still does). If she gets her way, supervision of children will be judged and enforced via the federal government, which will supercede the values parents hope to teach their children, ranging from decisions on religion to cosmetic surgery, etc.

UNSEEMLY POLITICAL MANEUVERS

Is there nothing the Clintons would not do to get the control and power they want? In Barbara Olson's book *Hell to Pay*, she tells of her investigation, along with five other people who worked on the FBI files the FBI and Travel Office scandals. They operated out of a tiny, window-less, cramped room, chosen after some of the documents on their work had mysteriously disappeared, working shifts in order to keep more records from mysteriously disappearing. Olson said: "It was here that I poured over details of Hillary Rodham Clinton's role in several of the Clinton administration's unseemly political maneuvers."

In time, through research and study of the documents, the group of six were in an agreement of their estimation of Hillary. "We came to see, essentially, Hillary is a woman animated by a lifelong ambition. That ambition is to make the world accept the ideas she embraced in the sanctuaries of liberation theology, radical feminism, and hard left. We came to see her as a politician who invented her own strategies of protective coloration, who learned to mask her true feelings and intentions. She has become a master manipulator of the press, the public, her staff, and—likely—even the president."

Unfortunately, an awful lot of people don't see through this master manipulator until after the fact—that is they look back and wonder what happened to the adoption idea? Or what happened to Hillary's allegiance to Yasir Arafat, to the Palestinian Liberation Organization (PLO)? Well, those of us who are onto the Clinton ways knew the adoption was a farce from the word go, meant to soften her image. However, things changed suddenly with the PLO when this particular stand was not beneficial to Hillary's climb for power—loyalty flew out the window.

Perhaps, loyalty is not the right word to relate to Hillary. I don't believe that is a part of her makeup; but, loyal or not, her record indicates long years of support for the Palestine Liberation Organization (PLO). As chairperson for the New World Foundation, a $15,000 grant was given to Grassroots International, a group which holds direct ties to the PLO. The kissup to Suha, Arafat's wife, and all other support for the PLO changed almost overnight—Hillary would run for New York senator, and she had to have the Jewish vote in order to win. Suddenly she was pandering to the New York Jewish population, speaking in behalf of Israel, speaking for Jerusalem as the capital of Israel, not Tel Aviv. This change of heart was a complete reversal of what the Clintons had planned for the Palestinians and against the Israelites only a short time before. Clinton had gotten Prime Minister Ehud Barak to literally give away the store to the Palestinians, including part of Jerusalem. Actually it was the best deal they had ever had, and Arafat and his terrorist groups responded almost immediately by sending suicide bombers into public places to kill Jews.

That wasn't all. No matter what it would take to get the Jewish vote, Hillary was up to it. In fact, no one but she would have the chutzpah to take her next chameleon step. Hillary became a "real, authentic Jew" herself. In August of 1999, she "came out of the closet," so to speak, and announced that she had just discovered that her stepgrandfather was a Jew. As we found out later, the President and the "New Jew" Hillary met with Hsadic Jews in the White House just before the election, and out of this meeting the Jewish community in Rockland County, New York was absolved of some financial indebtedness, borne out of an illegal scheme of which they were convicted. In appreciation of the favor, the Jewish community overwhelmingly voted for the first time in their history as a near 100% solid block for you-know-who, and their essential vote helped to put her over the top. However, previous to this pardon was another pardon to aid Hillary's run for the Senate: the pardon for the Puerto Rican terrorists in New York The Clintons are indeed, shameless, but what about the people who voted for her, and what about the American media who can muster absolutely no outrage over this kind of mockery of justice?

However, the shamelessness of Hillary's actions (or Bill's) do not fall entirely on her shoulders, but people who fall before her in idol worship, who, despite her falseness and hypocrisy refuse to see her for what she is, a person who will stoop as low as she needs to go to get what she wants.

Ms. Olson writes: "Over the years Hillary Clinton has assembled and skillfully used an arsenal of opposition researchers and private detectives that her one-time mentor, Dick Morris, now identifies as a 'secret police' that has been used in 'a systematic campaign to intimidate, frighten, threaten, discredit, and punish innocent Americans whose only misdeed is their desire to tell the truth.'"

GETTING RID THE "SPIES"

Hillary had exhibited all the characteristics from early adulthood to the White House that could easily qualify her for the title, "Queen of Mean," long before she met one of the people who had great influence on her thinking, the radical leftist, Saul Alinsky (author of *Rules for Radicals* and *Reveille for Radicals*), but nevertheless he was able to teach her some of the tricks of the trade that would strengthen and intensify her personal arsenal in trashing her opponents. Of course, this was right down Hillary's alley since she was predisposed to paranoia anyway. She trusted only her lawyer buddies from Arkansas and the Hollywood couple Harry and Linda Bloodworth-Thomason.

Olson talks about Hillary's paranoia in *Hell to Pay*: "It wasn't long until the Clintons became paranoid about the constant hovering staff, a fear that extended to a press corps that also seemed to appear in too many sensitive places. In short order, Hillary ended the practice of allowing reporters to stroll unescorted to press secretary Dee Dee Myer's office.

Her paranoia spread further: "Unaware of the statutory role the Secret Service plays in protecting the president, the Clintons naively asked Harry Thomason to investigate the possibility of replacing them with private security guards or the FBI." This is where former bar bouncer Craig Livingstone entered the picture, the man no one in the White House could "remember" who hired him. Nevertheless, it was obvious that Livingstone felt himself commissioned from the highest level. He told an FBI agent: "I wrote this memo, this four page memo, and I recommended that the Secret Service be dumped in favor of the FBI....Someone got a hold of the memo, leaked it to the Secret service, and they went ballistic." Olson writes; "The project of 'privatizing' the Secret Service function was mercifully short-lived."

The fear that spies were everywhere extended to the White House telephone system, so a new system was installed at a cost of $27 million to the taxpayers, thus giving the president privacy to place his own calls without interference of an operator. Olson writes: "This would later give him the false sense of security he needed to call Monica Lewinsky for phone sex and, undoubtedly, countless other equally willing associates."

Next on Hillary's purge to rid the spies were the ladies in the White House correspondence office. They were fired. A Bush White House aide said: "Of all the things the Clintons did, this was perhaps the most sickening. Most of them had been there for many years, some were close to retiring. They were hard-working, dedicated, and good-humored. It was like beating up the town librarian." But it wasn't long until this irrational behavior backfired on the Clintons: "Soon mail was piling to the ceiling, and there were tales of mail being thrown out by the bushel. But room had been made for patronage employees, people who could be trusted."

White House usher, Chris Emery, was the next to go. He was fired for speaking to former First Lady Barbara Bush on the phone about a computer he had programmed for her. The Clintons did not realize that staff members often took calls from former first family members, but had they known, it would not have made any difference. Olson goes on to say that the paranoia extended to the firing of White House chefs, and to requiring gardeners, cooks, ushers, etc. to fill out a 33-question form, which included their political affiliations.

Hillary's problem was more than paranoia; it was tyranny. If nothing else, the Travelgate fiasco proved the mental state under which she operated. Instead of giving the employees of the travel office notice of termination and replacing them with her own people, they were first to be trashed and then fired. Catherine Corneilus, supposedly Clinton's cousin, was brought in to write up reports on the crew—reports of poor bookkeeping, poor handling of money, and strong hints of "sticky fingers." The reports were then transferred to David Watkins, a former Little Rock ad man operating in the White House as director of administration, who would in the end find himself as the target to take the fall for Hillary over the Travelgate firings. Evidence clearly showed Hillary as the chief architect of the fiasco, but of course, in usual Clintonian style she denied knowing anything about it. In a memo to Chief of Staff Mack McLarty, Watkins wrote: "...At that meeting you explained that this was on the First Lady's screen. *The message you con-*

veyed to me was clear; immediate action must be taken....We both knew that there would be hell to pay if, after our failure in the Secret Service situation earlier, we failed to take swift and decisive action in conformity with the First Lady's wishes."

In the meantime, Billy Dale's career was ruined. "He ended up pleading to a misdemeanor to keep his legal bills down, and after a brief deliberation was found not guilty by a D.C. jury." The screwups that followed for the next year in the travel office are similar to those of the mail pile ups mentioned above, and ultimately caused some big liberal reporters a lot of inconvenience in scheduling flights, so that they spoke out in favor of Billy Dale and his crew.

GIFTS FOR THE "NEW BRIDE"

I think it is impossible that people do not pick up on the hypocrisy of Hillary—the lady who soundly denounced the 80's as the "decade of greed"—unless they are brain dead, or just don't care so long as they have a liberal Democrat in the White House. Dick Morris, former strategist for the Clintons, and who probably knows the Clintons as well as anyone, said that "Hillary craved luxury." There is a crassness and arrogance of those who do not know how to handle fame and fortune, and Hillary certainly fits well into this category. Olson writes in her book *Hell to Pay*: "The Clintons are...public officials, accustomed to influence, respect, and privilege. People listen to them...flatter them...do things for them, like feeding them, paying their bills, and giving them gifts....They can thus disparage the wealthy and rail against the "decade of greed" without any sense of shame at never having had to pay bills, meet a mortgage, or fix a roof.

"For more than twenty years the Clintons have enjoyed the very best in food, entertainment, housing, care, housecleaning, transportation, security, and staff, virtually all of it at the expense of others: ordinary taxpaying Americans." With huge staffs at their beck and call, a personal Boeing 747, and their every desire accommodated, Olson says,

"Hillary was not in a mood to walk away from her cherished lifestyle simply because the Twenty-second Amendment forced her husband from office on January 20, 2001."

A phrase that we often hear applied to Hillary is her "sense of nobility," that everything is owed her. We saw just how much brass this woman had when she registered with the most exclusive stores in New York City so her Hollywood friends and the well-to-do, who were willing to commit to her "trousseau," would know exactly what she would like to have in order to furnish her two new homes in lavish style.

The scheme was well-thought out. Donors to the "new bridal" shower were told everything had to be gift wrapped and in by January 3 so as to avoid the Senate rules that would limit their gifts to $100 per person, per year. Well, they came through with everything just in the nick of time.—clothing, jewelry, furniture, paintings, art works, china, silverware, and more. Olson writes: "Mrs. Clinton pulled in over $50,000 worth of china and flatware…The spectacle of a woman who had just received an $8 million advance for a book she hadn't yet written and who was about to become a U.S. Senator, soliciting china, furniture, pant suits, and cashmere sweaters…was too much for the public to take."

9

He Speaks with Forked Tongue

Neither Hillary nor Bill Clinton have ever been willing to verbalize their "social engineering" goals for what they really are. Their strategy to"sell" their programs is to replace the harsh truth with a nice acceptable homey spin. That is how "social engineering" became "community building," increasing taxes became "investments," and so on. But no matter how much twisting and turning to redefine words, the Clinton's biggest problem remained right up to the 1996 election (and beyond): a false facade of humility. Instead of hiding a sense of self-righteousness, it translated into arrogance.

POLITICAL SOUL MATES

In the 1992 election the Clintons had presented themselves as "mankind's best hope." There was the promise of equality for all, beginning with a tax cut for the middle class and a cleaner more ethical government than we had ever seen before. Nevertheless, Clinton's problems mounted quickly while the pundits tried desperately to explain them away. He was merely "unfocused," they said. But the truth is, he was focused. His number one priority was staffing the White House with gays and other minorities so as to be "politically correct," rather than selecting the best qualified person for the job. As a result, after more than three years of occupancy, the operation of running the White House was in chaos, and had not yet been fully staffed nor fully cleared for security purposes. Also, we witnessed a parade of the Clinton's fallen buddies as they had been forced to leave for one reason or another, while others opted to fall on the sword for him.

Furthermore, the promised middle-class tax cut was quickly discarded in favor of tabling everything imaginable as a possible tax increase. Apparently the "new Democrat" felt the middle classers were not only able to take care of themselves, but also anyone who was lower than they on the financial scale (an attitude which helped the Democrats lose in a big way in the 1994 election). In the case of increased taxes, though, Clinton's poll reading to see what he believed in worked to the advantage of the taxpayer, and some of the potential government looting of John and Jane Doe's take-home pay fizzled out, like the value-added tax. Hillary's words of wisdom warned us of the "ugliness of greed—" the "acquisitive and competitive corporate life is not the way of life for us," she said. But her "noble" rhetoric would set up the middle class for the bulk of funding for the administration's liberal policies. Martin Gross explains why she so often uses such carefully chosen "noble" words. He says she "does not want to appear radical in her [radical] views."

However, Bill Clinton was as guilty of the same deceptive practices as his wife; she just had a larger bag of euphemisms to draw from than he. Anyway, whether noble or not, it turned out that the Clinton venture has always been an ugly conquest for money and power, the very things that both of them denounced over and again, especially just prior to an election.

During the 1992 presidential campaign, the image Clinton presented was that of an ordinary wage earner, making only $35,000 a year—but he left out the extras he got as governor of Arkansas. It happens state-paid childcare was not one of them. Nevertheless, our two

Yale lawyers did not let that minor detail stop them. Instead, they listed their babysitter as a security guard and let the taxpayer foot the bill. To sweeten the deal, the slick Clinton's paid no social security taxes for their sitter, and topped it off by getting a tax credit to boot (hmm, worse than Zoe Baird?). Other monies expanded the perceived $35,000 salary to well over $100,000. The list is incomplete, but a sampling makes the point: $51,000 for food, $19,000 for public relations, and a Lincoln Town car (hmm, Willaim Sessions?). Of course, governorship packages are legal and expected. I mention some of their special extras here simply because of the perceived low salary Clinton wished to project during the campaign.

I also think the "conscious-raising awareness" agenda Hillary had planned for us could stand a little more scrutiny. Although she made more in her profession as a lawyer than the average doctor does, she never missed a chance to use their high incomes against them. Given the Clinton's political theme during the campaign that all of us must sacrifice, along with the fact that Hillary lived high in considerable wealth, one would think she would have been more than happy to sacrifice a tad. But still, she was not satisfied with her lot. To help make ends meet, she collected the family cast-away clothing, including Bill and Chelsea's used underwear (charging one dollar per undie) for the purpose of tax deductions. (Oh, would that we could all sacrifice as Bill and Hillary have!)

The key word in understanding the politics of the Clintons was/is "deception." Gross outlines the many avenues they sought to finance and control their destinies as leaders of the "politics of meaning," which they intended would create a new American culture based on their personal concept of relevance, and to be maintained by government control.

As for Bill Clinton's style of vagueness, he left everyone guessing to which poll he had adopted as his core belief. Not even anyone in his own party could successfully argue that he is a man of his word. He said whatever would further his cause at the moment, and often reversed his stand, even the next day. Michael Kelly talked about this character flaw in his article "Why the President Is in Trouble in the November 1994 issue of *Reader's Digest*. "In mainstream journalism and even more so in popular entertainment, President Clinton is routinely depicted as a liar, a fraud, and an indecisive man who can't be trusted to stand for anything—or with anyone."

Why would Clinton purposely and habitually make promises that he knows he will not keep? Kelly finds at least part of the answer in his mother's autobiography. She writes that Hope, Arkansas, the town he grew up in, is "a town in which the con job was considered an art form….Rules were made to be bent, and money and power—however you got them—were the total measure of a man." Kelly suggests that this environment, plus the character trait Bill got from his mother, "an obsessive need for adulation," had much to do with the way he turned out.

What happened to Hillary, who came from a conservative upper-middle-class family, isn't as clear. But who knows the complex workings of anyone's mind? The point is that Hillary has proven herself to rank high on the list of the greediest of power hungry people. Kelly implies the same of Bill, however he seems to give Hillary an edge over her husband. As more and more news leaked out over time from a very reluctant media, preferring to keep the character issue under wraps, we saw that both Clintons were more than willing to pull unethical levers at every turn for the money and power they sought for their personal American dream, the highest office in the land. The worst of it is all these things were known and available to the media during the 1992 campaign, but in their eagerness to get Clinton elected, they often hid the true characters of the Clintons, making light of damaging information, even rationalizing for them, and continually saying that the public was not interested.

THE MONEY SUPPLY

Almost immediately after Bill Clinton became the attorney general in Arkansas, connections to insure money and power for the Clintons were being put in place. Hillary was hired as an attorney for the famous Rose Law Firm. Reports are that she spent very little time at the office, yet drew a full-time salary. Later, when Bill was elected Governor of Arkansas, she was given a full partnership in the firm, plus a 20% increase in salary because, as she said, she was "doing public service work for the governor." However, her hours remained the same as before.

Shortly after this first appointment Hillary got another influential position as staff attorney for the Little Rock Airport Commission, making her politically influential from two offices in Arkansas Business. Martin Gross quotes John Harmon, former City Attorney of North Little Rock: "If her [Hillary] husband had not been attorney general, she wouldn't even have been considered for that job. At the time, she had not established any legal credentials." Gross goes on to say. "This windfall, among others, set up the whole question of conflict of interest involving the spouse of a powerful politician."

Eager for more money and a way to influence the politics of Arkansas, Hillary decided to team up with William Wilson in a criminal defense practice. (Records show that she only went to court five times in fifteen years.) Gross writes: "Once again, Hillary's activities became a bone of contention. Opponents pointed out that her criminal work could be a conflict. As attorney general, Bill might have to rule on cases she handled. Would he rule against his wife?" One of Clinton's opponents charged that "her presence in the Rose Law Firm gave them a front door to the governors office."

Conflicting reports of her salary in this capacity range from $8,000 (stated by Bill) to as much as $54,000 (stated by Clinton's opponent). However, the matter apparently cannot be cleared up since the Legal

Service Corporation in Washington D.C., keeper of these kinds of records, reports it has no record on Hillary Clinton.

These special favors done on behalf of the Clintons were only the beginning. There was the $1,000 investment in cattle futures, urged by James Flair, attorney for Tyson Foods, a company which later contributed to Clinton's campaign for governor. The story goes that Hillary lacked savvy in these matters, and so Blair told her that "she wouldn't have to be the expert—he would be." But Hillary was not consistent with her story as to what took place. Evidently the media was charmed with her non answer when she said "woulda, coulda, shoulda," in answer to questions on this matter. As we now know she netted $100,000 from a $1,000 investment—an extraordinary feat that pros in the business do not believe, as they say, it is next to impossible. Evidence seems to support the theory that Blair was motivated with this gift to the Clintons so they would show good will toward Tyson Foods, one of Rose's clients and a reliable campaign contributor to Clinton.

Because of the money supply for his political campaigns, Clinton not only ignored Tyson Foods' abuse of environmental laws—laws which he had a part in drawing up—but also excused $9 million in taxes the company owed because of so-called "development programs." Tyson Foods had been cited by state regulators as polluting the Arkansas rivers and drinking water several years before the situation was declared a disaster. Gross writes: "The strange connection between money and power ended up sending tons of extra chicken feces into Arkansas rivers and ground water, forcing at least one town to close down its polluted drinking water system.

"In 1977, the state pollution regulators reissued the license for a Tyson plant in the town of Green Forest. But the order was never enforced, and in May 1983, the waste seeped into the drinking water."

Hillary's position with the Rose Law Firm didn't help matters either. Gross lists the bond among the wealthiest and most influential in Arkansas who were clients of the Rose Law Firm. "Tyson Foods; Stephens, Inc, the nation's largest investment firm outside of Wall

Street; ARKLA, the natural gas utility (whose former head, Thomas F. 'Mack' McLarty, became President Clinton's chief of staff); TCBY; the Arkansas Gazette; the Worthen Bank, the state's largest, whose major stockholder was the Stephens organization. They even handled public agencies, from the Public Service Commission to the Little Rock Airport Commission."

Gross goes on to say that Hillary, as the wife of the Governor, was the "glue" that held "a quartet of lawyers who stuck together through thick and thicker." These included Webster L. Hubbell, Vincent W. Foster, Jr., William Kennedy II, (and Hillary)—"the Famous Four, as they came to be known, joined inexorably in loyalty." Regulating was done by individuals appointed by her husband, often with Hillary's advice and counsel, even comment. All members of the Famous Four ended up in some capacity as White House staffers (all fell by the wayside with the exception of Hillary).

Despite the tight public-relation controls the administration held, by the end of his first term, Clinton was in trouble with the voters. He had burdened the people with heavy taxes, and reneged on deals with Arkansas utilities, timber interests and trucking companies, costing him the governorship in the 1980 election. But failure for the Clintons simply meant then, as it does now, that they would get into the chameleon act and remake their image.

This time for Hillary Rodham's big transformation, Hollywood producer Linda Bloodsworth Thomason came to the rescue—out went the granny glasses and hippy clothes, and on went the Clinton name. The new "Mrs. Clinton" was reinvented, hair and togs, Hollywood style. Meanwhile, Clinton apologized publically for the mistakes he had made and spent the next two years buttering up to bank and other important business executives, all of whom could help him financially to take on the 1982 run for governor. Hillary's assignment in the meantime was to win over John Robert Starr, editor and columnist of the *Arkansas Gazette*. Gross writes that even though Hillary was not known for her charm or tact, "she managed to dredge it up and turned it on full force for this one target." Her strategy included taking Starr to lunch, showing interest in their education program (his wife a teacher), and flattering him by seeking his opinion and advice on a number of issues. It worked.

Along with the new image and flattering job, Bill Clinton came out swinging with a strategy now familiar to all of us, and accused his opponent of the very thing for which he himself was guilty. Michael Kelly says that he accused Frank White, his opponent and 1980 winner of the gubernatorial race, of being "a tool of moneyed interests," telling one audience, 'He's for a half-million dollars because the people who wanted decisions from the governor's office paid for them. But off-stage, Clinton established a lucrative relationship with the big-money interests against whom he was railing."

As the usual Clinton campaign pattern goes, he proceeded to follow up with promises he knew he would not keep. Kelly quotes Scott Trotter, who campaigned for a referendum to change the state's utility regulations: "We had a flat commitment from him that he would enact our reforms if he got back in." Once in office, Trotter says, "He was completely dilatory. He and I argued about it in his office, and he just said that he didn't need the utility issue anymore. He was going in education....He quickly earned the reputation as someone who didn't understand that a handshake deal was inviolable."

Another broken promise was for a rebate of the sales tax poor people paid on groceries. Once back in office, Clinton told reporters that his promise had been only "a 24-hour commitment." Kelly quotes veteran Little Rock liberal activist Edwin Dunaway regarding another broken promise. "He talked big ideas, but he never followed through on anything. His word is no good."

THE "NEW" DEMOCRAT

We saw this so-called "new" Democrat acting out the same strategies in the 1992 campaign for president, and also after taking office, but finally the voters caught on, at least to some extent. By the 1994 congressional election, both Bill and Hillary's popularity was at an all-time low, and the public diminished Clinton's power drastically by giving it to a Republican Congress. The defeat of Democrats in this election meant only one thing to the Clintons. Bill Clinton would do what had always worked for the two of them in the past—the old reliable chameleon act. So, he turned almost immediately into a "Republican," and began vacillating on his "core" beliefs. Not vetoing the budget bill the second time around is a good example, but it was nearing election time, and he felt forced to sign it. While Clinton crowed about this good bill, remember that he and the Democrats had blasted the Republicans on their first bill (which closely resembled the "good" bill) for supposedly being cruel to kids and favoring the rich—always a favorite theme for the Democrats. Michael Kelly seems to know what's behind Clinton's vacillating behavior. Referring to his loss in the Arkansas gubernatorial race, he wrote: "Bill Clinton's problem isn't that his past haunts him. It is that his past has made him what he is today."

One might have assumed that even though the Clintons presented themselves with a new image and a "commitment" that comes from taking polls and not from the heart, they would not be able to fool the people again. Surely the American voter had finally had his/her fill of situational ethics and cultural relativism. But this was not the case. The fact that the Clinton Administration was mired in one scandal after another didn't seem to bother the public much at all. If polls were accurate, Bill Clinton's approval rating climbed upward—unbelievable!

THE SCANDALS

In the beginning, we saw bimbogate, troopergate, and whitewatergate. According to the left wingers, these "mistakes" didn't count because they were past history. But it didn't stop there, and the pattern continued. Then came a flood of other scandals: filegate, Lincoln bedroom-gate, and the other highly scandalous China-financegate. In the meantime, all through the Clinton reign a parade of unethical charac-ters, buddies of the Clintons, filed into the White House, and one by one most had to leave under clouds ofsuspicion and allegation, or else to serve jail sentences (and possibly, some just couldn't take the Clin-ton ethics problems)—and this was the administration that talked so much about restoring integrity to the office of the presidency. Joe Biden, former chairman of the Judiciary Committee, announced shortly after the new president was officially installed in office, "We are adopting a new standard for appointments." But such a poor record was to follow, causing us to recall the hypocritical statements coming from so many Democrats on ethics. Senators Tom Harkin (D.Iowa), John Kerry (D. Mass.), Ted Kennedy (D. Mass.), George Mitchell (D.) all had spouted how nominees were to be extraordinary examples for "ethics and propriety," "sensitive" and with "good judgment" and having "especially high standards." Former Senator Howard Metzen-baum said: "There is no room for bowing to the privileged, no room for self-serving decisions…we must strive to find individuals who have demonstrated a consistent pattern of sound judgment and ethical sen-sitivity"—Farewell, Cisnero, Nussbaum, Kennedy, Elders, Hubbell, McDougal, Aspen, Myers, Altman, Hanson, Bentsen, Steiner, Espy, Stephanopolis, McLarty, the suicide of Vince foster—and the list goes on totaling somewhere around thirty.

Despite the unprecedented numbers of witnesses coming forth with damaging allegations against this administration, the major media was in no mood to see justice where the Clintons were concerned. After all, approximately 85% voted for them. Instead, any factual information regarding the Clintons was quickly squelched by diverting attention away from them and portraying the messengers as meanspirited, witch hunters. In some cases, the person who had decided to come "clean" may suddenly reverse his/her story, as did James B. McDougal of the Madison Guaranty debacle. Gross writes: "Speaking about the Clintons' supposed loss on Whitewater of almost $69,000—since scaled down to $47,000 by the White House—McDougal, who apparently made all the mortgage payments on Whitewater, let the President have it." Gross quotes Sheffield Nelson, Clinton's opponent in one of the Arkansas governor races, from a taped interview between McDougal and Nelson: "I saw that article in the *Post* where some guy just accepted the Clintons' $69,000 loss," said McDougal angrily. "I could sink it (the estimate) quicker than they could lie about it if I could get in a position so that I wouldn't have my head beaten off, and Bill knows that."

Having registered this cynical complaint, shortly afterwards McDougal became supportive of the president and insisted on his former friend's total innocence in the Whitewater affair on all accounts. (Are we to assume that McDougal had not gotten himself in a safe position before speaking out?) The strange thing is that he was a little more hesitant to speak up for Hillary—strange, because Gross' research indicates that she represented the S & L owned by her partner McDougal before state authorities which were named by her husband. Also, as an active policy maker in the governor's administration, she often helped select state supreme court justices to fill out terms. Some believed that she personally interviewed judicial candidates herself— justices before whom her law firm would soon be pleading cases. So the conflict of interest we saw with Attorney General Janet Reno is nothing new with the Clintons.

However, since McDougal's show of loyalty toward the Clintons did not last long, and he was scheduled and ready to testify against them, we might assume he had grown tired of bearing the brunt of some unlawful dealings in which they were a part.

Take the deal with the Whitewater Development Corporation in which McDougal tried to make money for the Clintons. Some sources claim the Clinton's put up $500 to get in the deal. Gross writes that the "latest theory is that they put up zero cash and were able to circumvent bank laws, since it was not likely that bank officials would question a deal in which the governor was a part.

Once the land was purchased, it was necessary to put a show home on one of the lots to attract buyers. Lot 13 was chosen, but since Whitewater Development could not borrow the money for the home because McDougal had operating control of the bank and the land, Hillary got a loan of $30,000 for Whitewater. From all outward appearances she owned the home, but records show that Whitewater paid all interest and principle payments. The company also listed Lot 13 as the corporation's asset, yet the Clintons never paid real estate taxes on the house, and when it sold, they kept the proceeds of the sale and reported a mere capital gains of $1,640 on their income tax return.

Former Arkansas banker David Hale, (later appointed judge by Clinton) was another person involved in Whitewater who decided to talk. He claimed he met with James McDougal and Bill Clinton to make a fake paper loan of $300,000 to Susan McDougal. However, the money went to both Clinton and McDougal. Hale quoted Clinton as saying: "My name can't show up on this." Of course, the White House spin was that Hale is a felon so he can't be believed. This is sure to be the response to James McDougal's testimony also. As long as Susan McDougal would not tell what happened, even though she, too, is a felon, whatever denials she would claim in behalf of the Clintons will most likely be counted credible.

It is questionable whether we will ever know the full truth of Whitewater. Records disappeared somewhere in the White House for years, and then suddenly reappeared in the Clinton's personal quarters (with parts blackened out). Special counsel for the Senate Whitewater hearings, Michael Chertoff, said Whitewater and Travelgate are "connected in a funny way because of Vincent Foster. Because Vincent Foster—we've lately come to learn—was really at the center of damage control not only with respect to Whitewater, but with respect to Travelgate."

The Vince Foster suicide controversy did not go away for a year or more because of the many inconsistences and unanswered questions regarding his death. Columnist Chris Ruddy for the *Pittsburg Tribune-Review* documents the things that don't "add up" in his book, *Vincent Foster: The Ruddy Investigation*. Though Foster supposedly walked 700 feet into Marcy Park to the edge of a steep slope where he sat down and shot himself in the mouth, evidence seems to contradict this scenario. Questions arise as to why there was no soil on the soles of his shoes, why his suit was covered with carpet fuzz; why there was very little blood, why there were no bone fragments or brain tissue, and why there were no damaged teeth. Also, there are questions about the gun as it did not have the gunpowder found on Foster's hands on its grip when it was fired; why were there no fingerprints on it; why it was in his left hand when he was right handed; why the .38 was made from two guns (called a "drop gun"), the type used to make murder look like suicide; and why no one in the park heard a gunshot—*and where were his car keys?*

Then there is the mystery of the briefcase which had disappeared. Upon its sudden reappearance six days later, a suicide note torn in 27 pieces (which went undetected on the first examination of the case), was found inside it. Added to the mystery is the fact that three handwriting experts came to the conclusion the note was not written by Vince Foster. Finally, there is the testimony Patrick Knowlton, who was in the park at the time of Foster's suicide and noticed a reddish-brown Honda with Arkansas plates. What got his attention was the man who rolled down the car window and glared at him, giving himthe feeling he was not welcome there. This occasion was followed by various scare tactics used against him for weeks to come, but most disturbing was the FBI's distortion of his and other witnesses' testimony when they appeared before the Senate investigative committee. Though most authorities believe Foster did commit suicide, they do not believe it took place in Marcy Park. The apparent cover-up, missing documents taken from Foster's office, and the fact that certain members of the White House knew about his death hours before the time they claimed they did, makes one wonder what the Clintons might be hiding. Another highly questionable deal involving Clinton was with Dan Laster, a local millionaire who contributed heavily to his campaigns. Laster was also the main bond dealer for the Arkansas Development Finance Authority (ADFA). Martin Gross, as a guest on *The 700 Club* said that Lasater "made a fortune because the governor gave him the business. Now who's Dan Lasater? Dan Lasater was a cocaine user who went to jail for cocaine use and (he) gave $8,000 to Bill Clinton's brother to bail out his drug debts and he gave him a job in Florida. And then as soon as Dan Lasater got out of jail, Bill Clinton pardoned him....Nancy Thomason ran Lasater's firm when he was in jail, and now she's one of the three who got the Whitewater files from Foster's office." In her testimony at the hearings, she conveniently couldn't remember anything to speak of.

The Great Whitewater Fiasco is a story that exposes the greed of the Clintons and how they misused their power and exploited people most of their adult lives in order to get to the top. Gross talks about much more than their political favors to pay off loans, irresponsible appointments of friends to high offices, conflicts of interest, and cover-ups. It is also about the misuse and theft of federally guaranteed funds, bank fraud, obstruction of justice, destruction of subpoenaed documents, and much more. There is an interesting story behind the nearly two year long investigation into Madison Guaranty by criminal investigator, Jean Lewis, and how she met with the stone-walling and the runaround Washington is noted for when she tried to find out what became of her reports on the Arkansas S & L, and then her sudden removal from the case. Actually, reading Gross' book puts one in the mind of the old western movies in which power was centered in one man who tyrannized the townspeople with his political will for his and his pals benefit.

As for Whitewater, Dr. Robert Lichter's Center for Media and Public Affairs reports that "media coverage on Whitewater has been lacking." Stephen Hess of the Brookings Institute says of Whitewater: "It snuck under the national press' radar screen." Reporters from two London newspapers, the *Economist* and *Sunday Telegraph*, having done a far better job in their coverage of Whitewater than American reporters, agreed. Christopher Wood of the *Economist*, did not understand the American press' failure to cover Whitewater. Commenting to *The Wall Street Journal* in regard to their "genteel distance" on this subject, he said he was "a little puzzled by my colleagues in the American media."

Well, up to now it appears that a lot more than Whitewater "snuck under the national press' radar screen," as the same stonewalling obstruction of justice exists throughout other scandals involving this White House. William Safire of *N.Y. Times News Service* talks about how Congress has been "systematically stifled" into looking into the Asian penetration of the Clinton campaign—12 key figures and 16 Buddhist monks havedeclined to testify by taking the Fifth Amendment. His solution as to how the Senate can break through this cover is to 1) "call all these witnesses to public hearing…Let those who wish to take the oath and then personally give their variations of "I decline to testify because anything I say may tend to incriminate me; and 2) counter the cabal of White House and DNC lawyers and Democratic senators determined to delay the proceedings until the committee clock runs out on Dec. 31."

That is exactly how White House security aide Anthony Marceca handled the situation regarding his involvement in Filegate. He left Craig Livingstone (former campaign man for Clinton and Gore) holding the bag, to explain how 900 confidential FBI files (remember Watkins and Travelgate) mostly on Republicans, ended up in the White House. Charles Colson in an interview with Pat Robertson said: "The whole time I was in the White House I saw maybe three or four…. They were carefully guarded by the FBI. I can't conceive of them leaving 700 files in anyone's office. Unless you were doing a wholesale search for dirt on political enemies, there would be no basis to do that." He went on to say, "The FBI would never turn over that many files unless they thought the president or the chief of staff wanted them." When asked specifically what he went to jail for, Colson replied: "I gave an FBI file to reporters. Leon Jaworski, the special pros-ecutor, said, 'We've been looking for a way to stop that abuse....Steal-ing, or looking at FBI files will not happen again if you plead guilty.'" I guess we can conclude that Colson was in the wrong administration.

Campaign-financegate is probably the mother of all "gates." It involves the Riady family of Indonesia which heads the Lippo organi-zation. One of its allege functions during the 1996 campaign was to act as a front for laundering money to the President and the DNC. According to *Investor Business Daily,* this organization donated millions of dollars toward Clinton's re-election. The infamous John Huang fits into the picture through his connections with the Riady family, and appears to have been the chief financial procurer of Asian money donated to Clinton and the DNC. Huang was given a lot of authority, along with top security clearance to the White House, which allowed him to come and go as he pleased. Evidence clearly shows he made 67 visits there, had access to America's military secrets, and was privy to daily briefings from the CIA (37 of which there is hard proof he was shown raw intelligence data.) What especially makes these discoveries of grave concern was the fact that Huang had an E-mail drop and tele-phone connections across the street from the government office. This was a room rented from Stephens, Inc. of Little Rock, Arkansas, one of the big money donators to the 1992 election of Bill Clinton. Also, there is hard evidence that Huang made as many as 237 calls in 14 months to his former Lippo associates during the time he held a sensi-tive trade post position (these calls do not include any calls from the Stephens, Inc. office.)

Sen. Joseph Lieberman of Connecticut is at least one bi-partisan Democrat on the investigative panel who looked into campaign fraud, and who found this information very troublesome. Even some of the talking heads on television made a few remarks about the seriousness of this situation, yet the TV media did a total blackout of the hearings, except for *C-Span,* and the press didn't do much better. Why? It allowed them to continually say, "The public isn't interested in the hearings." The truth is a lot of Americans did not even know the Senate Thompson hearings were going on.

Many in Congress believed the excessive money given in these campaigns did have an affect on Clinton's policy with Asian countries. The *Bulletin of the Atomic Scientist* gives one good example of a special deal with North Korea, which is definitely not a U.S. ally. Shortly after having received $5 billion for the construction of two light-water reactors, the president gave the North Korean government top-secret nuclear technology.

Nick Guarino, who heads the *Wallstreet Underground* writes: "According to FBI and CIA documents, Chinese military intelligence has been cultivating Clinton since the early 1980's. As governor of Arkansas, he helped the Chinese set up 'subsidiaries' that were used as bases for an elaborate industrial espionage operation.

Their mission was to steal industrial secrets from U.S. firms, and then use them to energize China's stagnant state-controlled economy. It worked spectacularly. Thanks to Clinton, there are now more than 1,000 fronts for Chinese government intelligence operating under the guise of legitimate businesses in the U.S."

It also appeared that Secretary of State Madeleine Albright might have aided the administration in coverups regarding these kinds of transactions. In her testimony before the Senate committee, she announced that the U.S. would ban trade with certain Chinese companies because of some of their deals with Iran, and was asked, in view of what she said, to explain how the administration could justify its eagerness to renew MFN status with that country. Her answer was that "there was no evidence that the Chinese government was involved."

William Rusher of *Newspaper Enterprise Association*, calls her remark "preposterous," saying that "it casts doubt on everything that preceded it." He goes on to say, "The chances that the Chinese government didn't know what those three companies and five businessmen were doing, handing over chemical weapons technology and raw materials to Iran, are exactly nil—zip, nada. Not a sparrow falls to earth in the

Peoples Republic of China without the government's prior knowledge and approval."

Rusher goes on to explain why it is so easy for anyone connected with this administration to be evasive. "We are told that a number of President Clinton's closest friends, as well as his personal lawyer, were well aware that former Deputy Attorney Web Hubble was in deep trouble, and indeed that several of them were raising hundreds of thousands of dollars to throw at him in the guise of legal fees (or hush money), but that (to use the Albright formula) "there was no evidence the president was involved.

But if Madame Secretary is allowed to get away with this one, there's no telling how widely the formula may be applied....

On China, the truth is that the Clinton Administration had no policy except maintaining MFN status for the People's Republic at all costs."

Well, if anyone has been able to accurately discover what really goes on in Bill Clinton's world, you would think it would be his biographer, Roger Morris. He says, "The current scandals aren't simply an aberration. These scandals are Arkansas writ large. The illegal fund-raising has been played as a sometime-vice when, in fact, it's the lifeblood of Clinton's politics."

The long trail of unscrupulous characters did not begin with Clinton's entry into the White House. He was associated with the drug dealer, Dan Lasater, The Lippo Group, John Huang, and other shady people and groups that supported him with donations for his election when he was governor of Arkansas—and the media chose not to bring it to the public's attention.

ABUSING THE PRIVILEGE OF EXECUTIVE ORDERS

In her book, *The Final Days*, Barbara Olson gives a detailed account of the massive land grabs and executive orders (EO)President Clinton enforced during his tenure in office, and most especially in the last days and weeks of his presidency. Presidents have the right and the authority to issue executive orders which are provided by Article II of the Constitution, but it is also the president's duty to enforce the laws Congress has passed, using discretion and respect for "rights, duties, and obligations growing out the Constitution itself...and all the protections implied by the nature of government under the Constitution." On the very last day, hours before he handed over the keys to the White House, Bill Clinton issued a torrent of 140 pardons and thirty-six sentence commutations. One television commentator said: "Not since the opening of the gates of the Bastille have so many criminals been liberated on a single day."

"Former presidents have used the power sparingly," Olson writes, "until the twentieth century." Franklin Delano Roosevelt made the most of this privilege, and possibly even abused it, but considering the fact that he served nearly four terms, and because of World War II being a time of crisis with vast and unusual needs to be met, we can understand to some extent his need to do so. "What is interesting," Olson says, "about William Jefferson Clinton's use of executive orders to make law is not the number of executive orders, but their content, objectives, and timing—and the employment by President Clinton of executive orders to reverse or repeal orders issued by prior presidents."

Almost immediately upon taking office, Clinton began reversing a lot of the Reagan/Bush EOs. Some of these reversals included "cost-benefit analyses for new government regulation...restraint in taking action that would result in federal preemption of state laws...[enacting] laws or regulations that interfere with the traditional family...a constitutional guarantee against uncompensated taking of private property…unclear rules that led to costly and unnecessary lawsuits."

Big Surprise! One of Clinton's first EOs reversed *Communication Workers v. Beck*, "a U. S. Supreme Court ruling that limited the union's ability to confiscate money of workers for political purposes. The form of forced worker contribution to Democrats, particularly Bill Clinton, is a blatant intrusion on the political rights of union members in favor of union bosses."

It was only a matter of days after his inauguration that Clinton replaced the existing policy of the military on homosexuals to "don't ask don't tell." Most of us could live by that order without objection, but the fact that Clinton wanted to go much further for gay "rights" was what caused the public outcry and forced him to backdown from his original objective. Olson writes: "That order responded to pressure from Clinton's homosexual supporters, who had raised $3.5 million for him. In the words of Clinton's openly homosexual adviser David Mixner, 'Clinton became the Abraham Lincoln of our movement.'"

Within two days of his inauguration, Clinton satisfied the feminist "cheerleaders" and the abortion lobby with the issuance of a memorandum "allowing abortions on U.S. military bases overseas, another reversal of the Reagan and Bush policy."

In the final days of his presidency, Clinton went into a frenzy, issuing executive orders right up to within weeks, days, and hours before his tenure was up. On January 10, 2001, he signed the "Responsibilities of Federal Agencies to Protect Migratory Birds," a new bureaucracy which would include "representation from the departments of Interior, State, Commerce, Agriculture, Transportation, Energy, and Defense, EPA, and other agencies. A peculiar action," says Olson, "for a president about to leave office—creating a brand new bureaucratic entity that would be part of a new president's government. But Bill was consumed about leaving his mark on the government he was about to leave." The same day he signed another EO, "The President's Disability Employment Partnership Board," which amended "one of his previous EOs that had countermanded one by George H. W. Bush. Boards, commissions, councils, committees, tribunals, and agencies are so plentiful in Washington that no one can even identify them all."

On January 12, Clinton added another EO to his long list: "Advisory Committee on Expanding Training Opportunities, another amendment of an earlier order." On January 15, it was EO "Federal Interagency Task Force on the District of Columbia." Two days later the "Implementation of the Africa Growth Basin Trade Partnership Act" and the "Lifting and Modifying Measure With Respect to the Federal Republic of Yugoslavia (Serbia and Montenegro)" became law. On January 18, he signed an EO for "Federal Leadership on Global Tobacco control and prevention; and in the last moments an EO to extend Secret Service protection for his daughter, Chelsea.

One of Bill Clinton's outrageous "midnight" EOs was to overturn the U.S. Supreme Court's decision. Under *Alexander v Sandoval*, the court "held that there is no civil right to force our government to use languages other than English." Clinton's order was just the reverse. Phyllis Schafly, president of Eagle Forum, said: "He ordered all executive-branch agencies to provide all federal benefits and service in foreign languages." A few weeks later "Janet Reno published 15 pages of 'Guidance' in the Federal Register, and the other executive departments then did likewise."

The reason we get so many options in foreign languages on our phone calls to businesses, as well as information in airports and other places, is because of Clinton's mandate, which includes all state and federal government to provide services in foreign languages. Clinton holdovers in the Department of Health and Human Services (HHS) are attempting to make doctors hire translators for their non-English-speaking Medicare or Medicaid patients. They are also giving small businesses trouble if they want their employees to speak English. But some doctors are fighting the HHS. They joined a non-profit organization, Pro-English, which promotes English as the national language, in hopes of getting a court ruling against enforcement of the HHS order.

English has been the tie that binds us together as Americans, and some in Congress are not too happy with our national language slipping in importance. Rep. Bob Stump (R-AZ) has introduced legislation to try to nullify all the department regulations that resulted from Clinton's EO.

One of the subjects Barbara Olson covers in regard to Clinton's quest for power and legacy is his "monument mania" (which includes the massive land grabs in Chapter 7 under the subtitle, "The Environmental Extremists"). Speaking of the "FDR memorial, she says: "The memorial shows the wartime leader seated in a wheelchair, a reality that was studiously hidden from the American people by FDR and his aides. And gone were Roosevelt's omnipresent cigarette and cigarette holder." Bill Clinton's attempt to make the memorial of Franklin Delano Roosevelt a memorial to himself also becomes transparent to the observer. "Clinton made sure that everyone who visited the FDR memorial would also think of William Jefferson Clinton. The plaque in the information center prominently features the name WILLIAM J. CLINTON etched just below that of Franklin Delano Roosevelt. Clinton's dedication is above and in larger characters than the names of the FDR Memorial Congressional Committee members, architect Lawrence Halprin, who worked on the project for more than twenty years; private donors; and the citizens of the United States who made it all possible."

THE PARDONS

Right up to the last minute before leaving the White House on January 20, 2001, President Clinton was busy issuing pardons and commutations for crooks of every stripe—drug smugglers, tax cheats, frauds, money launderers, embezzlers, international fugitives—the grand total for pardons reaching 140, for commutations, 36; and most of these done without the usual process of review by an attorney of the Department of Justice.

Barbara Olson gives a vivid description of Clinton's actions during this time in her book, *FINAL DAYS The Last, Desperate Abuses of Power by the Clinton White House*, "He [Clinton] set aside eight new national monuments and signed new executive orders like a rock star at an autograph session. On a last-minute spree, he launched enough new pages of federal regulation to fill a law library, dealing with everything from snowmobiles in national parks, to air conditioning, to the very definition of human existence. He also nominated nine new federal judges and packed every available board and commission with his pals, supporters, and contributors."

Most of us can probably figure out why alleged part time girlfriend of Bill Clinton, Susan McDougal, was pardoned. After all, she went to jail rather than give testimony against the Clintons, and repeatedly spewed hateful tirades against special prosecutor investigating several of the Clinton scandals—Ken Starr, whom the Clintons thoroughly despised. As for the pardons one of the Democrat's "rising stars," Henry Cisneros, and also his mistress, we might also figure this pardon was due to Clinton's soft spot for adulterers and their mistresses. The hush money in the amount of $250,000 in Cisneros conviction evidently was not enough to keep his secret from coming out.

Then there is *The reverend* Jesse Jackson, who falls into multiple categories of unsavory dealings, the adulterer/mistress being one of them. Since he had consoled and counseled the "broken and contrite" Bill Clinton after his affair with Monica Lewinsky, these two surely felt a kinship with one another. At least Clinton granted pardons for several of Jackson's shadowy friends.

One friend Jackson lobbied for was Mel Reynolds, "a former Democratic congressman," who in 1995, Olson writes, "was convicted for having sex with a sixteen-year-old campaign worker." Two years later, "he was convicted of…federal fraud charges," that is he hid his debts for the purpose of getting bank loans, and on a separate charge of "laundering union political donations that were intended for voter registration drives but were directed instead to his election campaign." With two years left to serve, Clinton commuted his sentence.

Friend of Jackson, Dorothy Rivers, "a Democratic Party loyalist and top official of Jackson's Rainbow/PUSH Coalition," also got a pardon for being a first-class crook. Olson tells of her guilty plea of "stealing $1.2 million in government grants following a forty-count indictment on charges of fraud, theft, tax evasion, obstruction, and making false statements." What makes the theft even worse was that Rivers used "federal money slated for homeless children to buy, among other things, a $35,000 fur coat, a Mercedes-Benz for her son, clothes for her live-in-boyfriend, landscaping, and $250,000 for a record company. She used the cash to hire a chauffeur and to throw parties. At one of these events, she ordered a champagne glass six feet tall. She also used federal money for political donations and to make payments on a six-unit apartment and a home on Lake Michigan."

In a summation of Rivers character, Olson writes: "Rivers, a kind of reverse Robin Hood who stole from the poor and gave to herself, showed absolutely no remorse at any time but received relatively lenient treatment by the court anyway....she received the least amount of time allowed under federal sentencing guidelines—five years and ten months. President Clinton reduced to time serve, which came to about three years."

Perhaps Clinton also feels a kinship with swindlers and con men, which may have led him to pardon three of his cabinet members. Secretary of Agriculture Mike Espy was convicted of lying about $22,000 he accepted from agribusiness friends, and John Deutch, his former director of the Central Intelligence Agency, was convicted of "transferring classified intelligence documents to unsecured home computers. American nuclear secrets were turning up in China."

Out of the twenty-one drug offenders whose sentences were commuted, one of the most undeserving was a Manhattan lawyer, Harvey Weinig. Weinig was involved in the Cali cartel, had helped in a kidnaping, and participated in "one of the largest drug money-laundering cases in New York history," and yet Bill Clinton commuted his sentence to the time served, 270 days. Olson writes: "Both the Department of Justice and the U.S. attorney in New York were stunned by Clinton's action....A reaction of outrage came from Columbia's government officials, calling Clinton's actions 'sordid.'" Olson goes on to say that Weinig had connections in the White House that pushed the deal for him: "In the end, the connections with Clinton trumped the connections with the Cali cartel."

Another Clinton gift was to cocaine kingpin Carlos Anibal Vignali, of Los Angeles. Vignali was convicted of drug trafficking and sentenced to fifteen years. Stunned that the president had commuted his sentence to time served, former U.S. attorney Todd Jones, who had helped prosecute Vignali said: "We considered it a no-brainer. I did not believe that there was any way [clemency] was going to be granted in this case." But Jones had not figured on the money connections to the White House. Carlos Vignali is the son of a very wealthy Los Angeles developer. He helped his son's case out tremendously by contributing $150,000 to Democrats in 2000, and later $10,000 to the Democratic National Committee. Olson writes: "As the Clinton administration wound down, the politicians whom the elder Vignali had befriended became a veritable phone bank and letter-writing committee on behalf of the son, the imprisoned drug smuggler." It all paid off for Carlos Vignali, but to law enforcement who put their lives on the line, it was a stunning blow.

Of course, the really big one that got away was Marc Rich, America's number one fugitive from justice. Rich was a man who traded with the enemy. Bans against trade with the Khomeini regime of Iran, with Colonel Gaddahi of Libya, or the Soviet Union during the Cold War did not hinder Marc Rich in the least. Neither did propping up the Castro dictatorship in Cuba, or wanting to buy oil from Iraq "when it was under an international embargo for the 1990 invasion of Kuwait." Olson writes: "For Rich, dealing with pariah nations and terrorist dictators became a lucrative way of life." And it paid off in billions of dollars for him.

Olson continues: "Morris 'Sandy' Weinberg "headed a team of prosecutors from New York's elite southern district U.S. Attorney's Office that eventually brought charges against Rich in a fifty-one-count indictment, in part under RICO, the Racketeer Influenced and Corrupt Organization statutes...." And Weinberg had this to say: "The evidence was absolutely overwhelming that Marc Rich, in fact, committed the largest tax fraud in the history of the United States."

Did Marc Rich figure that money and beautiful women might be the way to offer Bill Clinton a deal he couldn't resist? As Olson writes in her book, "Denise Rich was a regular visitor at the White House, especially during the final days, and so was Beth Dozoretz, a Democratic Party fundraiser—"Dozoretz was a familiar and dependable aide to the Clintons. Of course, Bill Clinton denies there was a *quid pro quo*, and Hillary never knew anything, but the bottom line is there was a lot of money that passed hands just before Marc Rich was pardoned.

Mary Jo white, President Clinton's U.S. attorney for the southern district of New York would investigate the Rich pardon, but so far she has done nothing but let time pass. I don't find this too surprising, as she has done the same thing with other cases involving party politics. Kelly Patricia O'Meara, and investigative reporter for *Insight* (12/31/01) writes: "Critics of departing U.S. Attorney Mary Jo White say she buried the Teamsters scandal and other cases out of concern that the political fallout would hurt her career." the convicted were fund-raiser and consultant for the Democratic National Party (DNC), Michael Ansara; campaign manager to Teamsters', Jere Nash; and political consultant to the DNC—both of whom pled guilty to mail fraud and embezzlement for DNC fund-raisers, but four years later they have not been sentence. Mary Jo White plays the clock out with one excuse after another.

The same thing happened with the New Square Hasidic Jews pardon so they would vote for Hillary. White said this case would be part of her investigation of the Clinton pardons. O'Meara quote Larry Klayman, president of Judicial Watch: "She knows that if she ever wants another job politically she's going to have to go through [Democratic New York senators] Hillary Clinton or Chuck Schumer." Sentencing anyone would be "a career-ender" for Mary Jo White.

Speaking of the passes White has given the Democrats and the Clintons, Charles Krauthammer of the *Washington Post* said: "There is no way to prove a *quid pro quo*, "but then, the Clintons have been especially diligent in covering their tracks in similar dealings over the past twenty years." Olson response: "Maybe there was no proof of a *quid pro quo*, but maybe there does not need to be. Another legal Latin phrase seems to cover it: *res ipsa loquitur*—the thing speaks for itself.

What I have written about the executive orders, pardons, land grabs and monuments—the quest for power and a legacy—is a mere speck compared to the whole. It would take tremendous research of a professional nature, perhaps an attorney, or even several, and another book to explain what went on in the political life of the Clintons. An excellent source is Barbara Olson's book *THE FINAL DAYS, The Last, Desperate Abuses of Power by the Clinton White House*, which I highly recommend to anyone who is interested in understanding what is the true character of the Clintons.

10

Does Character Matter?

○ ○

"A good name is better than precious ointment…"—*Ecclestiastes 7:1*

Once Mr. Clinton was installed firmly in the presidential chair—sometime inDecember of '93—and having had enough time to reflect on his core beliefs, I noticed he began saying that the real crisis in America was not economic or governmental, but spiritual and cultural. Candidate Clinton had run for office with all the energy he had, claiming, "It's the economy stupid!" Now, the second Clinton was saying, "It is the twisted values that are tearing society apart….It's due to the breakdown of the family." Seems to me when Dan Quayle said something about twisted values and the need for family values, the first Clinton had quite a different opinion. In fact, if my memory serves me, he said: "Unfortunately, the Vice President's address is, in my view, cynical-election-year politics"?

It wasn't long afterwards that the new president bravely confirmed his secondary stand and told Tom Brokaw that he had read Dan Quayle's speech (the one on family values), and that he thought "it has a lot of good ideas in it…it is true that America would be much better off if every child was born in a two-parent family." What a contrast to what the major media gave Dan Quayle!—they forgave Clinton; there was no hissing, no screaming, and no one dipped his/her pens in poison and wrote nasty, ungracious accusations about him. I found myself thinking, "Goodness, it is finally okay, and maybe even politically correct, to talk about family values now." And I was right. But still, I was curious. I couldn't help but wonder if the new president had forgotten what his wife said about Quayle's "Murphy Brown" speech just months before. She had attacked the vice president before a San Francisco audience during the campaign, saying, "I wonder if he lives in the same America we live in, if he sees the same things we see. He's trying to blame the Los Angeles riots and blame the social problems in this country on a TV sitcom."

Well, despite the hypocrisy, it was a little exciting. It looked as though America was about to be launched into the year of family values. My liberal newspaper got in on the act, too, and wrote about Mr. Clinton and related family value issues, saying, "President Bill Clinton continues to show that he's determined to put some real meaning into the hep new phrase 'politics of meaning.'" Guess what? It turned out that the hep new phrase had to do with family values! And our former columnist, Myrne Roe, who had not been too happy about hearing anything on family values previously, was silent this time on the subject.

The plus on this whole thing is that almost no one had to keep his/her mouth shut as they did in the previous administration. Before, the media, and liberals in general, had been so proud of candidate (the first) Clinton when he said, "I'm fed up with Washington lecturing us about family values!" I remember, the crowd had roared and cheered so loudly, I thought the house might come down.

These sudden conversions always leaves me confused as to how easily the public adjusts to them, hardly batting an eye. Maybe columnist Robert Novak had figured it out? In June, 1995, he wrote in the *Conservative Chronicle:* "Clinton thinks about tactics much more than philosophy, and his budget switch was essentially tactical." But that comment set me to thinking again—how about the President coming out for school prayer? The irony is that he even co-opted his speech in favor of school prayer, pretty much repeating verbatim what Jay Seku-low of the American Center for Law and Justice (ACLJ) had said on this issue. I figure the President surely had to be listening to Pat Rob-ertson's "Newswatch." After all, *The 700 Club* is about the only place you could get a speech like the one Mr. Sekulow delivered. The way I see it, the President must have kept tabs on Sekulow's progress, since he is the attorney who had fought the ACLU into a corner and won the battle on this issue. Seeing that he was boxed in, plus the fact that the issue was more popular with the public than he had realized, I sup-pose Mr. Clinton felt justified in claiming authorship for what some-one else had earned. It is no surprise that the media cared nothing about the ACLJ because it was founded by Pat Robertson, and so they decided to keep super mum about Mr. Sekulow's work and accom-plishment in this area.

With the Clinton pattern of misstatements, hypocrisy, and all the bad stuff that continually surrounded that administration, it was amaz-ing that he could deceive the American people again and get re-elected. Journalist and talk show host, Tony Snow, sums up the Clinton phe-nomenon this way: "Clinton won a second term in office because he divided and conquered in 1996. The Dick Morris strategy of triangula-tion helped frighten blacks into remaining Democrats, shocked women into abandoning Republicans, and persuaded the press not to look too hard at such things as Lippogate."

But as soon as things began to heat up a little on Campaign Financegate, it merely meant we would hear more from the President (also, from the democrats and the major media), trying to divert atten-tion away from himself and cast republicans as the real wrong-doers. And that is exactly what happened. The gall of the president never ceases to amaze me. In his June, 1997 visit to California, once again he played the innocent victim. Speaking of some "people in Washing-ton,"during one of his lectures on racism, character, etc., he said: "They wake up every day trying to think of some way to put us down, this whole country, and get us back to being angry and mad with one another. I just keep trying to get everybody to look on the bright side and go forward."

Editor of *The American Spectator*, R. Emmett Tyrrell, Jr., reflecting on public sanction of Clinton's tawdry behavior, wrote: "So what? Boy Clinton's knee has healed. He can golf again. He can vacation with the rich and famous on Martha's Vineyard. He has suffered no more embarrassments from his staff: no reports of drug use, of bankruptcy, of suicide. In fact, independent counsel Kenneth Starr, after suffering such cruel abuse from Hatchetman Carville, has delivered up his report that deputy counsel Vincent Foster did actually commit suicide in Fort Marcy Park. So why do I get these notifications that witnesses are being hassled?"

In the meantime, Paula Jones' law suit against Mr. Clinton for gross sexual misconduct was in process. When the time came for him to give his deposition, some people said, "The President is in real trouble," but I didn't think he had much to worry about. We can't say the media has ever shown any interest in Paula Jones—she's been called "trailer trash," "Dogpatch Madonna," and it has been implied that she would say anything for a hundred dollar bill. Given this description of her, liberals must figure no one could possibly think her testimony credible. Somehow I felt if she had only been an elitist of some sort, maybe like Anita Hill, she may have had some credibility—sorry Paula, you're from the wrong side of the tracks.

Well, that is the analysis I reasoned up to the time Monica Lewinsky entered the picture. I don't think she can be classified as an elitist, but we know that she wasn't from the wrong side of the tracks (and this is not to say I excuse Monica's behavior). But the Clintons never needed a good reason to smear anyone. They just had to tell the truth about them, and that was enough. Olson writes (*Hell to Pay*): "As it had been from the beginning, the Clinton spin machine went into high gear. The word went out that Monica was a mentally unstable, stalking, Valley Girl sexual predator. Hillary went on national television and blamed it all on a "vast right-wing conspiracy,'" and Bill Clinton was getting away with another one of his tawdry escapades, that is, until the blue dress turned up and proved him a liar. Suddenly the media were "shocked" that he *may* have lied!—but maybe they should have put some stock in what Senator Bob Kerrey of Nebraska said of his president earlier: "He's an exceptionally good liar."

The question became "would the so-called comeback kid survive this one? At least the House of Representatives had the courage to impeach the president for lying under oath, but party politics meaning everything to the Democrats, right down to the last man, they voted against impeachment. As for the major media, who showed all kinds of interest in the titillation factor a sex story would bring, and thus boost their ratings, they could not muster any outrage, preferring more a shady character in the White House than to see their man disgraced. The reality is Bill Clinton's affairs with women (as disgusting as they are) were not nearly as important as some of his other scandals. He should have been impeached, if not jailed, for his traitorous acts toward Asian countries for campaign money so that he could get re-elected.

Don Feder's take on the whole Clinton mess is that we should "expect a modicum of decency—that a president will have enough respect for his office not to comport himself like a drunken frat boy during spring break....so that parents won't have to explain to their adolescent children why the leader of the free world behaves like a barnyard animal during mating season."

Syndicated columnist, Joseph Sobran, talks about Michael Kellett's (author) pamphlet in which he summarizes Dr. Robert Hare's profile of a psychopath in his book *Without Conscience*. The description reads as follows: "The essence of the psychopath is his sheer absence of conscience. He lies and manipulates without remorse, often with charm and suavity. He isn't insane or delusional, but highly rational. He knows right from wrong but doesn't care. He's a proficient actor who can simulate emotions appropriate to the immediate situation, but he doesn't feel them deeply (if he feels them at all) and he abandons them when their utility has passed. He's egocentric, seeing others purely as instrumental to himself. He craves power. He is likely to be sexually promiscuous, with no stable attachment to any individual. He loves to take risks: he isn't embarrassed when caught in outright lies. He'll take amazing gambles, committing serious crimes to cover up lesser ones: For him, raising the stakes is irresistible.

Hare says the psychopath may strike others as a little too "slick," and argues further: "Psychopathy can't be understood in conventional terms of "mental illness," because it doesn't involve psychosis. On the contrary, the psychopath tends to be very perceptive, with a facade of perfect normality. He's hard for ordinary people to detect—except that he lies constantly, even when he doesn't have to."

The irony is that Dr. Hare did not have a particular person in mind when he wrote the profile of a psychopath. I leave it to the reader to determine whom this description puts him or her in the mind of.

So how will history record this President? In his last weeks in office it was clear Clinton wanted to be remembered for more than talking about his underwear on MTV, or the fun he had on the turf in the bed of his pickup truck, or Paula Jones and the rest of them, or packing in thousands of immigrants just in time for the election—derailing the usual procedures and qualifications for citizenship in order to get more votes for himself and other Democrats—or being head of a party that registered dead people to vote (with his blessings?), or the multiple scandals surrounding him and his wife.

DOUBLE SLEAZE

Both Clintons try to appear noble after they have reaped the rewards of their own unethical and criminal behavior. Then, and only then, did they suggest reforming all the avenues they took to beat the system. For instance, even though they did a lot of unethical and illegal tricks to get Bill his second term and Hillary elected to the Senate, on each occasion, they suddenly argued for campaign reform, but never once did they confess and do penance for the outlandish crime against the American people for bending the existing laws to benefit themselves. With the exception of Monica Lewinsky, Hillary has always been just as involved in the scandals as her husband was. In fact, most investigators believe her to be the chief engineer of them. Just because neither one of the Clintons were convicted of a particular case, means nothing. Some of the things they were alleged of having done are very difficult to prove, and we know that both Clintons have had a lot of practice in getting rid of evidence.

The question has often been asked in reference to Bill Clinton, "Does character matter?" but it is just as important to apply the same question to Hillary. In her book *The Final Days*, Barbara Olson lists several of Hillary's responses to any inquiries about questionable behavior on her part, or that of her husbands. A few of them are—

"If I had known about this…;" "I don't know anything other than what has now come out…;" "I did not know my brother was involved in this…;" "I did not know any specific information…;" "And as soon as I found out, I was very upset about it and very disappointed about it…;" "As soon as we found out…I was heartbroken and shocked by it…;" "You know, I don't have any memory at all of it…."

Speaking of one of Hillary's press conferences where she was questioned about the pardons and her brother's involvement, Olson writes: "Hillary's entire press conference was one long plea for pity. She was surprised, you know, and disappointed, you know, and, you know, hurt. Poor, poor pitiful Hillary." Hillary plays the victim when she is guilty of something, and the media will not rein her in.

Every time you thought you had heard it all, the Clintons always managed to come up with another revolting escapade. One could easily get the impression that they were in competition with themselves to see if they could outdo each of their previous sleazy acts with an even worse one. And worse than that was how press members are often willing to dismiss or make light of their latest indiscretion, like, for instance, the condition the Clinton administration left the White House on their departure from it.

Syndicated columnist Ken Herman is at least one of those media people who considered the disgraceful mess merely a prank ("Prank leaves only the Oval Office with its W intact," Jan. 24, 2001). He did a whitewash of the event and tried to put a positive spin to it by being humorous. But the so-called prank the Clinton administration pulled on the new administration by removing the "W" key from all typewriters and computer keyboards was not a joke. The childish "prank" was done not to be humorous, but to cause confusion and to delay the work of the Bush White House. That is why the "pranksters" hid the keys and destroyed some of them.

Well, some may think it petty to make a federal case out of a prank, but the destruction of government property went much further than lost and ruined keys. Masquerading in adult bodies, those juveniles severed telephone and computer lines, sprayed graffiti on walls, overturned desks, glued cabinet drawers closed, and put pornographic messages on computers.

After all the harm was done, the Clinton's hauled out almost $200,000 worth of furniture, china and flatware from the White House, boarded Air Force One where they carried on the looting, taking the glasses and hand towels embellished with the presidential seal. But nothing should surprise us when it comes to the former president, as this escapade was certainly not the first expression of his immaturity, and it is doubtful that it will be the last. However, the Bush Administration exonerated them from this alleged Air Force One theft and said it didn't happen. Given the Clinton's propensity toward believing that they are exempt from rules, regulations, and laws of conduct that apply to other people, I find this hard to believe.

Meanwhile, the Bush Administration played reaction to the malevolent act, "low-key," and filed no claims against the guilty culprits. Who knows why? Perhaps President Bush did not want to begin his administration on a bad tone. As a candidate, Bush had repeatedly said that he wanted to create a "new tone in Washington." But it must have been hard to follow through with that pledge, especially when DNC chairman Terry McAuliffe and a handful of Democrats came before the TV cameras, huffing and puffing and threatening to sue the Bush White House over the "untrue" reports of destruction left by the Clinton administration. As soon as the Bush White House called their bluff and said they had pictures, McAuliffe and his gang fell silent—their threat, gone with the wind.

In his mad search for a legacy, no one can say Bill Clinton didn't give it all he had to get a peace agreement between Israelis and the Palestinians—what a legacy that would have been! In fact, he worked Israel's Prime Minister Ehud Barak so hard that Barak literally gave away the store to the endangerment of his own country (and Hillary, as always, supported the Arafat regime 100%). But it was the legacy, the legacy that was important. And for all that effort, and the best deal the Palestinians have ever had, how did they show their appreciation? Arafat went home and almost immediately his suicide bombers began hitting civilians wherever they could find them in crowded social gatherings.

Perhaps the seventy tons of material Bill Clinton had shipped out of the White House to Arkansas for his library will help him to create the legacy he wants to have. And there can be no doubt that he is desperate to get a good name in the history books, but he went about it in all the wrong ways. By his very words and actions, he just naturally evoked a lot of questions in our minds. Are his gestures sincere? Are they the "politics of meaning," "ethos of caring," or what? Actually, the same can be said of his co-president, Hillary, who was involved in all the dirty work, right up to her eyeballs. My husband Ed asks a good one: "If character doesn't matter, how are we ever going to impanel our juries?"

Before leaving the subject of character and legacy, two comments sum up the Clinton administration rather well. One is from Barbara Olson's book, *Hell to Pay*, and reads—

"When told that he had become president, Harry Truman said that he felt as if all the stars and moon had fallen on him. Ronald Reagan, in his memoirs, recalled walking into the White House with Nancy, seeing the furniture from their home moved into the grand rooms of the mansion, and suddenly being overwhelmed by the realization that the presidency was truly his to command.

In their respective memoirs, the Clinton will one day each tell of similar emotions on their first day as president and first lady. Untold, likely, will be the real tone and tenor of that day, or the reason for their very public fight that day as reported by *Time* magazine. Standing on the steps of Blair House on Inauguration Day, 1993, Bill Clinton yelled at his wife through the cold morning air. "F—ing bitch!" he screamed, causing Secret Service agents and well-wishers to cower. "Stupid motherf—er," was the reply from our first lady."

The second example comes from a statement I will never forget. It was a speech Bill Clinton gave in California, lecturing on racism, educational excellence, and high character. He said: "As we observe this special week, I ask that all Americans demonstrate in their personal and public lives, and teach actively to our country's children, the high ethical standards that are essential to good character." And I ask: "Did this President ever have a clue?"

PART IV
Tyranny of the Gods

11

Piling on and Getting Too Tough Policy

o o o o o o o o o o o o o o o o o o o o o o o o o o o o o

"Behold, I send you forth as sheep in the midst of wolves: be ye therefore wise as serpents, and harmless as doves. But beware of men: for they will deliver you up to the councils, and they will scourge you in the synagogues..." Matthew 10:16.17

I cannot think of anyone in my lifetime that has had as cruel a job done on him/her by the media as what was done to Vice President Dan Quayle. The "Dan Quayle story" is a classic example of pure hatefulness perpetrated on one person, and illustrates perfectly all the mean-spirited strategies and campaign management (discussed in detail in previous chapters) the liberal media utilizes to make or break a person. In all my 50 years of watching the political scene, I have never seen anything to compare with the insults and vicious attacks that the former vice president endured at the hands of this group. The fact that he came through, with his sanity in tact, is a testament to his strong, moral character.

STRIKING OUT FOR "IMPARTIALITY"?

Hoping to cover for the poor job they did during the 1992 election, the media began making attempts to show their "impartiality," but they still couldn't get the job done right. I am reminded of what Nancy Traver, *Time* reporter, said on *C-Span* in June of '93, after having done a cover story on the Zoe Baird nomination. She said, "This week, we considered running another really tough cover story on Clinton about gays in the military, and we decided, no, that was too tough, that's too much, that's piling on. So we'll move that story inside. We just didn't want to come across as beating up on the President."

Apparently, Nancy Traver did not feel the same policy she expressed on *C-Span* should apply to everyone. For instance, remember Clinton's changing draft story, and how his Uncle Raymond pulled strings to keep him from being drafted. Brent Bozell documents the course of events that took place in the media during the 1991 campaign in one of his columns entitled, "Reporters aren't tough enough on Clinton." He wrote: "None of the networks led its newscast with the controversy. Each only did one story—except for *NBC*, which did nothing. *Times* dedicated four paragraphs, and *Newsweek* gave it the second-to-last paragraph in one story.

Then comparing the Clinton "coverage" with that done on Dan Quayle and the National Guard controversy, she said: "On August 18, 1988, all four networks led off with the news and aired an incredible 15 Quayle stories on one night. Print stories, both in magazines and newspapers, were endless." In his book *Standing Firm,* Quayle talks about the comparisons the media tried to make between him and Clinton on this issue. "I resented the comparison, because there's not much of a parallel. Clinton, who during his college years wrote a letter admitting that he 'loathed the military,' sought every way to get out of serving: I did not. I did not base my choices on some hypothetical future political career, whereas he did. As his letters home from Oxford show, with their reference to future 'political viability,' Clinton clearly was thinking about standing before a press conference twenty years later. And when he did, and was finally called upon to explain his actions, he was evasive: I was not."

It should be remembered that Quayle did serve six years in the National Guard, and that there was no evidence strings were pulled for his benefit. However, Clinton suffered from his choices, but not so much because he opted not to join the military (as so many young men did at that time), but more because he would not tell the truth of how he managed to escape the service, and still more because he protested on foreign soil duringthe Vietnam War. His actions amount to something similar to what Jane Fonda did in turning her loyalty away from the American fighting men and women and consorting with the enemy.

COILED AND READY TO STRIKE

On the fly cover of Dan Quayles' book, the first paragraph reads: *"Standing Firm* leaves no doubt that Dan Quayle is the most misjudged figure in modern political history. Prior to 1988, Quayle had never lost an election. Not for Congress. Not even for the Senate. Heading into that year's Republican Convention, Quayle was considered one of the party's 'bright young stars'—a man of unusual political instincts who, when it came to campaigning, had a reputation as a giant killer."

That Quayle had proven himself an effective campaigner had been established as early as 1976 when he ran against the longtime incumbent, Ed Roush, whom many considered unbeatable. At the time, Quayle's father told him he would lose, saying, "Nobody can beat Ed Roush." But the 29 year old Quayle did beat him and was sworn in Congress in January 1977. Two years later he ran against another Democratic incumbent. Birch Bayh, a former presidential candidate who was also considered a political giant. Despite the fact that the odds were against him, and that Bayh had outspent the Quayle campaign by several hundred thousand dollars, Quayle was confident he could win on the issues, which he did by a margin of 10 percent.

Given Quayle's impressive background, we can only ask, "Why was the major media so bent on humiliating this man?" If anyone thinks he/she has a clear picture of the mean job the media did on Dan Quayle when he was vice-president (as I did), read *Standing Firm*. I found myself in utter disgust with the media and their inability to report news objectively. Quayle's book should be a must read for every student of political science and journalism.

In the following examples we see a tactic used over and over by the left—presenting gross exaggerations or falsehoods as fact. However, it is not my intent to rehash all the hatchet jobs here, but to give a few of the predominate media themes created to destroy Dan Quayle. One that dominated their coverage of him early on was that he was a rich boy who had everything handed to him on a silver platter, and that he had acquired his wealth through inheriting vast sums of money from his grandfather. If the media has such a hatred of people who inherit great wealth, then they should definitely find the Kennedys, the Rockefellers, and others fair game (not to speak of the many talking heads themselves who are extremely wealthy), but for some reason they and the Democrats are very selective in their torturous "reporting" on this subject.

In *Standing Firm,* Quayle says the media portrayed him as the "$600 million man," but that his actual net worth at that time, including his house, was $854,000—information which was available to the media by looking at his financial disclosure forms from his twelve years in the House and Senate. As for his inheritance, Quayle says it consisted of "a small portion of the trust fund his grandfather had set up," and that the principle to his grandfather's estate "would not be distributed to the heirs for nearly 100 years." Clearly, we can assume that neither Dan Quayle nor his children will be around to receive the big bucks then.

Though far from a pauper's life, Quayle's childhood was neither luxurious nor idealistic as the arrogant media portrayed it. "What was lost in this exaggeration of the fortune my grandfather made in the newspaper business was that he believed in people having to earn their own living. He knew the dangers of inherited wealth. My parents made their own way through the middle class, and I attended public schools. My dad became sick with lupus when I was growing up, and he was in and out of hospitals for two years. I can remember my mother, when I was about ten or eleven, telling me that I was now 'the man of the house.' I changed a lot of diapers and helped my mother through some very difficult times. I had jobs throughout college and law school. I've always lived off my salary and paid a mortgage."

THE PRESS BEARS ITS FANGS

Quayle gives two main reasons why the media were determined to characterize him as a spoiled and pampered person. The first one had to do with the fact that he being a babyboomer is also a conservative, and one thing the secular media cannot handle is one of their own being both conservative and in a position of authority. The second reason is that the media were motivated by revenge.

During the 1988 campaign, Dan and Marilyn Quayle, along with the President and the First Lady, attended a rally in Dan's hometown, Huntington, Indiana. Knowing that his friends and neighbors would be out to cheer him, this event was one in which he particularly looked forward, thinking that if seen in a different light, it might end the negative press he had been getting. What happened was the press made every attempt to discredit him, but it backfired on them, and they were not able to take what they so loved to dish out. Quayle writes:

"The press was booed getting off the buss…some in the media wanted to go for the kill and their questions grew more combative. The harder they pushed, the madder the crowd got….The campaign people decided to crank up the microphones so the crowd would hear all of

the give-and-take between me and the press. We wanted to create a little healthy antagonism, to force the press to recognize that not everyone was buying into the media-created image.

The little skirmish we were hoping for turned into a battle royal.
The press's questions were often outrageous. Ellen Hume of *The Wall
Street Journal*, for example, screamed at me, wanting to know how I
had felt when 'people were dying in Vietnam while [I was] writing
press releases (one of my desk duties in the Guard). This absurdity was
answered by angry shouts and name-calling from the crowd, who followed my own replies with deafening cheers....

The press-which has at least as much vanity as politicians—was furious....Len Downie, the *Washington Post's* executive editor, told me
years later that the media's 'searing' experience in Huntington was one
factor keeping them closed-minded about me during the years of my
vice-presidency. They were not used to feeling the public's scorn."

THE DEBATE

Quayle tells how most people thought he had gotten the best of Lloyd
Bentsen in their first debate. For this reason, and that he was also well
up on the issues, Quayle said he felt confident and wasn't nervous
going into the second debate. Unfortunately, this time it was to be
judged by one single exchange, the "no Jack Kennedy" response. Had
it been scored on points, as it should have been, there are some legitimate doubts that Bentsen would have won.

The irony of the situation was that Quayle had been warned that if
he brought Kennedy's name up, it might backfire, which he said he
never intended to do in the first place: "Because I was young and such
a new face on the national scene, my opponents were arguing that I
lacked the qualifications for the vice-presidency. When they made this
argument, they often weren't talking about stature of vision...but were
trying to indicate that I lacked any basic experience in government.
And this was ridiculous. I had served four years in the House of Repre-

sentatives and eight in the Senate—a considerably longer and more challenging stretch than that served by the Democrats' nominee for vice president, Geraldine Ferraro, whose genuine lack of experience was a non-issue....

I made the comparison out of frustration, in response to a question the panel kept asking over and over: 'What would you do if you suddenly found yourself having to assume the presidency?' Bentsen was never asked the question, but I was asked it three times. I felt I had answered it satisfactorily the first two times....Trying to answer it in some new way, one that would put it to rest, I said what was true; that at the heart of the question lay qualifications and experience. And that's when I mentioned Kennedy—strictly to compare our length of service in Congress. I didn't say I was like President Kennedy, a man of great talents and great flaws, in any other respect." (Here again is the badgering strategy the left uses to keep their opponent from talking about issues—the "objective" chauvinistic media.)

A VINDICTIVE PRESS TRIES HARD TO FIND DIRT

The story of Dan Quayle's supposed drug usage is a classic example of how obsessed the media were to wipe this guy out. Quayle writes: "The media had been tantalized from the beginning by the possibility—I'd even call it their certainty—that I had used drugs when I was in college. After all, this was part of the boomer profile. The truth is I hadn't used them....Had I gone to school a few years later, I would have been much more exposed to them....While I am adamantly opposed to the legalization of even so-called soft drugs like marijuana, it's foolish to think we should write off a whole generation for having flirted with the stuff when it was all around them. Four years later I never cared much about whether Clinton had inhaled or not."

Quayle goes on to say, "In the last weeks of the campaign a convicted felon bent on exploiting the system cooked up just the story some of them wanted. Brett Kimberlin was a perjurer doing a fifty-one year federal prison sentence for terrorizing the town of Speedway, Indiana by planting eight bombs in seven days. The explosions maimed several people....Suddenly, just before the election, he was claiming to have regularly sold me marijuana. He said he wanted to show how 'hypocritical' my antidrug positions were."

Despite the fact that Kimberlin had no real credibility, or that there was no evidence or a single witness to back his story, the media having no conscience did what they could to create doubt in the voter's mind. Quayle writes: "But the media in the frantic final days of the campaign didn't care about facts and ran with the story anyway."

By no means would Sam Donaldson and Diane Sawyer be left out of the ambush to discredit Dan Quayle. They invited him on their show, *Prime Time Live,* for a supposed interview; instead, like coiled snakes, they sat ready to strike out at their "guest" with a whole passel of "Quayle jokes." Quayle writes: "In fact, the whole purpose of the thing seemed to be to give them a chance to entertain their viewers with them. This was in the days when that program actually was live, and some friendly observers pointed out that both Donaldson and Sawyer made their own slips of the tongue that night. Diane—who at that time reportedly made $1.6 million a year—also asked me about my 'easy' life. The pampered rich boy image was once again reinforced. I tried to be as pleasant as I could, and I joked about all the work I was providing for comedians, but I was fuming. I had accomplished as much, both at home and abroad, as the office of the Vice President permits any of its occupants to. Almost none of it was getting through. I had to resign myself to the possibility that it never would. The media had put too much of their own credibility into creating the caricature to abandon it now."

Quayle tells of another time Donaldson struck, which took place at a big luncheon rally. Just as the Bush and Quayle families made their entrance, Quayle said, "I can remember Sam Donaldson charging across the hall like a Santa Ana wind, trying to fan the flames that were engulfing me. 'Are you going to get off the ticket? Are you going to get off the ticket?' He was more or less screaming hysterical, and I can remember Barbara Bush turning to her husband and saying serenely, 'Gee, I've never seen Sam so exercised.'"

A PLOT FOILED

One of the biggest reasons Quayle spoke out for tort reform in the legal system was because of the time and money spent on cases that do not belong on court dockets. He gives a hypothetical situation that explains an all too common scenario: "Today a baseball comes crashing through a window, and instead of picking it up and returning it to the neighbor whose kid knocked it through—and who pays the glazier's bill in a reasonably, neighborly way—the 'victim' hangs on to the baseball as evidence and sues the neighbor. (Or the baseball's manufacturer. Or the glass maker. Or usually all three.) Several lawyers are soon billing hours and the civil docket has been crowded with one more pointless case....American businesses and individuals spend more than $80 billion annually on the direct costs of litigation and higher insurance. Include the extra costs and that figure could top $300 million."

Finally, after two and one half years into his vice-presidency, Dan Quayle got some good press. It was the annual convention of the American Bar Association held in Atlanta, and he was to be a guest speaker there. However, he was warned that a plot was in the making to discredit whatever points he might make in his speech. Quayle describes the situation he was up against: "The ABA, a partisan organization, was out of touch not just with American people but with many American lawyers as well. Its leaders tend to be glibly fond of the cameras...they raise a lot of money, and they contribute heavily to Democrats."

First off, Quayle said that the greeting he received "wasn't even polite." Almost immediately he was approached by ABA's president, John Curtin, Jr., who asked him to stay after his speech so that he could respond. Since there were no chairs on stage and only one podium, Quayle said it meant he would "either have to stand by him at the lectern or go out and sit in the audience. Either way, he [Curtin] would have the last word and I would look like a schoolboy being reprimanded."

Originally, Quayle decided not to stay after giving his speech because of the set-up, but made a snap decision after he had finished: "I would stay and listen after all. I was going to stand there, right at his elbow, while he trashed what we'd worked so hard to develop. I would do it because whether he knew it or not, I wasn't going to let him have the last word....His rebuttal was more like a diatribe—a whole bushel of red herrings."

Quayle's decision to stay and get the last word paid off. He writes: "Suddenly, what would probably have been a page 20 story was page 1. And I had the extraordinary experience of enjoying the morning papers....The mail I got was as heartening as the press."

One cannot read *Standing Firm* and not come away with the realization of the intelligent, political savvy and insight Dan Quayle has on the issues. Yet, his accomplishments as vice-president were largely ignored and unreported by a media who considers "foul is fair." For instance, his successes and proven ability as an able diplomat for his work in Latin American countries where he promoted free markets, trade, and democracy, or his work to limit the regulations on business did not attract the media. He did get notice for speaking out on family values, but the result was that the media saw it as a means to make fun and criticize him. However, once Bill Clinton discovered family values was a popular concern of the people, he began talking about it in positive terms—but when has this man not cashed in on any idea that ran high in the polls and claimed it as his own? In fact, all the liberals in the Democrat Party and in the media who trashed the "silly idea of family values" couldn't seem to get enough of throwing the term around to show just how "virtuous and caring" they are.

The unrelenting media blitz to ruin Dan Quayle has gone a long way to insure public cynicism and an intense dislike of the mainstream media. It would be difficult to judge which was their "unkindest cut of all," but returning from his first foreign trip, where progress and press were good, to such pettiness and mean spiritedness exemplified by a headline "FIRST FOREIGN TRIP: QUAYLE FAILS TO SCREW UP," has to be somewhere at the top of the list. But is that one worse than the theme the media hammered on after the Bush/Quayle ticket won the election?—"The education of Dan Quayle," followed by things like the lead story, "Why Danny Can't Read," put out by the-conservation *American Spectator* (on its cover, a Quayle cartoon figure in a propeller beanie). Shame on the *Spectator*! Or what about the "Quayle Watch" in the *Washington Post*, whose writers apparently had nothing better to do than to search through everything he said with a fine-tooth-comb—winding, twisting, convoluting all facts so as to write their daily inanities. It is like Quayle says in his book that if he gave a ten page speech and erred on one word (and even after immediately correcting himself), that would be the focus on page one of the newspaper. It is the kind of stuff that makes people like Sam Donaldson, Al Hunt, Margaret Carlson, Eleanor Clift, and smooth talking, sneaky Daine Sawyer become hyperactive and make fools of themselves with some unfounded point they try to make. The "superior" elite, at that time, had attained that exalted state of the ego where they felt it their duty to push "self actualization ala secular-humanistic style" onto the rest of us, and they succeeded much more than a lot of people, myself included, would like to think. However, the liberal media influence on public thinking was definitely on the decline before 9/11, but it has sunk even more so since that date.

The summary statement on the fly cover of *Standing Firm* reads: "Throughout [the book], the portrait that emerges of the former Vice President is that of a man whose good humor is exceeded only by a competence for which he has never been fully credited." The former Vice President had several unreported successes. A few of the more important ones were his coordination of America's response to a coup attempt in the Philippines, his diplomatic accomplishments in Latin American countries, and his work to curtail harmful overregulation.

It might be an education for the elitist media to have to take some of the same medicine they dish out. Actually, Dan Quayle did not make very many gaffes. Most of the bad press was a desire to damn him. If the media were impartial in reporting gaffes, then Al Gore would had kept them pretty well supplied with material—you know the cheetah with spots, "who are these people" (the bust at Monticello), etc. Getting lost in the woods is understandable, but Quayle is fortunate that it didn't happen to him—the media would have had a heyday with that one. Top the gaffes off with a monotone voice, accompanied with stiff gestures, and name calling and making threats—yes, Vice- President Gore gave the media a lot with which they could "pile on" and have funinflicting pain.

I have seen Dan Quayle several times on television this year (2002), and he is always up on the issues. He also knows his history very well. He is articulate, and never hesitates on any question asked of him, regardless of what the issue is. One could almost get the impression that he holds a position in the White House with access to everything that is going on nationally and internationally. This man is not the buffoon the media made him out to be. It is too bad, at such a time as this, that his insight and intelligence are not being given some thought as to the various problems our country faces.

12

Pros and Cons on the Religious Right

○ ○

"The wisdom of the prudent is to understand his way: but the folly of fools is deceit."—Proverbs 14:8

It appears as though Jesse Jackson has the same low opinion of Christians and conservatives, in general, as does Hollywood. But perhaps he qualifies his bias to mean only members of the Christian Coalition—it's hard to tell just how far and wide the span of his hatred is for these people. In November, 1994, he went on the attack, saying: "…The Christian Coalition was a strong force in Germany. It laid down a suitable scientific, theological rationale for the tragedy in Germany. The Christian Coalition was very much in evidence there." (The Christian Coalition was founded nearly 50 years after Hitler.) *The New York Post* quoted him as saying: "If this were Germany, we would call it fascism. If this were South Africa, we would call it Here we call it conservatism." I wonder how Jackson would square Hitler's attitude— "Antiquity was better than modern times, because it didn't know Christianity and syphilis"—toward Christians with his own toward the Christian Coalition. (I find Jackson's extreme bias ironic since in 1988 Super Sunday, he used churches and had offerings taken up for his own campaign for president—and no one on the left objected at all.)

However, Mr. Jackson only succeeded in turning off a lot of people, as well as showing extreme ignorance on his part. What he does not seem to understand is that the Christian Coalition would not exist today if it had not been for the left's extreme agenda, which has, in the words of nationally syndicated columnist, Linda Bowles, "successfully enshrined promiscuity, drugs, obscenity, personal failure, sexual perversion and cowardice as virtues while discrediting patriotism, loyalty and religion."

In response to Jackson's bitter tirade, Abraham Foxman of the Anti-Defamation League, said: "Nothing about the movement would justify comparing it to such evil institutions as Nazi Germany or apartheid South Africa." and Joseph A. Morris's column in the *Chicago Sun Times* said that Jackson should apologize for his remarks, and furthermore, that "the Christian Coalition is profoundly anti-totalitarian; conspicuously opposed to bigotry and racism, and deeply suspicious of state power....What the Christian Coalition much more closely resembles is the very movement that elevated Jesse Jackson: the civil rights movement."

There have been plenty of nasty remarks coming from the left in regard to Christians. On June 9, 1994, the left virtually exploded, hissing and spinning out envenomed remarks against Christians. Vic Fazio (D. Calif.) referred to them as the "fire breathing Christian right;" Ann Richards as "mongers of hate;" Jocelyn Elders as having a slave mentality, and "those people are selling our children out in the name of religion;" an anonymous voice from the White House as "a cancer in the Republican party;" Bill Clinton as "fanatics" embracing a message of "hate and fear." But as soon as it was determined that the public was not receptive to their hate language against Christians, all of a sudden the President began turning up at various churches trying to get back in their good graces, preaching and making pious remarks about what is right and what is wrong (violation of separation of church and state)?!

Michael Weisskopf of the *Washington Post* also thought he had an accurate description of evangelical Christians who tune in to Pat Robertson's *700 Club* when he wrote that they are "largely poor, uneducated, and easy to command." Little did he know how wrong he was. The *Post* was deluged with phone calls and letters from regular viewers of the show enumerating their intellectual credentials. Statistics show this group is actually over average percentage-wise in comparison with the rest of the country in regard to higher education—meaning, as a group, they are well read and well informed. The male answer to Veronica Lake, columnist Al Hunt, blamed Pat Robertson for violence against women, but the magazine *World* corrected him: "Hunt took out of context a sane discussion by Robertson which emphasized the need for men to love their wives with the same tenderness Christ showed for the church."

The tiresome criticisms from people who—by their very remarks give evidence they do not watch the person or his show—know next to nothing about what they are saying, unwittingly expose their ignorance. Invariably, to incite a negative emotional response in their readers, these complainers rely on buzz words and a lot of hatefulness in hopes to carry the message they themselves are unable to support with fact.

They seem to have the peculiar belief only non-Christians have the wisdom to decide what is best for Americans and so brand Christians as unfit to judge anything in the political arena. If they could only have their way, they would demand that Christians should sit idly by and leave social issues to the discretion of the secular humanist, in other words, the atheists. And this is why we have had so much of their brand of "compassion" legislation, which, more than not, negatively impacts the lives of the rest of us.

It is unfortunate when a columnist/editor has such access to express and spread his own misconceptions to vast numbers of people on this issue. David Awbrey of *The Wichita Eagle* is one such person (now retired from that paper). His column on September 26, 1994, had a great sounding title: "Political left needs to get religion"—but there was a catch. Any good common sense ideas he had, he countered in his usual manner, straddling the fence, hoping he would look good to both sides. The gist of his commentary was that "conservatives often misinterpret the influence of Christianity on America's Founders." But Awbrey was the misinterpreter since history does show that the Founder's religious beliefs did profoundly influence their political thinking. No doubt Awbrey has been influenced by the rewrites of history in which all information about how religion had impacted the Founder's political life has been eliminated by liberal humanists. Many of us are old enough to remember the history on this issue before the redacting process was put into operation.

Next, Awbrey threw in a qualifier so that he didn't appear to rule out religion altogether. He wrote: "The theology of the Founders who were devoted Christians was scarcely like that proclaimed by Roberston or Falwell." What Awbrey didn't take into account is the different situation that exists between two periods—that is, during the Founders' time our country was *not* under the direct assault of left-wing organizations whose aim was to totally eliminate God from nearly every aspect of their lives, as they are today. If that had been the case, I think it is safe to say they would not have waited for decades to retain their religious freedom, as many of today's Christians have, but would have taken immediate steps to remedy the injustice.

The fact that most of the Founders were guided by the moral principals and absolutes of the Bible in drawing up federal documents, certainly should motivate all conservatives who want to preserve the original intent of their work, and therefore politically defend it. Unfortunately, a lot of Christians are ready to condemn their fellow brothers and sisters for getting politically involved. They, too, don't seem to realize that being complacent for four decades, their heads buried in the sand, got us where we are today. They seem to be content to just sit back and gripe about how terrible things are.

Awbrey expressed another of this ideas regarding the religious right. This time he accused them of confusing political ideology with spirituality. Referring to Christians who voiced their opinions on various social issues, he made this statement: "The Bible says nothing about school curricula, tax rates, or a national health plan." So what? What is his point? Neither does the Bible specifically use the terms "child pornography," or "teen pregnancy," so does that mean there is no biblical standard of right and wrong in these areas?

Notice again Awbrey's confusion when he said, "Perhaps the greatest contribution the religious right can make to U.S. politics is to revitalize the religious left." He seems oblivious to that fact that it was the religious left (the secular humanists) and their doctrines that have dominated politics, culture, etc., and caused such destructive tendencies in our society. Thanks to the religious left, everything is up that needs to be down—broken families, teen pregnancy, crime, drugs, violence, pornography—you name it. I believe the 1994 change of power in Congress spoke more for the conservative view than Awbrey was willing to admit. It illustrated an understanding among a large segment of the population that a welfare state is emotionally crippling, and that diversity divides, antagonizes and undoes a good deal of progress made to eliminate racism (see The Legacy of Liberalism, Chapter 4).

Syndicated columnist Tom Teepen has much the same complaint against the religious right as Awbrey. In his column entitled "Christian right awaits days of glory," he implied that because he cannot find anything in the Bible where Jesus talks about balanced budgets, term limits, or tax cuts, that the Christian Coalition had no right to express political opinions. It may come as a surprise to Teepen, but neither did Jesus talk about computers, automobiles, K-Mart, etc. (I wonder, is Teepen suggesting that everything not mentioned in the Bible should be exempt from Christian thought?) The Bible doestell us to pray and seek wisdom and guidance. Also, it is important to remember that Jesus did not exclude anyone. The only outcasts were by choice, and the same thing is true today. Certainly it would be false to suggest that

Jesus was a wimp where politicians were involved. He stood up to the politicians of His day with just the right comeback, and they were unable to respond. They hated him for it, and decided to kill him. That same contempt for Christians keeps raising its ugly head today. But then, Jesus said we would be persecuted for following Him.

In another commentary Tom Teepen makes one of the silliest arguments I have ever heard against Christians: "These Christians know bigotry," August 16, 1994—and I'msurprised *The Wichita Eagle* gave it space in their paper. Attacking Pat Robertson's stand on Christian bigotry in America, Teepen's premise is that since Christians have it much worse in Iran than they do in the U.S., there really is no Christian bigotry here.

Assuming his argument is valid, why doesn't he make a case against the feminist movement in America when women complain that they are mistreated, restricted, or whatever. After all, Iranian women have it much worse than American Women. Iranian women are subjected to a lot of do's and don'ts, and they are in serious trouble if they cross the forbidden line. If Teepen is consistent in his theory, then he needs to repeat what he said about Christians and apply the same to the feminist movement in American—that it "mocks the very real martyrdom of [women] elsewhere by dramatically starring themselves in a staged political parody of the bigotry that is harming and tyrannizing them."

Also, if Mr. Teepen really thinks there is no Christian bigotry in the U.S., he needs to check with the American center for Law and Justice, to find out about the hundreds of cases they receive each month of the year on Christian bigotry across the U.S. Also, there are the alarming number of persecutions around the world. In the meantime, my husband Ed says, "Hopefully, someone will explain to Mr. Teepen that just because something isn't as bad as something else, doesn't make it good."

No examples of Christian bigotry would be complete with the liberal humanistic "reasoning" of Myrne Roe, retired columnist for *The Wichita Eagle*. To the point of petty nitpicking, she has often bitterly attacked Christians and conservatives, and anyone whose view did not parrot her own.

In September 24, 1994 issue of her paper, she wrote: "The religious right wants to make everyone believes as they do....They try to shove their beliefs down the collective throats of all the rest of us: voters should repudiate the righteous right's tyrannical notice that our democracy should become a theocracy." Okay, but why did she have nothing to say about the religion humanism that is daily forced on the public. (At least five of their tenets in *Manifesto I* affirm their religiosity, and how its leaders plan to immerse the world in it.

The irony is that Mrs. Roe's statements accurately express how many Christians feel about the media, how they continually shove their agenda (religion) down our "collective throats" by giving a one-sided coverage of the news, and by careful suppression and special editing of the content of conservative material. These kinds of methods are, in truth, how tyranny begins—reminiscent of the communist governments who controlled the presses and gave their people only the slanted, biased, and outright lies they wanted them to believe. However, no one suggests that members of the press are communists, but the practice described above is seen by many as definitely undemocratic.

Nevertheless, the media's strategy to sway our thinking should be familiar to any high school graduate, since everyone was required to take literature courses. There we learned all about the art of connotation, selecting just the right nouns, adjectives, and verbs, using innuendo and emphasis to present characters in favorable or unfavorable ways. And we can spot the reporters who consider themselves omniscient speakers with supernatural powers, enabling them to tell us exactly what is in the mind of their particular "chosen one," as well as their opponent's mind, exactly what is behind their actions, and exactly what their motivations are. But we were also taught that subjectivity is a technique for writers of fiction such as novels, plays, poetry, and short stories, but that news reporting should be as factual and objective as possible. As Sargent Friday used to say in the 50's TV show, *Drag-net*, "We just want the facts, Ma'am."

Conservatives wouldn't mind the "heat" so much if it were not for the double standard. Democrats, including the President, have been known during the Clinton reign to preach politics in church. There seemed to be no objection to the Rev. Martin Luther King's involve-ment in politics in the 60's; and it is certainly now okay for (Rev.?) Jesse Jackson to blather their political views anytime the mood hits him, but a no-no for Pat Robertson, who really does have a degree in religious theology.

However, the big cop-out Democrats use against him is the separa-tion of church and state, but these restrictions are for conservatives only. Cal Thomas gave an interesting bit of information in his column, "Cal's Corner," in the *Christian American* regarding Clinton's pastor and his political views. The Rev. I. Philip Wogaman of Washington's Foundry Church usually preaches a sermon that mirrors the Clintons' political views. So, then, it isn't surprising to learn that he advocates higher taxes and more welfare.

In 1985, Rev. Wogaman criticized President Reagan for lowering taxes instead of using them to bring more equity to social programs. Wogaman believes it is the government's job to look after the poor, and pretty much matches his actions with his philosophy. From his church budget of $900,000, only $35,000 was allocated for social pro-grams. The following year he called for "revenue sharing on a world scale." He also criticized Reagan for having relied on the free market, but then he doesn't think much of the free market system anyway. Thomas says, "In 1990, he warned that drug abuse, murder, unethical business practices, family breakups and homelessness were created by 'unrestrained laissez-faire capitalism,' and encouraged people to listen to the socialist's critique of the free markets 'brutalities and idolatries;'" and in 1992 he said that U.S. free markets "must not prevent us from using aspects of socialism." Apparently, the media didn't mind if the

President's minister preached politics from the pulpit, but they cannot tolerate Pat Robertson expressing his political views outside the pulpit.

It should be remembered that Pat Robertson is not a pastor of a church; he is a Christian with degrees in religious theology and law, and chooses to speak his political mind on social issues and religion. Though it appears as this is acceptable discourse for Democrats, they and the media do not find it acceptable for Robertson since he is in the "wrong" party. On this subject Robertson had this to say:

"When I was a Democrat, I was considered one of the good old boys. People in the party would say isn't it nice this nice Christian man has come in. I was welcomed to kiss babies and shake hands. Suddenly, when I changed parties, the head of the Democratic party in 'Virginia called me the new extremist.'"

Judge Robert Bork summed up the liberal's bias against Christians in his book *Slouching Toward Gomorrah* this way: "Liberals of the modern variety are hostile to religious conservatism in any denomination. They realize, quite correctly, that it is a threat to their agenda. For that reason, they regularly refer to the "religious right," using the term as pejorative to suggest that anything conservative is extreme."

WHAT'S THE RELIGIOUS RIGHT UP TO?

The fact is Christians owe Pat Robertson a great deal of thanks for his years of arduous work in the battle for their rights, which has involved countless hours of relentless pleas to his millions of viewers to pray for the "soul of America" and its youth. There have been many twenty-four-hour and week-long-prayer telethons over the years, but it has paid off very well culminating in many victories for Christians, especially in the last decade, as we shall see in the section "The Future and Christianity."

I have been a regular viewer of Pat Robertson's show, *The 700 Club*, for several years, and I do not recognize the negative descriptions the media in general attributes to him. Too bad more people do not serve

God and humanity in the mighty way he does, myself included. The fact is Pat Robertson is the biggest humanitarian story going, and the media says nary a word about him in this regard.

-The Pat Robertson I see is a man who each month sends several tractor-trailers loaded with food into various cities, via "Operation Blessing," an outreach program of *The 700 Club*. This caravan of trucks delivers tons of food to the poor, traveling from New York to Los Angles.

-At the beginning of each school year I see shopping trips for needy children in which they are decked out with new clothes, shoes, and school supplies.

-I see healing seminars for Vietnam veterans and seminars that put marriages back together.

-I see hygiene and medical supplies, blankets, clothes, and food distributed to disaster victims of floods, tornadoes, and earthquakes—and Wichita's neighbor, the people of Andover, were not forgotten when the tornado hit there in 1993. By the way, Robertson and a team of doctors were the first in Zaire to give aid to the Rwanda refugees, but all other groups were shown on TV except them. Although they continued sending more doctors and other medical people and supplies to assist in the rescue work of the suffering people there, mainstream media chose to ignore their life-saving work. At present, the "Operation Blessing" team are giving food supplies to the people of Afghanistan, and school supplies to the children.

-I see the gospel being spread to all parts of the world. Bibles are distributed by the millions to people in Russia, Romania, the Philippines, Africa, etc., and Bible stories via television for kids in formerly communist countries. And in 1996, the impossible became possible—Robertson's Christian Broadcasting System was shown regularly in the heart of Israel, yes, Jerusalem, as well as Libya, Iran, Iraq, Turkey, and India.Unfortunately, times have changed drastically in that part of the world since the 9/11/01 terrorist attacks on America. At the present time, it is doubtful that much headway is being accomplished there as far as the Gospel is concerned.

-I see decent programming for families on the Family Channel, something pushed by Pat Robertson and various conservative organizations.

-On a political level, I see the work of the American Center for Law and Justice, established by Robertson, getting graduation prayer and Bible clubs back in schools, as well as making available various facilities for Christian meetings, just as they are made available to every other organization that wants to use them.

-I see the Christian Coalition (which Robertson founded and now retired from) sent out voter guides which informed citizens how our representatives in Congress voted on the issues, so they could make up their minds for whom they wanted to vote—incidentally, it is the same information non-Christians and atheists look for, and for the same reason.

What I do not see is Robertson stooping to sleaze, or being a money-grubber, as one writer claimed in my local paper. True, he does a telethon twice a year to finance these and many other good causes not listed here. When the scope of his outreach work is taken into account, the fact is his humanitarian aid ranks right up there with the Salvation Army in terms of cutting middle-man costs. But all this information is available to the public; nothing is hidden. You just won't find any of it on the nightly news.

However, the liberal media's hatred of Pat Robertson is understandable. After all, in recent years he has had tremendous success in helping to turn the political tide in a more conservative direction, and the media sees their power hold on the public mind being diminished. All the low insulting remarks directed at Robertson after the 1994 congressional election, I suspect, had a lot to do with the media's favored party losing its position in the "catbird seat." Peter Jennings of ABC typified much of the childish behavior liberals often exhibit when they lose the "catbird seat: "It's clear that anger controls the child and the other way around. The voters had a temper tantrum…the nation can't be run by an angry two-year old." Wasn't that a stereotypical description—meanspirited and intolerant, directed toward the "wrong" people—and from an elitist who embraces political correctness that forbids stereotyping anyone? I do not always agree with Pat Robertson on everything he says, but I do know he is a great humanitarian and deserves better than he gets from the press. My guess is when he goes through those Pearly Gates, our Savior will welcome him with open arms, as well as bless him with the wonderful words, "Well done, good and faithful servant."

THE ACLU SHOWS ITS WARTS

Based on the obvious destruction the humanist movement has caused, we can say with confidence that its theories are not the answer to freedom and happiness. But, despite the negative effects these "freedoms" tend to promote, we continue to see many of its ideals being carried out in dramatic ways by several liberal, leftist groups, especially the American Civil Liberties Union (ACLU), which has a habit of protecting and rewarding irresponsible and immoral behavior. For instance, this organization is quick to support the actions of almost anyone and anything in the name of "freedom of speech"—Nazi organizations, child pornographers, flag burners, criminals, and any other perversive behaviors. It seems the ACLU fights hard for their clients as long as their problems do not involve Christians, or if they are victims of a criminal act—here they draw the line.

But once we know the history of the ACLU, we can understand why its people fight against Christianity, but energetically fight for all that is unwholesome. The following are some of its official policy positions, published by Coral Ridge Ministries: The ACLU supports legalization of child pornography, but opposes voluntary school prayer; supports legalization of drugs, but opposes sobriety checkpoints; supports tax exemption for satanists, but opposes tax exemption for churches; supports legalization of prostitution, but opposes religious displays in public; supports abortion on demand, but opposes medical safety regulation and reporting; supports mandatory sex education, but opposes parental consent laws; supports public demonstrations for Nazis and communists, but opposes public demonstrations for direct action pro-lifers; supports legalization of polygamy, but opposes teaching "monogamous, heterosexual intercourse within marriage" in the public schools.

This extreme leftist organization claims to be "wholly non-partisan," neither Republican nor Democrat." Its founder, Roger Baldwin (deceased 1981), gave us an idea of his "non-partisan" views when he said: "I am for Socialism, disarmament, and ultimately for abolishing the state itself as an instrument of violence and compulsion. I seek social ownership of property...Communism is the goal." It is important to note that this so-called non-partisan organization led the fight against a highly qualified judge for the U. S. Supreme Court, Robert Bork. The ACLU's politics is based totally on the religion of secular humanism.

Baldwin also founded the *Bureau for Conscientious Objectors* in 1917, but whenever the organization ran into trouble, he changed its name. It soon became *Civil Liberties Bureau*, and soon after that name change, it became the *National Civil Liberties Bureau.* An FBI raid in 1918, produced material that incriminated its leader, Roger Baldwin, and sent him to prison for one year for the crime of sedition. When he was released, he renamed the organization to the name it carries today. Although the ACLU claims to be for freedom of speech, for free press, for free assembly, it protects only the left. Let us call a "spade a spade"—the ACLU is secular humanistic to the core.

Do liberal organizations like the ACLU have an agenda to deny Christians their civil rights? On his television show, *The 700 Club*, Pat Robertson told his audience, "The ACLU is working hard to insure a secular society. This doesn't make sense! It was an atheist society that brought the Soviet Union to ruin—is that what we want for America?"

There is a lot of undeniable evidence that supports what Robertson says. For instance, the ACLU and other leftist groups began several years ago by getting prayer eliminated from the schools; next, they zeroed in on doing away with all Christian symbols and displays in parks and public buildings; and then they went to work, trying to stop prayer in locker rooms of pro baseball and football leagues, in sports arenas, and in graduation exercises.

The ACLU wasted no time to move into the public schools. Within a few years we began seeing an even stronger impact the disciples of humanistic philosophy would have on children. In a Minnesota school district teachers were not allowed to say the word "God" or "Christmas" or to sing Christmas carols. Apparently, some of these liberals thought poinsettias were Christian symbols as they were forbidden in the classrooms too.

THE NEA CHANGES ITS SPOTS

The National Education Association (NEA) is another organization with a left-wing agenda. But the shame is it once embraced teachings based on traditional family values, good citizenship, and patriotism. That was back in the 40's when recommended reading for students included documents like the Magna Charta, the Mayflower Compact, the Declaration of Independence, the Gettysburg Address, and others. At that time religious references made in these documents posed no problems for the NEA. In his book, *The Death of Ethics in America*, Cal Thomas quotes a passage from the NEA Handbook of 1941 which states the organization's belief in religious principles: "The American concept of democracy in government had its roots in religious belief. This ideal of the brotherhood of man roots down into the fundamentals of religion. The teachings of the Hebrew Prophets and of Jesus Christ inculcate the idea of brotherhood. The growth of the idea gave us the concept of democracy in government. It ennobled home life. It emphasized the sacredness of human personality."

Thomas also gives "The Code of the Good American" according to the NEA handbook—students were to learn control of their thoughts, their tongues, and their actions. They were encouraged to listen to older and wiser people, and to show loyalty to family and community, and to God.

But today we see a total reversal in the NEA's goals. They authorize "situational ethics," "outcomes based educations," and explicit sex education—all are humanistically based indoctrinations that go against the moral absolutes of the Bible.

HISTORY AND RELIGION

The one thing that has brought victory to these leftist groups in so many cases is the issue of separation of church and state. Dr. Francis A. Schaeffer believed these "thinkers" would lead us down the path to atheism and, subsequently, to ruin if their power went unchecked. In the same interview mentioned earlier and on the same subject, he had this to say:

"The Constitution to the founding fathers' intent meant two things and nothing else. One, they would not have a national church. They didn't want a Church of England, a Church of Sweden, etc. Two, the state would not interfere with religion—that's all it meant! But today it has been tuned over and made the absolute opposite, so that what is now is the state is interfering with religion—the very opposite thing. And now religion is ruled out of any real impact on our thinking. Notice, I am not saying 'Christianity'; I am saying 'religion'. The craziest thing of it is that Congress opens every day with a prayer, but you can't pray in school. How schizophrenic can you get?"

Nevertheless, despite what many informed and concerned people believe is a deliberate misinterpretation of the First Amendment, along with a process well underway to rewrite history, they feel they can eventually win the battle. On their side is the original historical record which clearly shows the importance of Christian principles to the

Founding Fathers and to their ancestors in general. Our governing documents were drawn up by men who relied on God and prayer in making major decisions, and they made no bones about it. In fact, until recent years, history books have been replete with examples that prove this to be the case.

A good example stated by Benjamin Franklin, who was commenting on government policy, spells out clearly and to the point the prevailing spiritual climate of early American history: "Except the Lord build the house, they that labor in vain that built it. I firmly believe this. I also believe that without His concurring aid, we shall succeed in the political building no better than the builders of Babel."

Also a foreigner who studied the American people and their leaders, and whose books have been required reading for many college courses for several decades, understood how important religion was to the American people and to their leaders. Alexis de Tocqueville, French political writer and statesman, became one of the best known writers on the American character. Before the Civil War he wrote:

"America is the place where the Christian religion has kept the greatest power over men's souls: and nothing better demonstrates how useful and natural it is to man, since the country where it now has the widest sway is both the most enlightened and the freest." And further on, he wrote: "...I am certain they [Americans] hold it [religion] to be indispensable for the maintenance of their republican institutions."

However, the elitist press has felt it their duty to program our minds in the belief that our religious heritage is dispensable, and unfortunately a lot of people bought the lie. Ironically, in 1821, Daniel Webster described the situation we find ourselves in now.

"If truth be not diffused, error will be; if God and His Word are not known and does not reach every hamlet, the pages of a corrupt and licentious literature will; if the power of the Gospel is not felt throughout the length and breadth of the land, anarchy and misrule, degradation and misery, corruption and darkness, will reign without mitigation or end.

THE FUTURE AND CHRISTIANITY

If we compare the era before the 60's with the present time, it seems we can only draw one conclusion: In striking God from our way of life, we unwittingly brought much of the strife and turmoil we see in our society today on ourselves.

But are most Americans willing to give up their religious freedom without a fight: Christian leaders such as James Dobson, Pat Robertson, Jack Hayford, Bill Bright and countless others say, "no". Though they acknowledge the fight ahead will be a hard one, they are optimistic about the future of Christianity. They say there is a revival going on in the United States that is unparalleled in the history of our country. And they are encouraged further by the successes of the American Center of Law and Justice (ACLJ) in restoring some Christian rights. It is important to note that the revival they talked about occurred months before the 9/11 terrorist attacks. Since then, religious fervor and a turning back to God has multiplied throughout the country.

The ACLJ is an organization founded by a fighter of many years for Christian freedoms, Pat Robertson. Though he has received nothing but negative-press distortions of what he says, he has never given up the battle for the soul of America. Many of the victories we have seen in the last several years for Christian causes are a direct result of his efforts, along with the groundwork laid by the ACLJ's, which made these wins possible.

Apparently the seed was sown in fertile soil. Chief Counsel for the ACLJ, Jay Sekulow, is an aggressive, dynamic lawyer, accomplishing what most of us saw as an impossible task—standing up to the ACLU. In the early '90's, he won every case involving Christian rights, and has continued from that time forward in achieving many victories for Christians. But the fight is never-ending, as the ACLU keeps pushing even when a ruling goes against them.

In the 1991 school year, the ACLJ began a concentrated effort to put an end to the double standards against Christians by sending a letter to every school superintendent in the United States, informing them of the many permissible activities relative to religious celebrations. These freedoms included the right to sing Christmas carols, todistribute Christmas cards, and to read biblical passages if done in the context of comparative religion or literature—the premier fighter in these activities, Jay Sekulow, affectionately called "The Hammer" by his colleagues.

How successful has Jay and his team been? One of their victories was in regard to a little girl in Las Vegas, Nevada who was denied her choice of songs after having been asked to select any song to sing at the school's winter concert. The reason for the denial was simply because she chose a Christmas carol. ACLJ attorneys worked on her behalf and she was allowed to sing "The First Noel" in the school program. Other victories concerned bans on displays of nativity scenes, references to Jesus Christ, wearing Christian jewelry, or saying a prayer at graduation, were also reversed by the ACLJ. With all the progress the ACLJ has made in standing up for Christian rights, there seems to be no end to the cases pouring in. The ACLU never stops, and of course, Mr. Sekulow and his team do not always win every case.

Another important ACLJ success story took place in Nazareth, Pennsylvania when a high school student asked that his club, The Teens for Christ, have their picture in the school yearbook. All of the school's clubs had their pictures taken for this yearbook, but the principal told Joseph that "due to the religious nature of the Teens for Christ Club, they could not be included in the yearbook." Immediately, the ACLJ sent a demand letter to the school lawyers in that district, and the decision was overturned. "Personnel at the high school indicated that they would be able to have the photographer return and that inclusion would not be a major problem."

Then there was the case of the little second-grade girl who had typed the word "Jesus" on her computer while waiting for the teacher to check her work. For that dastardly deed she was whisked off to the principal's office where she had to fill out a disciplinary report, writing out the crime and then writing that it was unacceptable to write Jesus on the computer—signed and dated. However, the ACLJ saw to it that she was apologized to by both teacher and principal, as well as having her record as a person "uncooperative to teacher and students" eliminated.

The ACLU's allegiance to "justice," (justice, supposedly being their trademark) in many instances has been to fight for other religions in the schools, including satanism—their books, symbols, and in some cases, their meetings—but to fight against these same things for Christian students. If the ACLU truly sought justice for all, then the ACLJ would not be receiving hundreds of calls every month that have to do with harmless things like a child saying a prayer of thanks over his or her lunch, and then receiving detention for doing so; or a child sharing a storybook of her choice with the class, as assigned by the teacher, but then being denied to do so simply because it had the word "God" in it.

Has the ACLU, with all its financial backing and political clout, met its match by a non-profit organization, dedicated to traditional values? Well, because of his victories in the United States Supreme Court, some lower courts, and numerous ones settled out of court, Jay Sekulow has gotten the attention and finally some long overdue good coverage of his record by the *New York Times, The Washington Post, USA Today, The Washington Times,* and *The Wall Street Journal.*

One cause for the attention was the case, *Jones v. Clear Creek Independent School District,* in which Mr. Sekulow won a major battle (fought in the U.S. Supreme Court) for student-led and initiated prayer at graduation ceremonies, accomplished despite the challenges of the ACLU, People for the American Way, and Americans United for Separation of Church and State. Another case, *Planned Parenthood v. Duval Country Board of Education,* having to do with the adoption of a curriculum called "Teen-Aid," was challenged by Planned Parenthood because it taught abstinence as the best method of birth control. Again the Supreme Court ruled in favor of the ACLJ, which said: "The curriculum was not in violation of the constitution prohibition on the state established religions."

The ACLJ also sent 19,000 letters to mayors of towns and cities all over the country, informing them of citizen's rights to erect religious holiday displays such as nativity scenes on public property, and that any organization renting its facilities to community groups must not deny the same privilege to church groups.

A pertinent case and a major victory in terms of precedent setting is *Lamb's Chapel v. Center Moriches Union Free School District.* The school district made its facilities available to a variety of groups but disallowed any religious programs in their facilities. Justice White wrote the decision: "The government violates the First Amendment when it denies access to a speaker solely to suppress the point of view he espouses to an otherwise includable subject." Another case, *Jews for Jesus v. Jewish Community Relations Council* (JCRJ), was about denial to rent hotel space to Jews for Jesus, and the cancellation of their contract. The U.S. Supreme Court of Appeals ruled unanimously that "This kind of boycott against religious groups is unlawful and unprecedented." Furthermore, the JCRC was ordered not to engage in any future acts of discrimination against Jews for Jesus, and also to pay them $15,000 damages.

But gains Jay Sekulow and his team have made do not end here. There have been several offenses on the abortion issue as well, especially involving "speech zones" surrounding abortion clinics. One of the most significant cases was *Black v. The City of Atlanta.* This case involved 24 people who were arrested for praying in front of an abortion clinic, even though no blockades were set up. The court ruled in favor of the ACLJ, resulting in required special training for police officers so that they will in the future respect pro-lifer's First Amendment rights. This order also includes new courses in their training manuals which teach that pro-lifer's have the right to pray, to protest, and to hand out literature on public sidewalks and streets. Furthermore, the

City of Atlanta was required to pay damages of $37,000 for its unlawful actions.

Given the ACLU's past record of denying Christians the right to free speech, one of the most unlikely events occurred on September 15,1993. "See You at the Pole" was a tremendous victory for Christians. This event had begun three or four years earlier when a few kids met at the flagpole to pray before classes at a high school in Texas, and has since spread across the country to an estimated two million kids participating at their schools. Just before the time the event was to take place, Keith Fournier, Director of the ACLJ made this statement in his article, "A Little Child Shall Lead Them: (Isa. 11;6). "We at the American Center for Law and Justice are honored to support 'See you at the Pole' and to offer our legal services, should they be needed, to any student subjected tothe brunt of censorship regarding the exercise of his or her constitutional rights".

One of the worst cases I've read about yet is one involving Larry Phillips, a case worker for the Division of Family Services (DFS) in the Missouri Department of Social Services. Mr. Phillips' job was to screen foster parents, interview children, and follow up with both parents and children. In January of 1998, the ACLJ filed a federal lawsuit against the DFS, due to Mr. Phillips' dismissal from the organization.

Mr. Phillips had been harassed and intimidated by his supervisor and others in the department shortly after he had questioned some material sponsored by the organization "Act Up," which was being given out to foster children (what a terrible thing to do to any child, but for children in the foster program who already have problems they cannot handle, it is downright vicious). The material showed graphic sexual practices and encouraged the children to experiment accordingly. Phillip's discharge came later after he refused to place foster children in homosexual homes. Jay Sekulow cited three reasons the case was critical: First, to defend the rights of believers to express the Christian beliefs in the workplace free of harassment and ridicule. Second, to expose anti-family activists who are using government agencies to advance their own purposes. Third, to bring to the public's attention the tragic plight of children who are too often used as pawns by activists whose main goal seems to be redefining the family in an attempt to advance their own misguided agendas.

This case reminds me of Hillary Clinton's crusade against the American family. She supports the gay agenda to infiltrate public schools with their indoctrination of their life style, using the film, *That's a Family*, as one of their sources. Chairman and founder of Concerned Women for America, Beverly La Haye, writes: "This movie is a subtle attempt to break down your children's and grandchildren's moral defenses, and teach them that homosexual "families" are just the same, and just as moral and right, as real families. It's a dangerous, destructive message. And the makers of *That's a Family!* have publicly sworn to get their film into every classroom in America!"

The above cases are a mere handful of the actual caseload that the ACLJ deals with every day throughout the year. It is important to note that the ACLU has plenty of hustlers that are more than happy to help push the same agenda as mentioned above. It is obvious in many of these cases, victims are often created by overly zealous, politically correct liberals, who have the same agenda as the ACLU, The American Way, the NEA, Planned Parenthood, and others. Also, the liberal media works subtly in the background to advance the left's liberal agenda.

PART V
National Destiny

13

One Nation Under God

o o o o o o o o o o o o o o o o o o o o o o o o o o o o o o o

"Righteousness exalts a nation, but sin is a disgrace to any people"—Proverbs 14:34

I cringe when I hear a Christian say the Bible does not talk about the United States—"We're not in it," they say. For that matter, not many nations are mentioned by name in the Bible. But the term "all nations" is mentioned, and to my way of thinking "all" includes the United States. Are we to believe God did not know the North American continent was in existence, or that it would become the United States of America? To say otherwise is to say that God did not create everything and was not able to see the future. The Bible was written to include all people, all nations, past, present, and future.

CARRIERS OF THE LIGHT

Peter Marshall, Jr. and David Manuel, in their book, *The Light and the Glory*, give a clear picture of how the earliest arrivals to our shores placed their trust and faith in God to guide them in the establishment of a new life under a government that was divinely inspired. Their story begins with an account of Christopher Columbus' discovery of America. According to entries in his journals, diaries, and other sources, the authors came to the same belief held by Columbus, which was that he had been chosen of God "to carry the Light of Christ in the darkness of undiscovered heathen lands and bring the faith of Christianity." And so the conclusion the authors drew was that the discovery of America was not an accident, but an event guided by "the invisible hand of Providence." While Marshall and Manuel admired Columbus' belief in his mission, they did not paint him as a saint: "To know Columbus was to know one's own desire for the rewards of this world: fame and power and all manner of ego gratification." Dominican and Franciscan friars, inspired by the words of the prophet Isaiah (49:6): "...I will give you as a light to the nations, that my salvation may reach to the end of the earth," dedicated themselves to spreading the Gospel in the new world. Likewise, the Pilgrims firmly believed that America was the Promised Land, the New Israel of the Bible, and they were the Chosen People of God to spread the Gospel.

The heartwarming story of the Indian Squanto in many ways parallels the biblical account of Joseph. Through his interpreter, he taught the white man how to overcome the hardships of wilderness living, helped establish good relations between them and the Indian tribes, and ultimately saved the Pilgrims from starvation.

Being a people in search of freedom and God's will in their lives, the carriers of Light were on a path that would eventually lead to the *American Revolutionary War*. At the signing of The Declaration of Independence, Samuel Adams echoed the Light carriers vision: "We have this day restored the Sovereign to Whom alone men ought to be obedient. He reigns in heaven and...from the rising to the setting sun, may His Kingdom come." And later, the first President of the United States, George Washington, conveyed a similar message to the citizens of America in his inaugural address:

"It would be peculiarly improper to omit, in the first official act, my fervent supplication to that Almighty Being, who rules over the universe, who presides in the councils of nations, and whose providential aids can supply every human defect, that His benediction may consecrate to the liberties and happiness of the people of the United

States….No people can be bound to acknowledge and adore the invisible hand which conducts the affairs of men more than the people of the United States."

Some 50 years after the Constitution of the United States was drawn up, William Gladstone, Prime Minister of England, called it "the most wonderful work every struck off at a given time by the brain and purpose of man." And Marshall and Manuel, speaking of its systems of balances and checks, wrote: "…the amazing thing is how smoothly such an elaborately interwoven and interdependent system works. And (aside from God's grace and inspiration) it works for one reason: It takes into account what the Puritans termed 'the utter depravity of man.'"

Years later in 1835, Alex de Tocqueville, in his study of what made the American system work, wrote: "Not until I went into the churches of America and heard her pulpits flame with righteousness did I understand the secret of her genius and power. America is great because America is good, and if America ever ceases to be good, America will cease to be great."

BLESSED OF GOD

Had the Light carriers been right? Was America, indeed, the City blessed by God? Even the skeptic has to admit, it seems history has been on America's side.

During the Industrial Revolution of the 19th Century, America rose quickly and dramatically to a position of power and influence in the world. In a historical sense, the young nation was catapulted into a position of international preeminence almost over night. Many people believe the seeds for such rapid growth had been sown much earlier—the major reasons being a strong belief in God and the freedom to dream, build, and own property. They felt we were blessed by a loving God who afforded us with many advantages: an abundant supply of natural resources—vast tracts of fertile land, virgin forests, furbearing animals, gold, silver, coal, natural gas, fossil fuel, iron, minerals, etc. All of these things combined with a "can do" spirit, soon placed the young nation in an enviable position around the world. Whether it was coincidence or destiny, America surpassed, or at least held its own with every developed country, especially in technology and industrial areas.

My husband Ed says that, "from the end of the 19th Century, our country has been blessed with the immigration of family-oriented, hard-working people from all countries of the world. This group is what we call the "melting pot" of America. From this integration of our common language and traditions comes our American culture."

The odd thing is that a lot of Americans seem to recognize other cultures, but not our own. For instance, my niece, Laura Lee Garrigue, e-mailed an editorial published in a California paper to me, which speaks to the point of our American culture better than I could ever do. I would be more than glad to give credit to the author, but somehow the name was lost. It reads:

IMMIGRANTS, NOT AMERICANS, MUST ADAPT! I am tired of this nation worrying about whether we are offending some individual or their culture. Since the terrorist attacks on Sept. 11, we have experienced a surge in patriotism by the majority of Americans. However, the dust from the attacks had barely settled when the "politically correct" crowd began complaining about the possibility that our patriotism was offending others.

I am not against immigration, nor do I hold a grudge against anyone who is seeking a better life by coming to America. Our population is almost entirely comprised of descendants of immigrants. However, there are a few things that those who have recently come to our country, and apparently some born here need to understand.

This idea of America being a multicultural community has served only to dilute our sovereignty and our national identity. As Americans, we have our own culture, our own society, our own language and our own lifestyle. This culture has been developed over centuries of struggles, trials, and victories by millions of men and women who have sought freedom.

We speak ENGLISH, not Spanish, Arabic, Chinese, Japanese, Russian, or any other language. Therefore, if you wish to become part of our society, learn the language!

"In God We Trust!" is our national motto. This is not some Christian, right wing, political slogan. We adopted this motto because Christian men and women, on Christian principles, founded this nation, and this is clearly documented. It is certainly appropriate to display it on the walls of our schools. If God offends you, then I suggest you consider another part of the world as your new home, because God is part of our culture.

If Stars and Stripes offend you, or you don't like Uncle Sam, then you should seriously consider a move to another part of this planet. We are happy with our culture and have no desire to change, and we really don't care how you did things where you came from. This is OUR COUNTRY, our land, and our lifestyle.

Our First Amendment gives every citizen the right to express his opinion, and we will allow you every opportunity to do so. But once you are done complaining, whining, and griping about our flag, our pledge, our national motto, or our way of life, I highly encourage you to take advantage of one other great American freedom, THE RIGHT TO LEAVE.

Despite all the blessings bestowed on America over the years, we began drifting away from our identity with God, until today we are number one in many areas that tarnish our national character. Government documentation shows the decline in education, morals, the breakdown of the family unit, and the increase of crime has multiplied dramatically from the 1960's on.

Is it coincidence that there has been a systematic endeavor to get God out of the picture from the 60's to the present time? This is something Dr. Schaeffer warned us about in a 1982 interview with Pat Robertson. He said that the further a nation gets away from biblical absolutes, the more chaos there is. From this point on, conditions worsen until a police state is established, thus placing the people under a tyrannical government. This is what happened to the Roman Empire and all fallen nations, just as we have seen happen in recent years to several communist countries.

Hmmm…police state…tyrannical government. Sound a little fanatical? Well, I just read an e-mail my niece, Laura Lee, sent me. It is called "The Law," and is a statement which was read over the PA system at a football game by school Principal Jody McLoud at Roane County High School, Kingston, Tennessee, on September 1, 2001.

"It has always been the custom at Roane County High School football games to say a prayer and play the National Anthem to honor God and Country. Due to a recent ruling by the Supreme Court, I am told that saying a prayer is a violation of Federal Case Law.

As I understand the law at this time, I can use this public facility to approve of sexual perversion and call it an alternate lifestyle, and if someone is offended, that's O.K.

I can use it to condone sexual promiscuity by dispensing condoms and calling it safe sex. If someone is offended, that O.K.

I can even use this public facility to present the merits of killing an unborn baby as a viable means of birth control. If someone is offended, no problem.

I can designate a school day as earth day and involve students in activities to religiously worship and praise the goddess, mother earth, and call it ecology.

I can use literature, videos and presentations in the classroom that depict people with strong, traditional Christian convictions as simple minded and ignorant and call it enlightenment.

However, if anyone uses this facility to honor God and asks Him to bless this event with safety and good sportsmanship. Federal Case Law is violated. This appears to be inconsistent at best, and at worst, diabolical. Apparently, we are to be tolerant of everything and anyone except God and His Commandments.

Nevertheless, as a school principal, I frequently ask staff and students to abide by rules which they do not necessarily agree. For me to do otherwise would be inconsistent at best, and at worst, hypocritical. I suffer from that affliction enough unintentionally. I certainly do not need to add an intentional transgression.

For this reason, I shall "Render unto Caesar that which is Caesar's," and refrain from praying at this time. However, if you feel inspired to honor, praise and thank God, and ask Him in the name of Jesus to bless this event, please feel free to do so. As far as I know, that's not against the law—yet."

AND…one by one, the people in the stands bowed their heads, held hands with one another, and began to pray. They prayed in the stands. They prayed in the team huddles. They prayed at the concession stand. And they prayed in the announcer's box. The only place they didn't pray was in the Supreme Court of the United States of America—the seat of "justice" in the one nation under God."

AMERICA YESTERDAY/TODAY

Former Speaker of the House of Representatives, Newt Gingrich, contrasted the phenomenal America of "yesterday" with the America of "today" in both his TV class and in his book *To Renew America.* He attributed much of America's "glory" days to the romantic view Americans have always held of their country. For example, the people of "yesterday" believed more in the virtues of responsibility, perseverence, self-reliance, and patriotism, while many of today's people seem to view themselves as victims and are constantly on the outlook to see if their rights are being violated.

Gingrich attributes much of this attitude to what he describes as "the practical, democratic culture" that has been "overlaid with an elite culture." Speaking of this new culture, as well as the re-write of history, he writes: "Predominant in American history is nothing but a story of racism, oppression, genocide, disenfranchisement, and constant violation of the norms to which we all thought we subscribed." At one time, Americans subscribed more to the view that "power comes from God and is loaned to the state," while "today" the opposite view seems to hold sway, that is "power comes from the state and occasionally is loaned to the individual." The commitment to God and country, along with the ingenuity of the American people, have largely disappeared from the pages of revised history books. The result Gingrich believes has created two entirely different models that have molded American thought.

One is the welfare-state model of today, which he says is responsible for "turning citizens into clients" It is a model that demeans and saps the energy of its "clients;" it creates static conditions, stifles competition in world markets, and loses opportunities because its supporters believe change is dangerous. Its participants tend to blame society for their plight, often operating on the premise, "I can't do anything unless you subsidize me," and too many cannot see any advantage in starting at the bottom and working up. The bottom line is that the welfare state creates huge bureaucracies and waste and tremendous tax loads, done under the guise of compassion, but all too often for the sake of appearances and keeping certain national cliques in office. This model tends to create problems, not solutions.

The second model is the opportunity model of yesterday in which people were more apt to take the first low paying job because it might lead to something, and they were more apt to look to the future where world markets were concerned. Gingrich says they had a more entrepreneurial spirit, or at least, "I will do what I can to help myself." Much of their energy came from combining their dreams with action. This is the model that recognizes the importance of absolutes. Even with all its flaws, it tended to build stability, and leaned heavily toward family unity. In this model, the idea is to think solutions, not problems.

According to Gingrich, solutions to problems begins first by recognizing that there are "absolutes set forth by our Creator," and next by "reasserting the value of American civilization," which means teaching children the satisfaction that comes from responsibility, perseverance, commitment, and self-reliance. Also, he feels it is important to integrate working people into the totality of the manufacture of their products—"People naturally take pride in their work when they feel a part of it." It not only lets them know their input has some value, but also greatly improves production output as well as the product itself."

Although Gingrich was able almost single-handedly to win majority for Republicans in the House of Representatives with common sense ideas of his "Contract for America"—ideas to get the country back on tract, the Democrats and the press were not able to bash him enough. Their strategy to constantly tell the American people that he is the most disliked and unpopular politician in America. This, of course, is exactly the same technique they use on any person or issue they are against.

Columnist Stephen Chapman said of Gingrich: "He knows what he believes, much of what he believes is sound, and he has shown daring, resolve and skill in pursuing his goals—most improbably, the stunning 1994 Republican takeover of the House, ending a 40-year drought."

Chapman goes on to say that Americans "owe the balanced federal budget largely to Gingrich. Shortly after the GOP takeover, he surprised his own Budget Committee chairman, John Kasich, by setting a goal of eliminating the deficit by 2002. At a meeting of the House Republican leaders, Kasich objected: 'Where is it in stone that we have to balance the budget in seven years?' Gingrich replied, "Let's put it to a vote. 'Who wants to put it in stone?' Kasich was the only dissenting vote—and even Bill Clinton, who once proposed $200 billion deficits from here to eternity, was forced to go along."

POLITICAL CHRISTIANS

This book begins with the question "What role, if any, does Christianity play in solving our social problems." Regardless how convincing the evidence that our governance is lacking spiritually, some people will always say that Christians should stay out of politics. That is the stand columnist Peter Wehner (Assoc. Press) takes in his column "Political Betrayal of Christianity (April 28, 1996).

One big flaw in his argument is that he paints all political Christians with the same brush, saying that they feel "inoculated against the seductions of the world"—quite the contrary. If any people are truly aware of their humanity, their vulnerability, it is Christians. They are very much aware that they have the same temptations as non-Christians. If they are successful in not succumbing to them, it is because they are grounded in the Word. Whether or not political Christians 'vulgarize their testimony," as Wehner claims, is like everything else; it depends solely on the individual.

How does Wehner justify his bad opinion of political Christians? He says the disciples were not involved in a political movement, and that Jesus came as a humble servant, "the antithesis of worldly power." We probably all agree on Jesus' mission. Nevertheless, He was not cowered by the politicians of His day. Throwing the money-changers out of the Temple is a good example.

In my opinion, a major flaw in Wehner's hypothesis exists largely because he has omitted an integral part of Christianity, the Old Testament. He needs to think about the politics of Sodom and Gomora, of the Tower of Babel, and of the hundreds of historical situations that brought doom and destruction to the people of that time. He needs to think further of the divinely anointed judges, prophets, and kings and their blessings or curses according to how they carried out God's government. He needs to include the Ten Commandments and all the Laws spelled out in Leviticus, Numbers, and Deuteronomy on care for the poor, widows, etc., and also of the specific actions to be taken against murder, homicide, robbery, and other wrongs perpetrated against society.

My point is that there was a moral government, not man-made, but divine, laid down by the Almighty. Furthermore, it is impossible to separate Jesus from the Old Testament, as there are allusions that point to Him throughout (and some believe actual appearances). This is possible because of the Holy Trinity, and because Jesus Himself said He is the "Beginning and the Ending," The Word," and "The Almighty."

Even though Christians are under the covenant of Grace instead of the Law, somehow I feel God does expect us to act responsibly and keep tabs on our government. Apparently, Wehner began to change his mind on this point before he finished his piece. He wrote that the "political arena undermines traditional Christian virtues—love, humility, forgiveness, forbearance, kindness, mercy and gentleness," and then went on to say, "Christians ought to be voices of decency, civility and moral sanity…speak out against evil…regard political power with suspicion and acknowledge its limits"—Yes! exactly what a lot of politically-minded Christians are doing!

Mr. Wehner would do well to review what some great political minds of the past have said. A few examples follow:

> *"We have staked the whole future of American civilization, not upon the power of government, far from it. We have staked the future of all of our political institutions…upon the capacity of each and all of us to govern ourselves, to to control ourselves, to sustain ourselves according to the Ten Commandments of God."—James Madison, 1778*

And—

> *"Our laws and our institutions must necessarily be based upon and embody the teachings of the Redeemer of mankind. It is impossible that it should be otherwise; and in this sense and to this*

extent our civilization and our institutions are emphatically Christian."—United States Supreme Court, 1892

It's a sad day when we find ourselves content to let secular humanists and atheists set the standards by which we live and raise our children.

AMERICA IN DECLINE

Jim Black, in his book *When Nations Die*, lists ten signs that have existed when a nation fell into decline, all fitting into three major categories: social, moral, and cultural—and America, he says, fits all ten categories. They are (1) A crisis of lawlessness, (2) a loss of economic discipline, (3) rising bureaucracy, (4) declining level of education, (5) weakening of cultural foundations, (6) lack of respect for traditions, (7) increasing materialism, (8) rising immorality, (9) devaluing human life, and (10) decay of religious belief.

With an increase of 560% in crime in the last 35 years; a 500% increase in government spending during the same period; a 3,000% increase in employees to staff government bureaucracies since the 30's; Americans ranking last academically in a study of 19 nations, or next to last in every category; nearly two or three generations raised without knowledge of the Christian faith in our history books; the cheapening of life, abortion on demand and assisted suicide; and the widespread acceptance of secular humanism and New Age cults, it would be hard to deny the parallels Black says exists between the fallen nations of the past and the United States.

Are we foolish not to heed the lessons of history? Peter Marshall, Jr. agrees with Black, saying that nations fall into decline because of their lack of moral standards and a loss of respect for cultural traditions. He sees the United States on a similar track with some of the once-great nations, whose blasphemy against God ended up as their downfall.

According to Marshall, America shares two weaknesses with these fallen societies: tolerance for abortion and homosexuality.

But Americans are not getting the full picture of what is going on. The media carefully edited the outrageous acts perpetrated by the gay community during the Gay Pride Parade a few years ago of which former President Clinton was so proud. *C-Span* was brave enough to show most of what actually went on during the parade, and Newswatch showed the full extent of what the public was not supposed to see. Also, some of the behavior by militant feminists would come as an eye opener to a lot of people if it were to be shown on the nightly news. However, since their membership has been in decline for the past three years, they have "cooled" it considerably. Many clergymen believe that the only reason God has not taken his protective hand completely off America is that we have the resources to evangelize the world—something many churches are in the process of doing now.

Columnist Armstrong Williams, syndicated through the *Los Angeles Times*, poses the question: "What should Christians do when confronted with our nation's increasingly amoral culture? First of all, understand that Christians will get no help or protection from the federal government. As many of you are aware, the God of Abraham, the father of our Savior, has long been banned from public places—schools, courts, the military and government buildings and agencies. Things have gone so far that proposals have been raised to even ban possession of Bibles and the display of religious images, even jewelry, on government property."

Williams goes on to say that businesses are being forced to give benefits to "domestic partners," and that homosexuals activists "are even pushing for laws that confer society's recognition of marriage in gay relationships." At the same time, "only Christian clubs are banned from using government facilities or classrooms, while other groups, including homosexual ones, are given benediction"

A TOUGH ROW TO HOE

Are liberals just blind, or are they stubborn? In my opinion, it is both. Historian Ronald Radosh, a former liberal for many years, is a person very qualified to explain the liberal mindset. One would think that the 9/11 attacks would cause many liberals to at least to rethink their ideology. But no. Radosh says: "They are trying to assert that the cause of all the evil in the world is still the United States and its expansionistic ways."

So what brought about the transformation of this man? He says, three things: One, his belief in the Cuban dictator, Fidel Castro, when he first came to power in the '70's, which he saw as a "vibrant, fresh humanist revolution." But Radosh got a rude awakening when he saw first hand the repression there, and the "frequent use of lobotomies in mental hospitals—"Socialist Lobotomies," he called them. His liberal colleagues' response to his report on the situation was hostile. Two, was his investigation of the Rosenberg Case, in which he set out to prove their innocence, but instead discovered they were actually guilty of the crime of treason—the left condemned his book on this case for exposing the truth. Three, was his opposition to U.S. policy in Central America. Radosh went there in support of the Sandinistas, and ended up supporting the Contras—again it was the repressive rule of the people that bothered him. He writes: "All of these things had an impact on me. In my book I say that they helped to end my long exile from America."

The bottom line is the left does not want the truth if the facts go against their agenda. This is an attitude that has allowed deceit and lies to become more and more acceptable, especially if it is packaged in "star Quality" status. The liberalism of the secular humanists have pushed their agenda through the movies, television, and into the schools to indoctrinate two generations of young people, and they have successfully been able to get much of their agenda enforced through the courts and other government agencies. Let us hope that not too many Americans have become so desensitized by explicit sex, violence, lies and scandals, that they are unable to choose right over wrong.

But with the entertainment industry largely bent on a liberal agenda—indoctrinating young impressionable minds, promoting trash and making big bucks, and generally being out of touch with the real world, it won't be easy to bring some sort of normalcy back to society.

With so many universities coming from mostly a Marxist or feminist perspective (Yale, a prime example); hiding Ophra-type classes under misleading titles; offering gay and lesbian studies on how to bring your child up gay, along with hard-core, graphic films; separating the religious heritage of our country from the history books; and subjecting students to the intellectual straight jacket of political correctness in order to stifle all conservative thought—it makes an already tough job that much tougher.

With liberals constantly seeking ways to bring about more dependency on government, so that incumbents stay secure in their positions of power, it puts a huge stumbling block on the road to recovery. No one says it better than Tom Adkins (Editor of **commonconservative.com**): "Liberals suck their power from failure, cannibalizing constituents and blaming everyone except their own foolish policies."

With powerful organizations like the American Civil Liberties Union (ACLU) and other liberal groups masquerading as "sheep in wolves clothing," and successfully duping vast numbers of American citizens, the job of restoration is HUGE. This organization is not a friend of the people, and we need to understand that in many cases it has not fought for our freedoms, but has succeeded in taking away many of our civil rights.

For instance, in 1973, the ACLU sat before the U.S. Senate, day after day, pleading their case for the "civil rights" of Americans against the FBI, CIA, and the National Security Council, and their efforts to track down terrorist organizations and bring them to justice. In a mood to be politically correct and to not hurt anyone's feelings, the

ACLU struck a willing cord in the hearts of the majority of Democrats and some Republicans—also, I'm sure the ACLU's considerable donations to the Democrat party helped get their agenda through. A series of bills followed for years afterwards, which successfully tied the hands of our law enforcement agencies to protect Americans in matters of national security. This is a major reason we were not prepared in the way we should have been to possibly divert the tragedy of 9/11, and why the set-back will take some years to correct. It is now known that these attacks were in the making for at least five years.

Also, it is important to note that since Franklin Roosevelt's administration, all presidents have had a daily briefing with the FBI and other security agencies, with the exception of Bill Clinton, who decided it was a waste of time to receive their input on national security. There was extreme lax security that prevailed in the first term of the Clinton presidency, as well as a bad attitude toward the military and the FBI's work for clearance for White House workers, and sometimes occasional interlopers.

And finally, with a media that picks up their poison pens and writes from a subjective angle; that campaigns for liberals at the expense of actual news; that has had an attention-deficit disorder on one of the most, if not the most, serious scandals in our history, they are the tin gods that hiss and rattle, the elitists, the know-it-alls—it piles on makes the path back one of the most difficult of our challenges.

It has been said that "the mills of God grind slowly, but fine," so our hopes and aspirations live on. Even so, despite all the oppositions to the pursuit of happiness, we do see many good signs that the tide is turning, not to the 40's or 50's, but to some of the values and principles that worked before we lost our way.

AND WE NEED TO GIVE THANKS

I think it is time Americans stop buying into the worn-out, wearisome, and witless harangue of the liberals who have given us just about everything that is not good for us. It is time to be thankful, and the good news is that we do have something to be thankful for, like acts such as the U.S. House of Representatives and House Majority Whip Tom Delay, R-Texas, and for any other persons regardless of their political party who had the good sense and wisdom to call our leaders to prayer for America. The act was long overdue, and has certainly been a part of our history in the past.

Unbelievable! We've got people praying in Congress. We've got people praying in the Justice Department! We've got a praying President, one who doesn't pretend to be pious for the cameras, but one who actually lives his faith, and one who is not afraid to speak the name Jesus in public—Awesome!!

Furthermore, we have "The Presidential Prayer Team" that anyone can access through the website (**presidentialprayerteam.org**) and sign up for the its weekly e-mail. Each week there are requests for prayer for the nation, the president, the military, etc., a presidential quotation for the week, and bits of historical information. An example of the latter follows:

"Our nation was founded on Christian principles and mostly by Christian men and women. Consider the witness of the Liberty Bell. In 1751, the Pennsylvania State Assembly called for the forging of a bell to commemorate William Penn's original charter of the state. They included instructions requiring that a scripture verse be included on the bell The verse is Leviticus 25:10, "Proclaim Liberty throughout all the land unto all the inhabitants thereof." Our Founding Fathers considered it important for all generations to know that God is the source of true freedom. The Liberty Bell is yet another example of our nation's godly heritage."

THE CHOICE

No matter what one believes about these assertions, or what one's religious beliefs are, the irony of the situation becomes increasingly clear:

The freedom "rights" programsecular humanists offer turns out to be enslavement. The facts are in and documented.Lord Acton's adage gives us some insight to what we are doing wrong. He said: "Power corrupts, and absolute power corrupts absolutely." We might touch it up a bit and apply it to our own situation: "Absolute" self "power, advocated by the secular humanist, does corrupt absolutely."

Then, should we not consider the missing ingredient that was present before the decline of family life, before the failure of our educational system, before a drug-ridden society, before rampant crime—the unsuppressed freedom of speech when God was in the equation? Christians feel to let such a philosophy of liberal, secular humanism prevail and replace wholesome standards and absolutes, that we surely will continue on a roller-coaster going downhill fast.

For whatever it is worth, it is my firm belief that there is a definite connection between the squalor and degraded life we see in countries where people choose to worship various false gods, sometimes as many as three hundred, and a country where God reigns supreme in the hearts of the people. The true path to national restoration, I think, is to take God at his word as stated in 2 Chron. 7:14:

> *"If my people, which are called by my name, shall humble themselves, and pray, and seek my face, and turn from their wicked ways, then will I hear from heaven, and will forgive their sins, and will heal their land."*

Sources

Magazines:
American Spectator
Forbes Magazine
Insight
Newsweek
Time

Newspapers:
Boston Herald, The
Conservative Chronicle
Chicago Sun Times, The
Detroit News
Human Events
Los Angeles Daily News
Los Angeles Times
New York Times
Seattle Times
Wall Street Journal
Washington Post
Wichita Eagle

Books:
Death of Ethics in America, The(by *Cal Thomas*)
Democracy In America(by *Alex de Tocqueville*)
FINAL DAYS: The Last, Desperate Abuses of Power by the Clinton
White House (by *Barbara Olson)*
Great Whitewater Fiasco, The(by *Martin Gross*)
Hell to Pay(by *Barbara Olson*)
The Holy Bible: King James Version

Light and the Glory, The(by *Peter Marshall, Jr.*, & *David Manuel*)
On the Edge: The Clinton Presidency(by *Elizabeth Drew*)
Standing Firm(by *Dan Quayle)*
Slouching Toward Gomorrah(by *Judge Robert Bork*)
The Turning Tide(by *Pat Robertson*)
To Renew America(by *Newt Gingrich*)
When Nations Die(by *Jim Black*)
Vince Foster: The Ruddy Investigation(by *Chris Ruddy*)

Organizations:
American Center for Law and Justice
Capital Research Center
Christian Film and Television Commission
Judicial Watch
Parent's Television Council
The 700 Club

Doctrines:
Humanist Manifesto I, II
Declaration of Feminism

Television:
Capital Gang
Crossfire
Dateline
Fox News Sunday
Good Morning America
Hardball
Larry King Live
Meet the Press
Prime Time Live
60 Minutes
The O'Reilly Factor

0-595-22844-5